THE JAZZ YEARS:

Earwitness to an Era

Leonard Feather

QUARTET BOOKS
LONDON   NEW YORK

First published by Quartet Books Limited 1986
A member of the Namara Group
27/29 Goodge Street, London W1P 1FD

Copyright © 1986 Leonard Feather

Feather, Leonard
   The jazz years : earwitness to an era.
   1. Jazz——History and criticism
   I. Title
   785.42'092'4   ML3506

ISBN 0-7043-2579-9
030680296 1 ✓

Typeset by MC Typeset Limited, Chatham, Kent
Printed and bound in Great Britain by
Nene Litho and Woolnough Bookbinding,
both of Irthlingborough, Northants

THE JAZZ YEARS

CONTENTS

To my sister Gweneth (Mrs David Cannon), with thanks for her love and understanding, and with admiration for her talent and courage

ACKNOWLEDGEMENTS

The author acknowledges with thanks permission to use material originally seen in slightly altered form in the following publications: *Down Beat* magazine/Maher Publications, courtesy John Maher, President; *Metronome* magazine, courtesy Robert Asen; *Los Angeles Times*, Times/Mirror Corp.; and *Esquire* magazine.

All music and lyrics reproduced are published by Model Music Co. except 'Mound Bayou', words by Andy Razaf, music by Leonard Feather © copyright 1942 by MCA Music, a division of MCA Inc, New York, NY. Copyright renewed. Used by permission. All rights reserved.

INTRODUCTION

Although the first few chapters follow a chronological pattern, these memoirs are intended less as an autobiography than as a selective retrospective.

In better than 19,000 days of professional involvement at one level or another with jazz, I doubt that there have been more than a couple of hundred days when I spent no time either listening to music or discussing it with a musician. During that time I have written several million words and read many millions more. Clearly all these experiences could not be covered in a single volume.

Instead, you will read here about some of the people I have known, the music I have heard, the records and concerts I have produced, the jobs I have held, the places I have visited. As a friend pointed out, *Earwitness to a Series of Eras* might have been an apter subtitle. More accurate but less pronounceable.

If there is a little less than you might have expected to find about Duke and Louis, Ella, Bird, Dizzy and Miles, Basie and Lester, the reason is simple: I did not want to repeat myself, and they were subjects of extended essays in one of my previous books, *From Satchmo to Miles*.

My thanks go to Dan Morgenstern, Ed Berger and Vincent Pelote of the Institute of Jazz Studies at Rutgers University for their help in researching some of my reminiscences; also to Frankie Nemko, my invaluable assistant for most of the past twenty years, and, of course, to my loving and beloved family, my wife Jane and daughter Lorraine in Los Angeles, and my sister Gweneth Cannon in London.

A special debt is due to Charles Champlin, arts editor of the *Los Angeles Times*. Had it not been for his decision to put me to work in 1965, much of the music I have listened to since then might well have gone unheard by me. Earlier editors, all of whom became good friends, were Jack Tracy, Gene Lees and the late Don De Micheal at *Down Beat*; George T. Simon and Barry Ulanov at *Metronome*; and very specially the late Arnold Gingrich of *Esquire*, to whom jazz and I owe more than I can express.

Finally, and with complete alphabetical logic, Mike Zwerin has earned my gratitude for helping to bring me together with Chris Parker and Quartet Books.

One closing caveat: I hope nobody will expect to find here a documentation of jazz history. All I have tried to do is recount some experiences the reader may enjoy sharing vicariously.

Sherman Oaks, California, 1986

PROLOGUE

The scene bore little resemblance to the dark, cramped after-hours London clubs where, ready to emerge from my teen years, I spent long nights soaking up the sounds of a music that had already become my permanent obsession. It was unlike the shoebox-shaped dives of 52nd Street where so many of my memories now lie buried beneath skyscrapers.

There was a resemblance only in the quality and quantity of the jazz that was being created in the brightly lit room that night, and in the wild enthusiasm that prevailed. Earl 'Fatha' Hines, with a slashing attack on 'Perdido', showed himself ready to outswing any man in the house. Paul Desmond and Gerry Mulligan engaged in a saxophone battle on 'Things ain't what They Used to be'. Clark Terry and Bill Berry exchanged trumpet phrases, waving their rubber plunger mutes, on 'Just Squeeze Me', J. J. Johnson roared through two choruses of aggressive trombone in 'Satin Doll'. Joe Williams, Billy Eckstine and Lou Rawls took turns belting out blues vocal verses.

Mahalia Jackson, Benny Goodman and Cab Calloway preferred to socialize rather than take part in the impromptu proceedings. Others among the 300 crowded in here were born to listen rather than perform; among them were diplomats, members of the Supreme Court, men and women of eminence from all over the world, black and white, young and old.

The great piano with its gold eagle legs was manned by a long succession of enthusiasts. Willie 'The Lion' Smith took a turn; so did Hank Jones, George Wein, Dave Brubeck, Billy Taylor. Even I sat in for a couple of choruses, principally for the pleasure of being able to remember for the rest of my life that I had briefly played an active part in this unprecedented evening.

Had someone told me, during my London years in the 1930s or

even my New York years in the 1940s and 1950s, that a scene such as this could take place, my response would have been ironic: 'That'll be the day.' But now that day had come. The scene was the East Room of the White House in Washington; the guest of honour was Edward Kennedy Ellington; the occasion his seventieth birthday, his host the President of the United States, and the climactic moment a presentation to Duke of the Presidential Medal of Freedom, America's highest possible civilian honour. (Even the fact that the President was Richard M. Nixon could not quell my enthusiasm.)

An art form created by black Americans, belittled or ignored or condescended to for a half century by most white Americans, omitted from music history books, long forbidden in colleges where there were severe penalties for practising it, was now being acknowledged on the highest social level through a tribute to its pre-eminent creative genius. How could everything have changed so swiftly and radically? And what unpredictable series of events could have led to my being present, playing even the smallest of roles in this supreme celebration?

PART ONE

Beginnings

LONDON

My life in jazz was in no way preordained. The family and friends among whom I grew up in Hampstead, a north-western suburb of London, had no interest in the aesthetics of music. If both my parents could play a few tunes at the piano, and if they encouraged my immediate interest in music, it was principally because of the pride they could take in a few small accomplishments. They liked to boast of my ability, before my second birthday, to distinguish in some unexplained manner between record labels and identify the contents of every one of those bulky 78s.

Few of the circumstances of my childhood were conducive to a career in any of the arts. In these upper-middle-class Jewish circles conformity was expected in every area of life. Your parents' friends were exclusively Jewish; if you brought a 'goyisher' friend home from school it was looked on with benign indulgence. The families went to synagogue with varying degrees of frequency. This was all considered to be an indispensable part of the way of life.

With thinly veiled reluctance, I dutifully climbed a hill off Finchley Road every Sunday to visit the home of a Hebrew teacher, who showed me how to read the words, but never to understand the meaning, of an alien language that would be of as much value to me later as if I were studying Urdu. My resentment of forced attitudes, beliefs and superstitious practices was best symbolized by these weekly exercises in futility.

It was in the synagogue that the seeds were planted, though I only dimly realized it then, of an attitude that would play a central part in my life and activities as an adult. The sight of women all seated in the balcony, like some lesser breed not fit to associate with men, taught me a lesson, not only about sexism but about segregation in whatever form it might appear. (Eventually, making my final break with the prejudices, taboos and divisiveness of sectarian religion, I became a devout lifelong agnostic.)

I suppose my subconscious rebellion against social and religious family values started early. Though my father's relative affluence during the pre-Depression years enabled me and my young sister Gweneth to live surrounded by servants, with a Daimler car and family chauffeur, I was never particularly impressed by these luxuries; as for my interest in Dad's chain of clothing stores, it was that of a bemused outsider.

It was a norm of Jewish middle-class life as I saw it for the son to 'go into the business'. By the time I was ready to contend with the problem, the business had dissolved with the Wall Street crash. My father eventually became involved in real estate. Possibly I was expected in due course to join him, but it soon became evident to both of us that other matters were occupying my mind and consuming my time.

An uncle visiting the United States had engaged my interest in things American, mainly by sending me copies of the comics, which resembled nothing that could be found in England. Before long I became intensely absorbed in American life, American motion pictures, American popular music. Listening did not soon lead to participation; my piano teacher all through the years at St Paul's High School was concerned only with my attempts to perfect a Grieg concerto or the latest Chopin assignment. He had scarcely even heard of the kinds of music that soon had a consuming interest for me.

A friend of the family who understood the structure of popular songs helped me to read sheet music (I subscribed to the service of a publishing company that sent out, every month, piano copies of its latest songs) and showed me how, in my clumsy way, to improvise along the same lines. Although for the first several years I was able to do this only in the key of F, it was comforting to become, on any level, an active part of something that had previously engaged me only as a listener.

During a lunch break at St Paul's School in Kensington a friend who played the saxophone, Laurence Goldrei, accompanied me to a nearby record shop, where he urged me to listen to a new release in the Rhythm Style Series on Parlophone Records, whose monthly releases had been inaugurated by the critic Edgar Jackson, founder of the London *Melody Maker*. The record was 'West End Blues' by Louis Armstrong. In those days Parlophone coupled its releases in the oddest ways; the tune on the back of 'West End Blues' was 'Freeze and Melt', played by Eddie Lang and a small band that included Jimmy and Tommy Dorsey. The Lang side had an immediate attraction in its hot, swinging looseness and the innovative lines of Lang's guitar; but 'West End Blues' penetrated deeper. Opening with a long solo arpeggio, it settled into a slow, languorous blues mood with Armstrong's horn in exquisite command. Later came Louis's gentle, wordless vocal, and a solo by Earl Hines that involved a series of rhythmic convolutions the like of which I had never heard. The final chorus began with Louis holding a high B flat for four incredible measures, before raining down dozens of blues-inflected tones, pausing momentarily for an interlude by Hines, ending on Louis's low E flat.

All these technicalities were unknown to me at the time; nothing mattered except the sheer, pure beauty. I was hooked. Though I was not to realize it for many years, this episode in the listening-room of a record shop, not long before I turned fifteen, would determine the pattern of my life.

'West End Blues' provided a sense of direction, a lifestyle, an obsessive concern with every aspect of jazz, as nothing had before. All that mattered from that moment was the next record release or the latest transatlantic news item.

College being economically impractical in the post-Depression years, my parents decided that my outlook would be broadened by sojourns in France and Germany. After graduating from high school I spent six months in Berlin, then several months in Paris. In London, Paris and Berlin alike, enthusiasm for jazz had elements in common with membership of a resistance movement. With the exception of the *Melody Maker* (then a monthly), the record review section in the *Gramophone*, and a French publication called *Jazz Tango Dancing*, there was no place to turn if one wanted to read about jazz. No *Down Beat* existed, nor any other publication that paid this music even the most casual attention, except for a rare article that might make some freak appearance in a magazine I was unlikely to see, such as the piece in *Fortune* about the economics of dance bands.

When Bix Beiderbecke died, twenty-eight years old and a legend, at least among musicians, not a word of obituary appeared in the *New York Times*. When an American musician such as Armstrong returned home from a European concert tour that marked a turning-point in the career of an artist normally confined to ghetto clubs and theatres, this too was greeted with total silence, except in the black press, the existence of which was unknown to me. It was as if a white curtain had been hung over an Afro-American art form lest someone on home ground become aware of its importance.

American jazz records were available in England, but of the small quantity of jazz then being recorded, an even more minute proportion was made available, much of it through the Parlophone Rhythm Style series. The releases were selected from the American Okeh catalogue. Edgar Jackson, a dedicated if somewhat narrow-minded critic, also wrote the *Gramophone* record reviews. Through his ministrations we might be granted three minutes of Armstrong per month, coupled with three minutes of Joe Venuti's Blue Four; or, if we were lucky, two tunes back to back both by Duke Ellington's orchestra, a band whose importance became so apparent that on learning it was to be seen briefly in a film called *Check and Double Check*, I went to see the film seven times. (The stars were Amos and Andy, and even in my teenaged remoteness from American society it was not hard to infer a travesty in the stars' burnt-cork portrayal of American blacks.)

Had it not been for a few men like Jackson in London, and Hugues Panassié and Charles Delaunay in Paris, there might have been no jazz records released in Europe; the consequent international spread of the music, which eventually boomeranged into an American cult, might well have been indefinitely delayed.

For those of us to whom this trickle of releases was barely a starvation diet, a special haven was Levy's, the record shop in Whitechapel, a Jewish district in the East End of London. Morris Levy made a speciality of importing unissued American records at what seemed to be prohibitive prices.

Nevertheless, it was worth the bus trip to Whitechapel to rummage through piles of new arrivals and invest four shillings and three pence (then more than a dollar) in a haunting new Ellington release called 'Mood Indigo', even though on the other side of the disc one had to settle for Benny Payne, a guest vocalist with the orchestra, singing 'When a Black Man's Blue' (written, of course, by three white men).

During the months spent in Paris and Berlin, I stayed with families known to my parents and was apprenticed to French and German movie trade magazines, *La Cinématographie Française* and *Film Kurier*. It was here that my first two bylined articles appeared, in 1932, entitled 'Europäische Zusammenarbeit' and

'L'Essor du Film Britannique' respectively.

In Berlin, where I lived less than a year before Hindenburg turned over the reins of power to Hitler, one shop kept a small supply of jazz records. Once I came across a new release by Ted Lewis, a notorious king of corn, but between his solos it was possible to hear the buoyant, rolling piano of a guest soloist, one Thomas 'Fats' Waller. The presence of a black man on the same record with a white band lent this item a rare significance.

With the disc under my arm I arrived at the *Film Kurier* office, where I ran into my boss, a man named Hans Rutenberg, and commented on a headline in the morning paper: though Hitler had won eleven million votes, Hindenburg had been re-elected.

'Great news,' I said, smiling.

Rutenberg looked at me indulgently. 'My boy,' he said, 'you don't understand these things.' He was showing his tolerance for the naive young English Jew, who failed to recognize what a powerful Führer could do for the fatherland.

Pre-Hitler Berlin remains in my memory as a city living in a giant shadow of which it was, to all outward appearances, largely unaware. The Kiwis, with whom I lived, did not seem fully conscious that as Jews they might be in mortal danger. My own life was that of a loner, picking out records for the gramophone or chords for the piano as I tried to master the technique of jazz.

Paris was no better; I lived with my hand-cranked portable and my slowly growing collection of treasures by Ellington, Armstrong, Venuti and Lang, McKinney's Cotton Pickers, Luis Russell, Bix and Trumbauer, Don Redman, Red Nichols' Five Pennies, Fletcher Henderson and other idols whom I vaguely hoped some day to meet.

The blues was a particularly deep and durable subject of fascinated study, performed not by Bessie Smith or the other race artists, but mainly in instrumental versions, with occasional vocals by Armstrong or Jack Teagarden. It was after I had discovered the twelve-bar blues form and had attempted to write a scholarly analysis of it for the *Melody Maker* (presumably the first to appear in print) that I received a warm congratulatory note from Hugues Panassié, who reacted to my essay in the manner of a man from Mars discovering a second Martian in the middle of the Place de la Concorde.

During my Paris sojourn the astonishing news reached me that Armstrong, by then a name to reckon with in Europe (thanks to

Jackson's reviews, John Hammond's *Melody Maker* news columns and the French critics), was due to play at the London Palladium. Indulging myself in a plane trip, my first, I arrived airsick enough to sit groggily through the opening-night show. As the curtains parted, Louis, fronting a sloppy, makeshift band of European musicians, mostly non-American blacks, went through the 'Sleepy Time Down South' opener. This was a moment to carry with me through a lifetime. A distant legend had become flesh and blood.

Through some devious connection I contrived to meet Louis and his future third wife, Alpha, at a nearby bar. That they were not merely approachable and affable but even treated me as an equal was almost more than I could comprehend. To be standing around chatting and drinking beer with the man whose record had set me off on a continuous adventure was an experience the measure of which Louis himself could not grasp.

Though I had slowly become aware of American racism, mainly through the writing of Hammond and a few enlightened English sociologists, it was impossible for me as an unsophisticated teenager to understand fully the enormity of the crimes visited on even the most prominent of Afro-Americans. This in turn left me minimally capable of understanding how Armstrong and Alpha reacted to the new identity England was now giving him as a mature and greatly respected artist. The realities of the legal, social and psychological subservience that had been his lifestyle from birth were not to be grasped until I had spent several years living closer to him, closer to Harlem, closer to a world that I would embrace sooner than I realized.

The black population of England in the early 1930s was negligible. Jim Crow was just a phrase I had read. Armstrong was the first American jazz musician I had met, the first black man, the first personal hero. The following year, when Ellington arrived on his maiden voyage, I knew nobody close enough to him to introduce me and could not summon the courage to introduce myself.

From late 1932, after my return from Paris, until the summer of 1935, I worked in a minor capacity (my name for the job was assistant-assistant-assistant director) at the British Lion Film Studios in Beaconsfield, outside London. During those years, an accidental chain of events propelled me into a professional relationship with music. A letter to the editor of the *Melody Maker*, in which I expressed amazement that no jazz had been written or recorded in waltz time, was published and led to considerable controversy. In one memorable phrase, the editor summed up the problem in a footnote: 'Asking for jazz in 3/4 time,' he stated firmly, 'is like asking for a red piece of green chalk.' Time would be slow in vindicating me, and I was to play a role in creating several of the recordings that would prove my point.

Another letter, in which I lamented the apparent lack of women jazz enthusiasts, turned out to be even more provocative. Predictably, angry letters from female jazz fans poured in.* By now the *Melody Maker*, and particularly an editor named Dan Ingman, seemed interested in meeting the writer of these circulation-stimulating letters.

At the magazine's offices I suggested a few ideas for feature articles. The publication's style in those days was essentially that of a fan magazine, with subject matter and writing style to match, though occasionally I was able to slip in an essay that attempted to be of some scholarly value. Many of my early articles were based on the venerable British tradition of the debate. An interview with Louis Armstrong used the premise that recordings were of greater artistic and historic value than personal appearances. Another debate was conducted with an adventurous twenty-seven-year-old composer named Reginald Foresythe, the London-born son of a black West African barrister and a German woman. Our discussion was headlined 'No Future for Hot Music'. I was assigned to take the negative stance although, as often happened in these debates, I felt that at least as strong a case could be made from the opposite point of view. (In one instance I wrote both sides of a purported debate.)

Somewhat more useful from the standpoint of the serious student were my blues analysis, and a later examination of the so-called 'Sixteen-Bar Swing', which I had heard in countless songs from Handy's 'Loveless Love' to Louis Armstrong's 'Ding Dong Daddy' and Ellington's 'Ring Dem Bells'. Variations of this hardy form are still in frequent use in such standards as Sonny Rollins' 'Doxy' and my own 'Heavy Hearted Blues'.

A curiosity with overtones of precognition, published as a Hallowe'en feature in November 1934, anticipated the advent of both LP records and videos. In the story, my Hallowe'en witch

*Perhaps I was not so far off the mark. In 1986, *Wire*, the English jazz monthly, conducted a survey of its readers' tastes. Just over 1% of replies received were from women.

produced a small black box on which she placed a reel of thin black cotton. 'This is a rather short record,' she apologized. 'It only runs for twenty minutes.' She set the reel in motion. On a screen appeared a picture of the band as it played. The same article preordained the arrival of electronic drums: 'The rhythm is produced by one of the latest model Mutzberger Metronomes – makes more din than a dozen drums. Rhythm has been automatic for years now.' I noted that on the wall during this mythical interview was a calendar dated October 1984.

I was off base in some of my other predictions: 'Well I don't think there are any all-Negro units existing,' my informant told me, 'they've mixed in with the ofays and lost their individuality. There isn't anyone darker than a mulatto left, anyway.'

The *Melody Maker* paid two guineas for a story ($10.50). Soon I was able to supplement this by fees for occasional articles in the *Gramophone*, *Tune Times*, the *Era* and *Swing Music*. My job with British Lion, which paid $12 a week, soon became secondary to my outside activities. Complaining to my boss, I was offered a $1 a week raise – a final insult which, added to the injury of long and fruitless working hours in the studio and commuting by train daily to Beaconsfield, led to my immediate resignation.

Felix King, a pianist friend, had been talking about going to America for a visit. Buoyed up by my new freedom, and helped by an assurance of financial aid from my father, I said, 'Why don't we go over there together?'

'Let's try the *Normandie*,' said Felix. The possibility of sailing on the great French liner, only weeks after its maiden voyage, reinforced the excitement of the prospect.

We set sail from Southampton. On the day before we docked, a cable was received on board from a friend I had met during one of his London visits: MEET YOU PIER TOMORROW: HAMMOND.

On 19 July 1935, a new world opened up for me. It was still unreal, almost surreal. Its buildings were vast and slightly intimidating, but I knew that this was my world. As I stepped off the gangplank and shook hands with John Hammond, the reality began to sink in. New York was no longer a postmark on a letter. Within hours Harlem was more than a name on a record label.

With the land of jazz right here under my feet, I headed for the hotel that seemed most logical, checking in at the President on 48th Street. I knew nothing about it except that its basement club was Adrian's Tap Room, where the bass saxophonist Adrian Rollini, whom I had heard on records with Bix and Venuti, presented small swing groups nightly. Where else in New York could you stay, at $12.50 a week, with music of that calibre just an elevator trip away?

NEW YORK

The America that greeted me in 1935 differed profoundly from the idealized image I had drawn selectively from reports in the British press. If this was my spiritual home, the breeding ground of a music that had become my obsession, it was also a country only two years away from repeal, and digging its way painfully out of an economic upheaval of which I had been only dimly aware; perhaps most significantly, the racial divisions with which I had tried to come to terms at long distance gradually became a startling reality.

This was an America in which lynchings often were dealt with casually enough to be relegated to the back pages; where segregation in New York City was more pervasive than it is today in Mississippi. New York in effect was composed of two distinct cities that were barely conscious of each other's existence. It was to the lesser-known of these two that John Hammond and I made our way within hours of my arrival.

The Apollo Theatre on West 125th Street was the last survivor of several theatrical landmarks that had provided Harlem with a steady diet of soul-food vaudeville. The Harlem Opera House and others had been victims of the Depression, but the Apollo continued to flourish. From the outside it could have been mistaken for any neighbourhood London theatre; inside, it had an exotic, funky appeal that transcended the seedy trappings. The comedy by Pigmeat Markham was raw and raucously funny; the orchestra for this week's show (Erskine Hawkins and his Bama State Collegians) was not the equal of the black bands whose records I had been collecting. The principal reason for our visit was that John knew of the presence, as a subsidiary attraction, of a former headliner, Bessie Smith.

Though she was billed as 'Queen of all blues singers', to many in

this audience hers was a name out of the past, for although Bessie Smith's empyrean voice had dominated the 1920s, with the collapse of the recording industry her career had been headed downhill for several years.

According to my innocent report to the *Melody Maker*, Bessie Smith 'proclaimed racy lyrics in a strange, throbbing voice . . . I was told that Bessie was not at her best; I confess to having remained unimpressed by her performance.'

This stuffy observation was my proper English way of implying that Bessie Smith was very drunk, as I soon realized when John introduced me to her after the show. She mumbled a half-intelligible greeting and hurried off to the box office, where she had some complaint to make to the manager about the orchestra.

It is ironic that my first and last glimpse of Bessie had nothing to do with the blues. I remember her in a gleaming-white dress, singing Duke Ellington's 'Oh Babe, Maybe Someday' and bouncing up and down during the second chorus in the closest approximation of a dance that her massive figure could assimilate. In the light of her death just two years later, one could construe something fey in her tragicomic demeanour.

Many years later I realized that this final opportunity to hear a woman whose records would outlive her by many decades was pathetically unrepresentative of her early grandeur. She was ten years beyond her prime, and at this stage there were perhaps a hundred Americans, ninety of them white musicologists, who had more than a vague comprehension of her stature in the history of Afro-American music. To John Hammond, who had produced her last record date in 1933, she was a figure who had always commanded his unswerving respect. To almost all whites she was unknown; to most young blacks she was an insignificant, half-forgotten vaudeville performer. What little success the Empress of the Blues might still enjoy depended on an appreciation of her simplistically risqué songs.

From the Apollo it was a short ride to the Savoy Ballroom at 140th Street and Lenox Avenue, where, skirting the elevated railroad tracks, we climbed up a steep flight of stairs. John, who seemed more at ease in Harlem than almost any other white American could feel, was greeted by Charles Buchanan, a tall, dour black man who was the manager of the ballroom.

The impact of the moment I walked into the Savoy was immediate and too startling ever to be forgotten. The sensation was one of removal from any world I had known. During the first five minutes I felt I had absorbed more music than I had heard in all my years of listening to jazz impersonalized by the obstacle of the phonograph.

The contortions of the dancers seemed unreal to my untutored eye. The jitterbugs had no knowledge of (or perhaps simply no respect for) the conventions of ballroom dancing as I had known it. An intense excitement suffused the room, ringed with booths at which beer and wine were served (the Savoy had no hard liquor). The parquet floor shook so visibly that I wondered whether it was safe to place a ballroom one flight up. Ironically, the music that made such a feverish emotional impact on my sensibilities appealed to this audience mainly on utilitarian grounds. None of the dancers showed any great concern; none formed a circle around the bandstand until John and I, joined soon by a few others who perhaps were encouraged by our initiative, stood in front of Teddy Hill's orchestra during a stomping arrangement of the tune that had just arrived as a Harlem novelty hit, 'Christopher Columbus'.

Leon 'Chu' Berry, the tenor saxophonist who, John and I agreed, was second only to Coleman Hawkins, was the composer of 'Christopher Columbus' and a principal soloist with Hill's band. Having never heard of Teddy Hill, I was astonished at the cohesion of the rhythm section, and by the solos, particularly those of a shrill, fearlessly innovative young trumpeter whose name, I learned, was Roy Eldridge. The band was of standard dimensions with three trumpets (the others were Bill Dillard and Bill Coleman), a trombonist (Dickie Wells, who would later enter the ranks of the early Count Basie band), four saxophones and the usual rhythm section: piano, acoustic guitar, bass and drums.

The orchestra worked half-hour dance sets as Hammond and I stayed riveted to our vantage point a few feet away. Playing the alternating sets until closing time (2.30 a.m.) was a group occupying the adjoining bandstand, Gus Gay and his San Domingans. The members actually were Cubans whose music brought to the rhumba colouration unknown to my London trained ears; I had been aware only of a generally limited level of musicianship among the very few West Indians and Cubans in Britain who attempted to embrace this idiom.

The Savoy engendered in me oddly mixed emotions of alienation (due to my British reserve rather than my whiteness) and of belonging, for it was at the ballroom, and at other retreats north of

Central Park, that I would quickly learn to feel more at one with my surroundings than anywhere else either at home or abroad. There was an immediate sense of being welcome in a community where, as Hammond and others had warned, people from downtown might expect to find themselves regarded with acute suspicion. Not being an American, as I soon found out, fortified my credentials.

Perhaps because of the degree to which I found myself identifying with the acquaintances I made through Hammond, and through the black friends to whom he introduced me, I balked at the suggestion from a white music publisher that a visit to the Cotton Club might be in order. The mob-owned Cotton Club represented a Harlem specially prepared for whites, who, in a mood of sophisticated slumming, patronized the club, unaware that they were tolerated in Harlem only because their presence was needed for the economic survival of the blacks who entertained there.

Most significantly, I knew that the Cotton Club admitted blacks only as performers. Except for the occasional celebrity, who was accepted grudgingly (nobody dared insult the gun-toting Bojangles Robinson by refusing him a table), blacks were not welcome as customers. Knowing this meant knowing that I would be uncomfortable. Consequently, and perhaps foolishly, since it would have been of sociological interest, I never saw the inside of the club.

During this first visit to New York my unofficial headquarters turned out to be the Mills Music office. I had met Mills briefly during his visit to England with Ellington. Al Brackman, a young song plugger and a cousin of Mills, who worked at the office, became my good friend and guide. Through him I met Alex Hill, a quiet and amiable man who at that time was a staff songwriter and arranger at Mills and a close friend and associate of Fats Waller, to whom he introduced me soon afterwards. It was with Alex that I did my willing share of rubbernecking when he took me to the top of the Empire State Building, then the world's tallest.

Others whom I met during the visit, or a few months later on my second trip, were Clarence Williams and Romeo L. Dougherty. Williams, by then a fairly prosperous publisher, whose name I had seen on early Armstrong records, was the first to encourage me by going to the trouble and expense of publishing some of my music; soon after our meeting he signed contracts for, and duly printed, two of my songs. Dougherty, the entertainment editor of the *New York Amsterdam News*, whose offices I visited, arranged for me to become the paper's London correspondent. Every two weeks my column, 'Uptown Lowdown', reported on the minuscule London Negro colony, dealing with parties held for such visiting celebrities as the Four Flash Devils at after-hours spots such as Jig's Club, the Shim Sham, and the Nest. There was no payment for these columns, but I was pleased to have my first byline in an American publication, and to be, according to Dougherty, its first regular white contributor.

One of my reports discussed black musicians in British bands. Historians seem not to have noted that before Benny Goodman hired Teddy Wilson, another black pianist with the same last name, Garland Wilson, was featured with Jack Payne's BBC band; Ellis Jackson, a forty-two-year-old trombonist from New Jersey, was a member of Billy Cotton's *palais de danse* orchestra, and Reginald Foresythe had pioneered in 1933 with his use of woodwinds in a jazz ensemble, leading his white sidemen at the chic 400 Club in London. Earlier that year he had recorded his music in New York with a group that included Benny Goodman, John Kirby and Gene Krupa.

Black musicians were not in evidence when I spent my second night in New York exploring 52nd Street. Although 'The Street', as we called it, is commonly associated with the World War II years, its jazz associations went much further back. Even during the last years of Prohibition the Onyx Club was in business as a speakeasy, with Art Tatum as a frequent visitor. Just two months after repeal the Onyx opened officially as a legitimate nightclub, with the Spirits of Rhythm and Tatum as the attractions.

By the time of my visit the Onyx, the Famous Door, the Hickory House and others were thriving, all in the two blocks between Fifth and Seventh Avenues. The two main attractions now happened to be Italian-Americans from New Orleans who played trumpet and sang: Louis Prima at the Famous Door, Wingy Manone at the Hickory House. The Onyx had a group organized by the singer Red McKenzie, co-led by Ed Farley and Mike Riley, who earned a questionable immortality with their novelty song 'The Music Goes Round and Around', recorded three months after my visit.

Novelty material was the crutch on which most of the 52nd Street artists had to rely. Manone was striking it rich with his raucous vocal on 'Isle of Capri', an English song by Will Grosz, but the patient listener, after sitting through these trifles, would be rewarded by some splendid solos, particularly by the clarinettist Joe Marsala, who in due course would lead his own group, also at the Hickory House.

Prima, all of whose records were built around his vocals, followed a similar pattern. A highlight of his performance was 'Rockin' Chair', for which he would play the dual roles of father and son, hopping from one side of the small stage to the other as he changed character with each line of the lyric. But here, too, there were compensatory factors: admirable clarinet by the glum-faced Pee Wee Russell, seated next to the grand piano, who would occasionally break into an inspired chorus. Prima, like Manone, used guitar and bass, dispensing with piano and drums. At closing time, 3.30 a.m., he paraded down the narrow gangway between tables in the shoebox-shaped room, followed by his sidemen, marching out into the street as they segued into his closing theme 'Way Down Yonder in New Orleans'.

Though the phrase was not yet in use, I was witnessing the birth of the swing era. Benny Goodman's breakthrough date at the Palomar Ballroom in Los Angeles, which set his orchestra on a path that managed to mix musical and commercial success, was only a couple of weeks away.

Jazz during the swing years, though far beyond its folk-music origins, was a relatively simple art form. Today it is divided and subdivided into a dozen disparate though sometimes overlapping idioms: traditional, swing, bop, modal, jazz-rock, fusion, electronic, funk and more. In 1935, big-band and small-combo jazz could both qualify as swing music; improvisation was frequent to total in the more intimate groups.

Fats Waller led a typical small combo of the period, using very little written music. One day Alex Hill took me to a rehearsal at a midtown studio. As we approached, the strains of 'Dinah', played with phenomenal intensity, could be heard through the door. We entered a small, bare room to find the enormous, cheerful Waller at a green upright piano on top of which were a straw hat and a bottle of gin. Never had I heard an upright piano yield such a shattering volume of sound.

Waller reached the end of the arrangement, paused to offer a hearty greeting, then explained that he was working out a new solo. I soon noticed that there was in his work far less improvisation than I had realized. He practised every phrase assiduously.

'Man, I've been busy,' he said, 'finishing up some recording down at Victor. Like to hear something new? Here's one I just wrote – probably use it on the next session.' He played 'You've Got

Me under Your Thumb' (which, perhaps due to Victor pressure to record commercial songs by other writers, he did not record until late 1937).

Waller's was of course a small swing band; swing was the motivating force also for Fletcher Henderson, whom I heard a few days later at the Roseland Ballroom, a typical dance hall in the midtown Broadway area. In size and appearance Roseland resembled the Savoy, but the intoxicating ambience of the Harlem dance hall was grimly lacking, and the attendance was sparse. Scores of blonde dance partners (this was still the 'ten cents a dance' era) sat patiently in orderly rows of chairs waiting for customers who seldom appeared.

Fletcher, very light-skinned, courteous and urbane, apologized (unnecessarily, it seemed to me) for the hastily rehearsed band. He assured me that he planned to lure such alumni as Red Allen, J. C. Higginbotham and Buster Bailey back into the ranks, but except for Bailey, who returned some four months later, he failed.

A limited pianist and always a somewhat ineffectual leader, Henderson considered his frequent assignments to write for Benny Goodman a godsend. Though he was destined to lead his own bands off and on until 1947, he was Goodman's pianist for the second half of 1939 and then became his staff arranger.

My chief impression of the musicians I met during this first New York visit was that artistry aside, they were accessible and hospitable. One evening, after attending one of Red Allen's frequent record dates, I accompanied him to his apartment near Sugar Hill. During dinner he played some records drawn from a large heap of sessions he had made over the years; afterwards, Mrs Allen showed me his press clippings, assuring me that Red was a regular reader of the *Melody Maker*, and let me glance at some of his fan mail, most of which, not surprisingly, was from Europe.

Red Allen took himself and his music fairly seriously. In sharp contrast, when I dropped in at Sally and Joe Venuti's hotel room in midtown, Venuti was mainly concerned with playing me a satirical record he had made for kicks at the end of a legitimate session. The tunes in this so-called 'Onyx Club Review' included 'Salvation Sal', the trumpeter Manny Klein introducing Venuti in Yiddish, Joe arguing with him in Italian and playing an out-of-tune version of 'Pagliacci', and a few passages of genuine jazz mixed in with the broad humour. Venuti also told me that he planned to make a record on which, through the miracle of overdubbing, he would play all the instruments. Had this project materialized, he would have anticipated Sidney Bechet by almost six years.

Another record for private distribution only was one I coaxed Mildred Bailey and Teddy Wilson to make, at a studio on 54th Street, as a souvenir of a delightful evening I had spent at the home of Red Norvo and Mildred on Long Island, where they enjoyed a quiet, away-from-the-Manhattan-madness life during their nights off. Though less than an hour's drive from town, they had a spacious country home where an evening might consist, as mine did, of a fried-chicken dinner, Mildred's gentle blues singing to Teddy's graceful backing, and Red tinkling on the xylophone. (Three copies were pressed of the record, with a blues on one side and a pop song on the other; all seem to have disappeared long ago.)

Another evening was spent at Wilson's own flat in Harlem. Wilson, to me, looked older than his twenty-two years, but at that time, to me at twenty, everyone seemed much older. Teddy was genuinely modest; he would not play until Felix King, who made the trip uptown with me, had warmed up the keyboard. Then, seated at the bedside piano (the apartment was too small to accommodate one in the living-room), Teddy played four hands with his wife Irene, herself a skilled musician. They next turned over the keyboard to Red Norvo, whose style at the piano was simple and refreshing.

Very late that night, Red and I went to Dickie Wells' Club (not the trombonist) on 133rd Street, where we heard the strangest group I had yet encountered. It comprised a rhythm section, with a nineteen-year-old drummer named Eddie Dougherty (who later recorded with Harry James and the Ammons–Johnson boogie-woogie duo), along with three or four others who played comb-and-paper-style kazoos.

To hear this instrumentation applied to a work as complex as Reginald Foresythe's 'Deep Forest' was an experience bordering on the eerie. On other tunes the band would play dozens of choruses without any let-up in energy or creativity. That this band never even recorded, except for one session that was rejected, leaves a curious gap in jazz history.

The most elite music venue I saw in New York was the Rainbow Room, sixty-four floors up in one of the Radio City skyscrapers, where Ray Noble was installed with his American orchestra (with two British exceptions: the drummer Bill Harty, and the singer Al Bowlly). I was mildly impressed, despite the surfeit of fiddles and muted brass, but felt that Bud Freeman on tenor was ill-at-ease in this sober setting, and was mainly impressed by the techniques of the presentation.

Noble was seated at a small white piano that continued gliding slowly around the edge of the dance floor; the timing was geared so that he would arrive back in front of the bandstand just as each number ended. The other effect involved a hookup between the amplification and the light system, through which various tone colours would change the lighting in the room. The reeds produced a pale green; open brass was bright orange; the trombones were a sort of mauve and baritone or bass sax a deep purple. During a complex arrangement the colours would change with vivid and dazzling speed.

'It's just a part of American ingenuity,' I observed in my bemused report to the *Melody Maker*.

One afternoon during my twelve-day stay was spent at a recording session on the fifteenth floor at Broadway and 57th Street, in a studio that resembled a living-room equipped for sound. John Hammond, who brought me to this date, was in charge, along with Harry Grey of Brunswick Records. This was the second in the long series of sessions under the name 'Teddy Wilson and His Orchestra'.

The musicians were Roy Eldridge, Cecil Scott (clarinet), Ben Webster, Hilton Jefferson, Wilson, guitarist Lawrence Lucie, John Kirby and Cozy Cole, with vocals by Billie Holiday ('daughter of the guitarist Clarence Holiday', I explained to *Melody Maker* readers).

There had been little preparation and virtually no written music; the men simply studied the sheet music of each song. After a rap session among the four horn players, a more or less straight opening chorus would be constructed, followed by Billie's vocal, a series of brief (mostly sixteen-bar) solos, and a half-chorus going out.

Teddy Wilson, seated quietly at the piano, set a figure for the coda. After the first playback, Harry Grey said: 'Maybe you better fix up some nice little figures behind those solos. Don't bother to write 'em down, Teddy; you can just play them.'

Ten minutes later the reed section had its series of phrases together, helping to give the results more body. There were a couple of trial runs before Grey decided to go for a master. Halfway through it, Hammond began waving wildly through the control booth; the accompaniment was drowning out Billie Holiday.

Placings were adjusted, a second master went well, and a third was made for safety.

Ben Webster, during his solos, reminded me of Coleman Hawkins, eyes tightly shut, shoulders hunched, producing rich and inspired melodic invention. Kirby revealed a subtle mastery of the bass; I remarked to Hammond how regrettable it was that Benny Goodman probably wanted both Kirby and Wilson to join him, but dared not take the chance, even though Kirby was light enough to pass for white. (Wilson, of course, did join Goodman to form the Trio the following April; the first Wilson–Goodman–Krupa record date had already been completed that month, 13 July 1935.)

My time in New York was so well spent, with so few moments away from music, that I arrived home with enough feature material to last me until my next visit.

This was accomplished a few months later under less favourable circumstances. I accepted an assignment to return to New York as solicitor of advertising for a special all-American issue of the *Melody Maker*. My immaturity and unawareness of the harsh facts of US business methods equipped me poorly for the job. Irving Mills came to my rescue; just as the trip seemed likely to end in failure, he bought four entire pages. Another friend was Milt Gabler, whose Commodore Music Shop at 144 East 42nd Street was a gathering place for the European and American cognoscenti. His large advertisement offered shellac records for twenty-five cents, other items at thirty-five cents, and special Commodore or United Hot Clubs of America reissues at $1 or $2. For orders totalling more than two pounds sterling Gabler offered to ship to England, post-free, these highly breakable discs in specially made wooden boxes. ('No wonder the Music Shop struggled for so long,' he remarked to me recently. 'We were crazy!')

This was not to be the last time Gabler would bail me out in an emergency. Though our musical tastes differed, he was immensely helpful to all of us, critics and musicians alike. His jam sessions, first at recording studios and then at Jimmy Ryan's on 52nd Street, became legends; he was even able to lure Bessie Smith to one, shortly before she died.

Socially, what little spare time I had during this visit was spent with Al Brackman, with his secretary Geraldine Stroback, and with Adrian De Haas, an arranger and copyist who had immigrated a few years earlier from Holland and who became a firm friend throughout the years until his return to the Netherlands in 1950.

Adrian, well liked by Benny Carter and other musicians, would later guide me in my first attempts to become an arranger.

During the months of my absence, the changes along 52nd Street had included a move by Wingy Manone to the Famous Door, where the intermission pianist was Teddy Wilson. Out of his element in this atmosphere of constant chatter, Wilson at least had some financial security, since he was now on the air five times weekly with the Charioteers, a vocal quartet.

Red Norvo had taken over at the Hickory House, heading a sextet that became instantly successful both musically and commercially. With trumpet, tenor, clarinet, Dave Barbour on guitar and Pete Peterson on bass (the room's no-piano-no-drums policy was still in force), Norvo had begun to establish the reputation for gently underplayed swing music that has served him for the past half century.

A few steps beyond the Hickory House I found the trumpeter Jack Purvis leading a quartet. A wild man, Purvis at various times was a chef, a carpenter, a member of Fred Waring's massive ensemble and a jailbird. I was fortunate to see him while he was still at large; he served ten years for rape in Texas from 1937–47 and died in obscurity in 1962. As his record of 'Copyin' Louis' indicated, he was one of the best of the white Armstrong disciples.

Standing out most sharply in my recollections of that winter is a Christmas night in Harlem, celebrated by one of the famous breakfast dances at the Savoy Ballroom, with Louis Armstrong as the main attraction.

Ever since Louis had left for Europe, then spent many months in Chicago, Harlem had been waiting for his return. At the Apollo, a placard that read: 'Coming Shortly – Louis Armstrong' made a promise that went unfulfilled for two years.

Late on Christmas Eve I arrived at the elaborately festooned ballroom. It was not until 1 a.m. on Christmas Day that there was any appreciable swelling of the crowd. The shouting and laughter, the noise of shuffling feet triggered by the music of Chick Webb's orchestra, all were intermingled as the hours slipped by. At 4.45 a.m. a roar went up that seemed literally to shake the foundations: Louis and his men had arrived. Five minutes later they swung into 'High Society'.

From then until well after six in the morning, ninety per cent of the crowd stood wedged tightly around the bandstand, consuming every inch of space. By now Louis had long been a consciously crowd-pleasing commodity, but aside from the dreary vocals by Sonny Woods and a young woman named Bobby Caston, I found in his performance a subtle mix of showmanship and artistry. There were no wild gesticulations to the band, no exhibitionism of the kind that had brought him boos and catcalls two years earlier at London's Holborn Empire.

If it was necessary to put up with a singalong during 'Old Man Mose', it was also possible to relish his superb sense of dramatic and musical values as he worked up to climaxes on 'Ain't Misbehavin'' or 'Confessin' '. The band, essentially the old Luis Russell Orchestra, played a couple of numbers on its own, notably the powerful and hypnotic blues 'Call of the Freaks'.

When Louis at last broke into the closing strains of 'Sleepy Time Down South' it seemed that the night must be over, yet for another hour or two, until breakfast time, hundreds of couples stayed on, dancing to a relief band as the supply of beer and hot dogs dwindled.

If this Christmas celebration was the supreme point, musically, among my evenings in Harlem during that chilly but bracing winter, the most remarkable aspect in terms of personal relationships was the beginning of a long and strange association. His name of course was familiar to me and I had heard his records, but meeting Mezz Mezzrow and growing to know and like him was perhaps the oddest chapter of all in the American side of my life.

MEZZ

The friendship between me and Milton Mesirow (better known in Harlem and wherever else he plied his trade as Mezz Mezzrow) was beyond any rational explanation. Musically and socially we were worlds apart. He was a traditionalist for whom New Orleans-style music was virtually the only true jazz; I was concerned with newer developments and, in later years, advocated the bebop he despised. The product of a rough Chicago neighbourhood, he had studied the saxophone while serving a jail sentence at the age of seventeen. I had grown up protected by a staid middle-class family in London.

Two forces, I suppose, brought us together: our intense opposition to racism and our shared love of the blues. Mezz, who considered himself a voluntary Negro, lived in Harlem with his bright-eyed, amiable black wife, Mae. A failed musician whose playing made him the laughing stock of the traditionalists (Eddie Condon was a particularly virulent antagonist), Mezz now performed only occasionally, having found that he could make a profitable living selling pot. So closely was he associated with this underground profession that a reefer was often known as a mezz or mezzroll.

I had been curious to find out what kind of man could make his living in this manner. Meeting him and Mae backstage one night at the Apollo, I was surprised to find an extrovert, easy-going fellow who talked with a quasi-southern-black accent and whose attitude towards this British newcomer was very much the same as that of the other musicians I had met in New York. He clearly wanted to make me feel at home.

Making the uptown rounds with Mezz, listening to Frankie Newton's singular trumpet with Charlie Johnson's band at Smalls Paradise and other such delights, was a special pleasure, since Mezz was well liked in the circles where his product was traded, which made us both feel welcome.

During a relationship that became more sporadic as our musical interests diverged, Mezz only once brought up the subject of his illegal livelihood. We were in his car, across the street from the Hotel Plymouth on 49th Street where I was staying. It had been a long night in Harlem and now, around 3.30 in the morning, conversation lagged until he came around to a subject that had evidently been on his mind.

'I heard they ran a big story in the *Melody Maker* about marijuana,' he said. 'They made quite a big deal of it, listing all the expressions associated with it, and they used my name to describe a reefer.

'Now I have some friends, some very powerful friends, that don't like that kind of publicity at all. I hope the paper don't do that no more.'

The implied threat was clear enough; I knew what kinds of friends Mezz meant. Not being the dictator of editorial policy at the *Melody Maker*, however, I could do nothing but nod wisely in implied agreement.

Our conversation turned to lighter subjects. When I mentioned that I had been studying clarinet and had my horn with me, Mezz insisted that I bring it down from the hotel room. Five minutes later we were seated side by side in his parked car, playing the blues on our clarinets. Why we were not arrested for disturbing the peace I will never know. It occurs to me that perhaps this was another reason Mezz and I got along so well: he was the one instrumentalist to whom I would never feel inferior.

Why did he never offer me a joint, never talk about pot again? Perhaps he felt he was on dangerous territory discussing it or sharing it with a journalist. However, just before one of my return trips to London, when he came down to the pier to see me off, Mezz remembered an old mutual friend of ours, the American clarinettist Danny Polo, who had been living for years in London.

Taking me aside for a moment, he said, 'Hey, Leonard, when you see Danny, give him this and tell him Mezz says hello.'

I took the reefer and put it in my cigarette case. A week later, just after my return home, I dropped in on Danny at the Mayfair, a very chic hotel where he was working with Ambrose's orchestra, and made my special delivery.

'Gee,' said Danny, 'that Mezz sure is a thoughtful cat.'

(My first experience with pot came several years later through my friendship with Charlie Barnet, whose band I greatly admired, and whom I came to know well enough to hang out with him occasionally. After one night on the town, Charlie shook hands and pressed a reefer into my palm. I took it home, tried it out alone in my room, and enjoyed it, but didn't have the pleasure again until an evening out at Louis Armstrong's Long Island home some thirteen years later. It was odd that Charlie and Satchmo showed their hospitality where Mezzrow feared to tread. But I never took up pot, for the same reason I have always been a very moderate drinker; I suppose my one true high is music.)

In 1946 Mezz's autobiography, *Really the Blues*, was published in New York. Although self-serving, with incredible claims that he had been a musical influence on everyone from Gene Krupa to Louis Armstrong, it was a vivid, often squalid story, well ghost-written by Bernard Wolfe.

Mezz inscribed a copy for me. He wrote: 'For my freind [*sic*] Leonard Feather, who sticks by his guns as a critic, plays the blues & likes the modern idiom. My dear Leonard – some day I hope to make you understand my point & analysis of the music, so till then – Best Wishes – Milton "Mezz" Mezzrow.'

The Mezzrow book was an intriguing document in which truths and fictionalized anecdotes are ingeniously intermingled. The story, for instance, of Mezzrow's attempt to form an interracial orchestra in New York begins with facts and ends in falsehoods. Mezzrow did indeed succeed in persuading a press agent named Jay Faggen, who in 1937 owned a club known as the Harlem Uproar House, to let him organize a mixed band.

Mezz lined up Gene Sedric, Frankie Newton, Max Kaminsky, Sidney de Paris, Bernard Addison, Zutty Singleton and others – seven white, seven black. I was not in New York, but the press reports of the opening were promising, with such headlines as 'Ofay–Sepia Disciples of Swing Shatter Big Town Traditions'.

Even John Hammond reported that the band, though young and rough, had 'one of the best brass sections in the country and a vitality that the Casa Loma band and Tommy Dorsey might do well to emulate'.

Business, however, did not hold up, and the club had already been in financial trouble. Ever the press agent, Faggen decided on a publicity stunt: he had swastikas painted on the dance floor and a display poster. A friend of mine, Mike Gould, who was in the club, saw Faggen at work on the alleged vandalism: nevertheless, Mezzrow recalled the incident in his book as if it had been genuine, and as recently as 1985 the notes for a Mezzrow album claimed that the Uproar House was 'vandalized by fascist hoods'.

The stunt aroused some curiosity and helped business for a while, but soon the creditors won, the room was padlocked and, except for a booking at the Savoy Ballroom, the Disciples of Swing were through.

Though Mezzrow's following as a musician was limited in the US he had a lifelong friend in Hugues Panassié, on whom Mezz had a growing influence. Although, in his watershed book *Le Jazz Hot*, Panassié had praised 'the personal genius of Jack Teagarden, Benny Goodman, Gene Krupa, Joe Sullivan and Babe Russin', by 1938, when he came to New York to produce a series of sessions for RCA with Mezz as his associate, his views had undergone radical changes: Benny Goodman was now guilty of a 'detestable clarinet style', his intonation was cold, his sonority saccharine, 'especially when compared to the tonal quality of Jimmie Noone, Omer Simeon or Milton Mesirow'. Mezz, in fact, had become almost the only white jazzman worthy of serious consideration.

These revised views, appearing in Panassié's book *The Real Jazz* in 1942, may have offered some consolation to Mezz, who was then serving a two-year prison sentence in New York for selling pot. After his return to civilian life, while he was running his shortlived King Jazz Record company and giving Bernard Wolfe the material for *Really the Blues*, our paths seldom crossed; we were on opposite sides of a barrier that had been erected in the jazz world.

Visiting Nice with a small group in 1948, Mezz became more and more enamoured of France, where Panassié and others took him seriously as a musician. Not surprisingly, he settled there in the early 1950s.

I saw Mezz and Mae for the last time during a visit to Paris, where, though separated for several years, they both lived, Mae working for a record company, Mezz playing the same old funky blues in a dank cellar cave, the Trois Maillets. By then Milton Mesirow Jr, born in New York, was twenty-three years old. Mae informed me that to Mezz's horror, the youngster had learned to play bebop trombone.

Mezz died in Paris at seventy-two. Mae also died in Paris, too soon and too young. Looking back, I remember the plaintive sound of those two clarinets awaiting the dawn, and Mae's fine home cooking, and the night when they came to see me embark on the *Aquitania* after my second visit to New York.

Leaving on that occasion was an even harder wrench. With Mezz and Mae were Arthur Karle, a tenor saxophonist, and my attractive New York companion, Geraldine Stroback. They knew how I felt about returning to a homeland where, because of a musicians' union ban, no American orchestra could visit us; where because of public apathy no genuine British jazz orchestra existed; and where it was almost impossible to convince anyone in the media – newspapers, magazines or radio – that jazz was a music of artistic value and possibly even commercially viable.

Fortunately, though, an event in the months to come would brighten the domestic scene and launch me on a stimulating new phase of my life in music.

BENNY

'*Vive la France!* From across the Channel every alternate Sunday night come the strains of music provided by Benny Carter, who is now playing sax, clarinet and trumpet, and arranging, with Willie Lewis's orchestra, the leading coloured band in Paris, at the Chez Florence nightclub. A great gang, vastly improved by the Carter orchestrations and solos.'

This item, in my 'New York Amsterdam News' column for 16 November 1935, was written before my second New York expedition. Soon after I returned, an idea occurred to me. Benny Carter, whose work I knew well through recordings he had made in New York over the years, would not be permitted to play in England, but what could stop him from entering the country as an arranger? And why not, say, with some firmly established group such as Henry Hall's BBC Dance Orchestra?

Impulsively I called Henry Hall, who seemed receptive. Spike Hughes, for whom Carter had assembled an orchestra to record Hughes's music in New York, called with an enthusiastic endorsement. I wrote to Carter and received, promptly, an expression of interest. A streamer headline in a February 1936 *Melody Maker* announced: 'Benny Carter May Become Orchestrator to Henry Hall'. Within days a deal was set; on 18 March I was at Victoria Station to greet a pipe-smoking young man, beginning what was to become a lifelong friendship.

Carter's arrival coincided with a plan in which I had become involved to start a new label in England, reviving the long-familiar Vocalion label, to issue some of the recordings by Teddy Wilson, Billie Holiday, Artie Shaw and others that had been in short supply in the UK. Carter and the record company worked fast; he was signed to an immediate contract (recordings presented no problem, provided he gave work to English musicians and made no public appearances) and made a deal with a music publisher for six compositions. Within nine days of his arrival, the first Carter arrangement for Henry Hall was on the air.

The dual importance of Carter's presence, for me, was that I learned more about music from him, quite informally, than I had from any other musician, and that, assigned to supervise his recordings, I enjoyed my baptism as an A & R man (known nowadays by the more pretentious title of producer).

In a country as thoroughly starved of authentic jazz as England, every move by Carter made a *Melody Maker* headline and even leaked into the general press. For his first session he made his debut as a tenor saxophonist, in his own elegiac ballad 'Nightfall'. Accompanying him was a group of Britain's best, a dozen capable musicians, with Ted Heath seated in the brass section.

We made six sessions with various large and small groups during Benny's sojourns in London, the last in early 1937. Because of labour-permit restrictions, he could remain in England only for a few months at a time.

Probably the best remembered session is a quartet date that produced the first recording of 'When Lights are Low', today Carter's best-known standard (Elisabeth Welch was the vocalist), and, more provocatively, 'Waltzing the Blues', which created a furore in the music press.

The conviction that jazz could be played in 3/4 time, first expressed in my 1933 letter to the *Melody Maker*, had remained an obsession. When I suggested to Benny that we try a blues in waltz time, he took to the concept immediately. The rhythm section had no problem dealing with a metre that was, as Benny himself put it, 'almost a more natural swing feeling than four'.

For the record we used long metre, i.e. a twenty-four-bar blues chorus. Benny played admirable solos on tenor, alto and trumpet, with solo interludes by the black American pianist Gene Rodgers, who was visiting London as half of the comedy team of Radcliffe and Rodgers, and by another American, the guitarist Bernard Addison, in town accompanying the Mills Brothers. We made two takes, both improvised from start to finish.

'REVOLUTION IN JAZZ!' was a typical headline when the controversial experiment was released. Predictably, most of the reviews were sceptical, some uncompromisingly negative. The *Melody Maker*'s anonymous writer known as 'Pick-Up' pompously observed: 'This is all very exciting, but if it is to be seriously regarded as a dance record, it fails, miserably.' But another review in the same paper began: 'Benny Carter has started something which others were either too scared or too unobservant to start.'

The most violent indictments were those of Spike Hughes, the British composer who doubled as a critic for the *Melody Maker*, and John Hammond. Writing in *Rhythm*, Hammond called the recording affected and clever 'in the most odious sense of the word . . . the blues is simple folk music, far too pure for defilement at the hands of sophisticates'.

Spike Hughes's comments are the most amusing of all in retrospect. ' "Waltzing the Blues",' he wrote, 'has as much prospect of posterity as a mule.'

So much for critical foresight.

The aftermath is curious. Another twenty years would elapse before jazz in 3/4 time became less than eyebrow-raising. Not until 1957 was there an all-waltz album, recorded and partly written by Max Roach.

In the long interim there had been to my knowledge only six other attempts to break the metre barrier: 'Jammin' the Waltz' by my own all-star jam band, with Bobby Hackett, Pete Brown and Joe Marsala, recorded in New York in 1938; Fats Waller's 'Jitterbug Waltz' in 1942 (surprisingly, this raised hardly a ripple; the tune did not enjoy general use in jazz circles until the 1960s); a short movement in Ellington's 'Black, Brown and Beige', Mary Lou Williams' 'Waltz Boogie', on a date I made for RCA in 1946; my own 'Bebop Waltz', written for an Eddie Shu session in 1949 and better known when it was issued on a Mercer LP as 'Waltzing the Blues'; a Neal Hefti arrangement of 'Tenderly' in three, for Woody Herman (Capitol, 1949); and in 1952 Thelonious Monk's arrangement of a 1928 pop waltz, 'Carolina Moon'.

Though the Carter record stimulated interest in Benny's series of British recordings, he had not intended to trigger a controversy. All the recordings made during his English incumbencies were grounded, like everything else he has done, in uncompromising musicianship. A few weeks after his arrival in London, having spent enough time with him to observe the man behind the music, I wrote an appraisal for the *Melody Maker*:

On a first meeting he appears quiet – almost unduly reserved, but as you get to know him the quality wears off completely.

There is neither conceit nor false modesty in Benny, but there is an animated conversationalist with a gift of sarcasm so subtle that sometimes you are unaware of it; and he is good company anywhere, being possessed of the ability to mix with success in the most sharply contrasted elements of society.

Fifty years later, these observations still hold good.

Benny eventually was allowed to play publicly, in a totally successful *Melody Maker*-sponsored concert at the London Hippodrome in January 1937, with an all-British band that included two black sidemen. After trips to Holland and France, he was back in London in May, seeking out talent for an orchestra he was to present during a three-month summer engagement in Scheveningen, Holland.

The history books have generally ignored the fact that it was Benny Carter, rather than Benny Goodman, who had the first interracial and international jazz orchestra. This was also several months before Mezzrow's ill-fated mixed-band venture in New York. Benny's twelve men included American and West Indian black musicians, along with whites. Perhaps the most important discovery was George Chisholm, a young trombonist from Glasgow whom Benny and I heard playing in a funky underground room called the Nest.

That summer I was dispatched to Holland to record this band, at The Hague. We did four tunes with the full band; for the second session I made a trip to Amsterdam to persuade Coleman Hawkins to take part. He was reluctant at first to appear in what nominally was a sideman role, though Benny assured me that there was no sense of competition between the two of them. Hawkins, in any case, did consent, and we cut four more numbers, using Carter, Hawkins, Chisholm, the clarinettist and tenor saxophonist Jimmy Williams and Benny's rhythm section. Recorded on this date was 'Mighty Like the Blues', the first composition I wrote on which I can look back neither in anger nor shame.

With Benny no longer available, the outlook for producing any meaningful jazz records in England seemed bleak. In May I had assembled a small group, using the device of turning two traditional English songs, 'John Peel' and 'There's a Tavern in the Town', into jazz vehicles. The results were only fair, not that the material was unsuitable (the songs, after all, were based on chord patterns that could just as well have had jazz origins), but mainly because there were no outstanding soloists. The following year Harry Sarton, an amiable executive at Decca, allowed me to try again. The results were superior, thanks to the presence of the West Indian musicians Dave Wilkins on trumpet and Bertie King on tenor (King had played in Benny Carter's band in Holland). On 'Early One Morning' I replaced Will Solomon at the piano to play the theme in what still sounds like a reasonable attempt at prehistoric blues-funk.

A problem we had all faced in England was that, despite the presence of a few genuinely talented jazz soloists, their artistry was largely hidden in commercial dance bands. Most notably, the American Danny Polo, though given limited opportunities as a soloist with Ambrose, had never been allowed to stretch out on a combo date of his own.

After presenting the idea to Polo, to Sarton at Decca and a few potential sidemen, I arranged to put together a seven-piece group, billed as 'Danny Polo and his Swing Stars', among whom were the Scotsmen Tommy McQuater on trumpet and Eddie Macauley on piano. An enthusiastic headline writer for the *Melody Maker* billed the first release ('More than Somewhat' and 'Stratton Street Strut') as 'Britain's First Real Jam Record'.

The general reaction was so favourable that three months later, in January 1938, we were able to add George Chisholm for a date with a similar group, this time with a second American on board, the guitarist Norman Brown.

Before returning to the States in 1939, Danny Polo spent a year in Paris. During that period we made what turned out to be his final session as a leader. We used a few French musicians, and brought in the extraordinary Argentinian Oscar Aleman to play a metal guitar that sounded as clear and resonant as if it were electric. It was my belief at the time that Aleman could outswing another, more famous Parisian resident of the day, Django Reinhardt. Certainly his brief appearances on the Polo date were impressive, but there would be no chance to reconfirm my conviction, since Aleman eventually returned to Argentina and to obscurity, dying there a few years ago.

On piano for this occasion we split the assignment between two Americans then resident in Paris, Garland Wilson and Una Mae Carlisle. (More about Carlisle when the role of women in jazz is discussed.)

Inevitably, George Chisholm in due course had been awarded a session of his own, produced in the autumn of 1938. Again we used McQuater and Macauley, but this time with an interesting addition in the person of Benny Winestone on clarinet and tenor sax.

Winestone was unique. With his dour face and Clark Gable ears he was visually unprepossessing. Though he looked as Jewish as a rabbi, his personality was as Scottish as a kilt; he was, in fact, the son of a cantor in Glasgow, with a broad Scottish accent that never left him even after he settled in Canada.

There was always something at once appealing and pathetic about Benny Winestone. He was a fair musician whose taste and enthusiasm exceeded his capabilities. He had a few good credits, first with the British dance band of Sidney Lipton, later with Maynard Ferguson and a few others in Canada, and all too briefly in the United States with the shortlived Jess Stacy orchestra in 1945.

A legal problem, supposedly due to a pot arrest in Canada, prevented him from settling in the States. This was a source of enduring grief to him. His visits to New York, and later to California where Benny Carter and I last saw him, were brief and fleeting, marred by financial problems.

As a fan, he always kept up with the times, idolizing Charlie Parker and listening to every new development up to Coltrane; but the last we heard of him was a report of continued ill health, of day jobs, and of his death in Toronto in 1974. Loquacious and likable, he was such a classic example of a failed artist that over the years 'poor Benny' came to sound like a single word.

Winestone played well on the Chisholm session, but Chisholm clearly dominated with his Teagarden-inspired solos. By now Benny Carter was convinced that the trombonist was Britain's foremost jazz soloist. Typically, Benny kept in touch with Chisholm and with several other friends he had made during his time in England. More than thirty years later, Benny persuaded Dick Gibson to invite Chisholm to one of his annual jazz parties in Colorado. Chisholm came, conquered, and was invited back repeatedly. I had seen him only once during the long interim, when he took part in the London segment of my international overdub album, *One World Jazz*, in 1959, for Columbia; this enabled Chisholm to play fours with J. J. Johnson, though they had never met.

Recording such men as Chisholm, Polo and Winestone was rewarding to me in the sense that it helped me to bring attention to artists who had been held back in their careers by circumstances unrelated to their talent; still, there was little in it financially for any of us and, worse, there were none of the expected consequences such as special nightclub engagements for these small groups. The sessions I had made were, in fact, dead ends.

It was in 1938 that I made two important steps, both destined to become signposts: the production of my first American record session, and the first tentative steps towards settling in New York. By now it had become clear that Britain was a musical blind alley and America represented the only way out.

SESSIONS AND EXCURSIONS

The month of March, 1938, was singularly eventful and auspicious. In addition to producing my first New York record date I was present at four others during a two-week period there; soon afterwards I flew to Chicago to confer with Glenn Burrs and Carl Cons of *Down Beat* about the possibility of becoming their New York correspondent. The magazine at that time had a basic Chicago orientation, with no representative in New York to supply regular news or feature coverage. Though they never offered a firm commitment, I convinced myself that the deal was as good as set.

No less promising were the results of my date, which had been arranged through the intercession of my friend Al Brackman at the Irving Mills office. Again I used the 'Ye Olde English Swynge Band' premise that had served me in London, but when the records were heard at the Mills office, the emphasis shifted, for I had again attempted a 3/4 experiment, this time using the title 'Jamming the Waltz'.

A press release quoted me as complaining that:

Jazz has been handicapped for too long by the limitations of a strict 4/4 metre. Swing music depends more on the inflections and expressions of the notes played, upon the use of syncopation and ingenious phrasing, and upon the Negro scale with the flatted third, than upon any particular time signature. When I suggested this idea at the session, the musicians took to it as naturally as if they had been doing it for years.

This was no exaggeration. I suggested an opening line to Bobby Hackett, based (as in the Benny Carter record) on a twenty-four-bar blues pattern. Pete Brown, with his good-humoured, ebullient alto, and Joe Marsala playing warm, Jimmy Noone-inspired clarinet, rounded out the front line. The rhythm section consisted of other musicians I had met along 52nd Street: Joe Bushkin, then twenty-one; a guitarist named Ray Biondi, who for the waltz doubled on violin; George Wettling and Artie Shapiro.

'Jamming the Waltz' was released coupled with 'My Darling Clementine'. The other two numbers had particularly delighted me, since I had set loose the manic scat vocalist Leo Watson, whom I had heard at the Onyx with the Spirits of Rhythm. The Columbia corporate masterminds decided these were 'too uncommercial' for release; fortunately Milt Gabler, disagreeing, took over 'For He's a Jolly Good Fellow' and 'Let's Get Happy' (based on 'Happy Birthday') and issued them on Commodore.

On the day after my own session I was invited to attend a Fats Waller recording at the RCA studios. I had known him since 1935, when I spent Christmas Day with Thomas (as his wife and intimates called him) on the outskirts of Harlem, sharing his 'libations' and hearing him try out a new piano. Now he was surrounded by his regular group, with Herman Autrey on trumpet, Gene Sedric on tenor and clarinet, Al Casey on guitar, Slick Jones on drums and Cedric Wallace on bass.

I had heard rumours that Fats recorded with the aid of a bottle of gin on either side of the piano. The myth was promptly dispelled: his requirements, I noticed, were a foxy young lady on one side and a bottle of brandy on the other.

Thus inspired, Fats began working his way through the piano copies of several songs perched on his Steinway grand. The combo now began rehearsing 'Lost and Found'. None of the happy abandon that characterized the typical Waller recordings could be found in the studio atmosphere. Musicians sat around quietly, talking only to check details of Waller's hastily sketched routines for the songs – all of them inferior pop tunes, unfamiliar to all the musicians, who were provided with skeleton parts consisting mainly of the chord changes.

Fats was faced with the tough task of reading the music and lyrics simultaneously. Autrey and Sedric shared one microphone, with Wallace just behind them while Casey and Slick Jones shared a mike of their own. The records, of course, were cut on wax masters.

The men ran through a single chorus. 'One thirty,' said Fats. 'That means we can stand about two choruses.' Again they played a chorus, and on arriving at the last measure, Fats called out, 'Take it, Sedric!' Within ten minutes a master had been made.

'Cigarettes!' called Fats, taking another swig of the rapidly diminishing brandy. 'Now watch out for that second chorus. In that last part I want it solid. No variations, no flowery embellishments, nothing.'

They tried it.

'Yeah, that's what I'm talking 'bout!'

Everything moved quietly and swiftly. On the next tune a voice from the control room said, 'Stick to the melody as much as possible, Fats, on your first chorus,' and then, as tactfully as possible: 'Is that your last bottle?'

'No,' Fats said, emptying it. 'This is my first.'

A playback was made. Fats commented, 'It needs a little more punch.' Next time, the rhythm section relaxed and a good master was made, with a humorous comment by Fats tagged on at the end. This was his trademark; he improvised a different remark on each take of every tune.

Then came an impasse. 'You Went to My Head', an oddly constructed song, had a twenty-five-bar chorus that baffled Waller. Time and again he tried it, then threw the copy aside. 'No time to learn that one,' he said. (Later on in the session, however, he did return to it and made a master.)

Next came 'If You're a Viper'. Sedric and Autrey worked out an engaging riff; Fats played celeste with his right hand, accompanying himself at the piano with his left.

We could all see that 'If You're a Viper' was going to be a knockout. All of us, that is, except the voice of commercial pragmatism in the control booth. To appease Waller, a wax was made of it, after which another pop tune was insisted upon. Fats struggled through it, with such difficulty that he did not even attempt to play piano during his vocal.

A week later I called Fats to check on 'Viper'. I was told that the master had been destroyed and that the pop song would be used. (The objection to 'Viper' presumably was grounded in the fact that a viper was common parlance in those days for a reefer smoker.)

Fats Waller resented the controls that were exerted over his musical and private life. He once told me that the wild times he had had were a direct outcome of the restrictions imposed on him in childhood.

'My father was a minister,' he said. 'He thought it was

outrageous to spend an evening at a dance hall. So as soon as I was
old enough to go for myself, I went right out and did all the things
I'd been held back from doing. Oh, the trouble I had in those early
days!

'I was playing organ at one of those silent movie houses in
Harlem, and they'd be playing some death scene on the screen, and
as likely as not I'd grab a bottle and start swingin' out on 'Squeeze
Me' or 'Royal Garden Blues'. The managers used to send
complaints, but shit, they couldn't stop me!'

Just a week after the Waller encounter, John Hammond invited
me to a session, the importance of which totally eluded me at the
time. I was told that the products of this date would be released
under the name 'Eddie Durham and his Base [*sic*] Four', and
certainly Durham was the central figure, but the title eventually
decided on was the Kansas City Five.

Durham's career was unique. He had four brothers who all
played various instruments; in 1918, before he was thirteen, he had
begun working professionally as a guitarist, and very shortly
afterwards doubled on trombone, in the Durham Brothers Orchestra in and around San Antonio, Texas. His entire career had
consisted of this unlikely double, coupled with composing and
arranging. During two years with Jimmie Lunceford he had begun
to experiment with ways of enhancing the guitar's sound, and very
soon bought one of the first electric guitars.

The Count Basie band, of which Durham was now a member,
provided the personnel for this session, with Buck Clayton, Freddie
Green, Walter Page and Jo Jones. There was no piano, and much of
the interest centred on the fact that Durham was featured as a
soloist on electric guitar. I was an earwitness to a precedent that
would have a tremendous impact on jazz and, a few decades later,
on rock; yet at the time, as the musicians quietly went through their
paces, this simply seemed like a relaxed small-combo gathering.
Durham was never accorded the recognition for his initiative; it has
often been stated in the documentation of jazz history that Charlie
Christian was the 'father of the electric guitar'. Christian was a
vastly more original soloist, but it was Durham who paved the way.

Only a few more days elapsed before I was at another session, the
importance of which did *not* escape me. Gene Krupa had left Benny
Goodman to start his own band; after Lionel Hampton filled in
briefly, Dave Tough had moved in as the replacement, and this was
to be his first session with the Goodman Quartet.

A few nights earlier, Goodman had told me: 'This is going to be the greatest thing we've ever done!' As the four men sat in the RCA studio discussing what tunes should be played, Benny showed little excitement beyond the typical puckering of his lips in a half-hidden grin. Tough looked forlorn, as he so often did; Lionel was jubilantly warming up on his vibes, and Teddy Wilson sat quietly, though a hint of excitement was detectable in his normally immobile manner.

After a few minutes of trying out a few standards, Benny said: 'How about this? What's it called? I can't remember the title. Anyway, let's make it.'

The tune was 'Sweet Lorraine', due for establishment as a jazz standard when Nat Cole recorded it a couple of years later. One trio cut was made, with Benny transferring his mouthpiece to an A clarinet and Lionel standing by.

Since it involved the hazard of taking everyone into some awkward keys, the A clarinet was laid aside and Lionel joined in, ad libbing on the blues. Tough, frail and silent, he looked straight ahead, motionless except for the slight movement of hands and feet as he conjured up an easy beat with his brushes.

'Hey,' said Goodman, 'that's a thought. Why not make a blues?'

Teddy Wilson took a bite out of a huge sandwich, pushed his hat a little further back on his head, and played gently, as if to himself. When the buzzer gave the cue to start, Benny leaned back on his chair, which remained in this position, on its hind legs, throughout the recording.

The first take went well, but Hampton suggested fixing up a definite melody for the first chorus, on which he and Benny could blend. Lionel's excitement was contagious, then as now. 'Yeah, yeah, yeah! That's it, Benny! Man, I could play the blues all day long!'

The next take came off so well, and found everyone so completely at ease, that Benny decided this was not enough for one day. I remarked to him, 'I wish you could make a fifteen-inch blues.' He replied: 'Well, why don't we make two sides? And let's have Lionel sing. I'll have them get a balance on his voice.'

Lionel's mind was a maze of all the blues lyrics he had ever heard. Sorting them out, he came up with a couple that seemed comfortable: one that began, 'Mama, mama, why do you treat me so?' and the long-familiar, 'Give me back that wig I bought you. . .' For good measure I dreamed up another: 'If my gal cried whisky instead of salt-water tears, I would never be sober for another twenty-five years.' 'Solid!' said Hamp. 'Let's put that in too!'

Within twenty minutes, two perfect takes had gone on wax. Benny was so inspired by Tough's support that he burst into a profusion of uncharacteristic compliments, which Tough accepted with modest reluctance.

'How about this for the next number?' said Benny, running through the first few bars of 'Sugar'. Everyone seemed satisfied with the choice and 'Sugar' was promptly dealt with.

'Four tunes in two and a half hours!' said Goodman with a quick smile. 'We have time to try out that tune of Lionel's, "Dizzy Spells".'

This was a complex piece by the standards of those days, involving a series of scales in descending thirds which even Goodman, with his limitless technique, had some trouble negotiating. He ran it over at least a dozen times before announcing himself ready for a take.

Goodman has often been characterized as a difficult and eccentric man; that was how he was seen by the music publishers, song pluggers and assorted sycophants who courted his goodwill. On a record session, though, and particularly in such compatible company, he seemed warm, human and as relaxed as I had ever seen him.

There was still another event at which I was a witness during that hectic month, but the memory has faded, principally because it was scarcely worth recalling. Bunny Berigan was at the RCA studios cutting a date with his band. All three tunes were trivial pop items, with vocals by Gail Reese. One, 'Downstream', proved so troublesome that Berigan seemed incapable of completing a take. I left, and heard later that forty-two masters had been used before 'Downstream' finally stopped floating.

This had been the most eventful and educational of all my visits to New York, providing me with enough material for a series of BBC broadcasts, features for the *Melody Maker* and various other publications, and friendships that were renewed when a couple of important visitors came to London that summer. On 19 July 1938, the *Daily Express* reported:

BENNY GOODMAN HIDES FROM BRITISH FANS

BENNY GOODMAN, £2,000-a-week king of swing and head-man of all the jitterbugs, crept into London last week looking fearfully bronzed and tired and timid . . . He jumped aboard the *Normandie* at the last minute with two suitcases he carried himself . . . To dodge the rush he caught the second boat train to Waterloo . . . Music publisher Jimmy Green said hello, but swing fan Leonard Feather said nothing, bundling the swing king into the oldest taxi in sight, driving off with him to visit friends.

Goodman's life this past year has been a mad kaleidoscope of flatfoot floogies (rabid jitterbugs, ma'am) and floy-floys (rabid jitterbugs in the process of enthusing at a swing passage). Mr Goodman has left his clarinet, at which he is an acknowledged world master, at home.

Less retiring than Benny Goodman was Fats Waller who, having qualified as an entertainer, was allowed to work in Britain, though he could not bring his musicians along.

Fats arrived in Glasgow after a week-long voyage, then headed for London, opening at the Palladium on 8 August. At first it seemed improbable that he would be able to record in England, not only because his substantial American sales had made him a high-priced performer, but also because of the absence of his band.

With considerable help from his genial manager, Ed Kirkeby, I managed to persuade the HMV executives that a suitable British 'jam band' could be assembled. A date was set, 21 August at the Abbey Road Studios. Rounding up the band turned out to be a tougher assignment than I had expected. David Wilkins, the trumpeter with Ken Johnson's band, rushed home from Glasgow and left immediately after the session for another date with Johnson.

George Chisholm seemed indispensable, but I was told he was on his honeymoon, in Jersey, where I reached him by phone.

'George, I really need you badly for a record date.'

'Sorry, man – impossible! I'm on my honeymoon.'

'George, it's with Fats Waller.'

'Ah . . . let me check the timetables. What time do we start?'

The rest of the job was easier: two tenor players, one doubling on

And Six of the latest masterpieces by "FATS" WALLER

Organ Records.

Water Boy (Convict Song) } and Lonesome Road.   **B 8845**   3 –

Swing low, sweet chariot. } All God's chillun got wings.   **B 8818**   3 –

Deep River. } Go down Moses.   **B 8816**   3 –

Piano.

Alligator crawl. } Viper's drag.   **B 8784**   3 –

I ain't got nobody. } Basin Street Blues.   **B 8636**   3 –

Beat it out. } Lost and Found (both with Orchestra).   **BD 5377**   2 –

"HIS MASTER'S VOICE"

Happiest picture ever taken! "Fats" Waller with a pair of "H.M.V." Portable Radios at the Studios.

"His Master's Voice"

clarinet, the other on violin; the Scottish guitarist Alan Ferguson, the West Indian drummer Edmundo Ros, and Len Harrison on bass.

I noticed that during the session Fats, though exuberant as always, took care of business a little more meticulously than he had in New York. Although he again used pop songs, they were his own choices. After the fourth number was wrapped up we adjourned to another studio where he played the pipe organ on a new version of 'Ain't Misbehavin' ' and the song I had written with him in mind, 'Don't Try Your Jive on Me', with easy blowing changes that gave both Waller and Chisholm a chance to shine.

'That organ,' he said later, 'reminded me of the Wurlitzer Grand I used to play at the Lincoln in Harlem. I had a ball! This session came easy.' He wound up cutting six organ solos of spirituals and two numbers accompanying Adelaide Hall.

Only two weeks after the Waller session, there was heartening news from Al Brackman: 'Mighty Like the Blues' had been recorded by Duke Ellington.

It was deceptively encouraging to have started at the top, with my first song of any consequence recorded by both Carter and Ellington; and I began soon to convince myself that life in America would not be intolerably difficult, and that when I made my move, the help of men like Ellington would play a crucial role.

Meanwhile, there were enough assignments to keep me busy: along with columns for *Melody Maker, Rhythm, Radio Times*, and the Swedish magazine *Estrad*, I had become the British correspondent for *Metronome* and more recently started a series of features for a new American publication that had cashed in on America's new craze by calling itself *Swing*.

Just before leaving for New York again in April 1939, I took part in a concert designed to introduce the Heralds of Swing, a ten-piece band I had helped to assemble, which the musicians and I innocently hoped could become Britain's first regularly organized jazz ensemble. The membership was drawn from the ranks of Ambrose's orchestra and other well-established groups: there were Dave Shand, Benny Winestone and Norman Maloney on saxes; an all-Scottish rhythm section with Archie Craig and Tommy McQuater on trumpets and George Chisholm on trombone; Bert Barnes, pianist and arranger; Sid Colin, guitar; Tiny Winters, bass, and George Firestone, drums.

The guest artists for this concert, and their billings, were: Fats

Waller ('World's Greatest Pianist and Master of Swing'), Adelaide Hall ('Swing Star from America'), Syd Phillips ('Noted Arranger and Composer'), Don and Jimmy Macaffer ('Scottish Brass Aces'), George Shearing ('Sensational Blind Pianist'), Billy Amstell ('Star Tenor Solist' [*sic*]), the Radio Revellers ('Novelty Vocal Quartette') and myself ('Gramophone Recital'). The MCs were Sam Browne and the American songwriter Eddie Pola.

The Heralds of Swing managed to land a gig at the Paradise, a well-publicized late-night rendezvous; but problems soon arose. Most of the men had conflicting and more lucrative jobs elsewhere. The band was theoretically a co-operative; my involvement was mainly that of a cheerleader and organizer, but the whole project soon fell apart; in fact, it was disintegrating during my absence, for a few days after the concert I was New York-bound again.

This time I assembled a different and stronger all-star band, for a date at Decca. Benny Carter and Pete Brown both doubled on alto sax and trumpet; Bobby Hackett played guitar on three tunes but picked up his cornet for the fourth; the pianist Billy Kyle, from John Kirby's elegant sextet, Benny's bassist Hayes Alvis and the superb drummer Cozy Cole completed the group.

During April and May I travelled a little, visiting Washington to catch Basie, then Lunceford, at the Howard Theatre, that city's counterpart of the Apollo. Again I flew to Chicago for a conference at *Down Beat*. The news was now more promising, though no firm date was named: 'Probably around the first of the year,' I was told. This meant that I had until the onset of 1940 to prepare my family. I had shielded them (even my sister, to whom I was close) from my plans, and from my involvement with a woman several years my senior with whom I had an affair in New York, and who had come to visit me in London. I knew they would approve neither of my desire to live 3,000 miles away nor of my girlfriend. She wasn't even Jewish, for God's sake.

My next relationship, brief and innocent though it was, would have struck them as doubly dubious: she wasn't even white, for God's sake. In London during June and July I caught the Dandridge Sisters' show at the Palladium and one night, at a club called Elma Warren's Nut House, met them: Dorothy and Vivian Dandridge, sixteen and seventeeen years old, protected by a chaperone who was on hand to preserve their virginity and keep them out of the clutches of predatory males; and a third girl, unrelated, Etta Jones (not the Etta Jones whom I would later record in New York).

Vivian and I found an immediate affinity. Somehow she was permitted to go out with me, and we spent a series of pleasant evenings together which we felt, in our self-deceiving way, were romantic. This was not hard to understand, at least from my point of view. I had felt isolated from the girls of my own social group: the nice, middle-class Jewish types who thought alike, acted alike, married alike. They had nothing to say to me, nor I to them. Vivian and I had something in common immediately – music – and mutual friends.

One night, after dinner at what may have been London's only Chinese restaurant, in Piccadilly Circus, Vivian and I organized a party at my Holborn studio as a farewell to Coleman Hawkins, who was due to leave in a few days for New York after five years in Europe. Among the guests were two or three of the already moribund Heralds of Swing; two of the Mills Brothers and their guitarist, Norman Brown; Dorothy Dandridge and Etta Jones; Ken Johnson and his trumpeter Dave Wilkins; and Coleman.

We were high more on the music than on liquor, though Coleman drank enough for all of us. I had a primitive acetate recorder on which we cut a few sides, none of which I had the sense to preserve.

Not long after the party, when the Dandridges had to go on tour, I decided to explore the Continent for a few weeks of music- and pleasure-hunting. I had not the remotest idea, when I left for Paris on that Bank Holiday weekend, that this would be the last I would see of England for almost exactly eight years.

PART TWO

Transitions

TRANSITION

Paris had been familiar territory since my summer there in 1932, followed by several briefer visits. It was still 'Gay Paree' and the source of musical and social satisfaction. In one evening I found time to drop in at the Swing Club, Frisco's, Fred Payne's and one or two other hot spots. The next afternoon I was strolling along the Place Blanche in the intense midsummer heat when I ran into Django Reinhardt and Charles Delaunay at a sidewalk cafe, and joined them for a *chocolat glacé*.

'Hey,' said Django, 'we'll see you soon. The quintet is going to London; we'll be making a record session there.'

'What date?'

'Oh, in a couple of weeks.'

'Well, maybe I'll see you, maybe not. I'm sort of ad libbing it over here.'

None of us could have guessed that a week after the record date (with a fourteen-year-old English girl, Beryl Davis, as vocalist), the original Quintette du Hot Club de France would be disbanded for ever.

The next day I ran into two friends who were driving up to Deauville. Accepting their invitation to join them I went along and continued with them to Knocke, in Belgium, and to Ostend, where I looked up Willie Lewis, whose band was no longer the illustrious group of stars he had led in the Benny Carter days.

A day or two later I sailed from Dunkirk to Esbjerg, and a few hours later was in Copenhagen, where I had spent some agreeable times with Baron Timme Rosenkrantz, the Danish nobleman, nicknamed 'the Barrelhouse Baron', and with Svend Asmussen, the young dentist turned violinist, whose performance at a London Rhythm Club session had convinced me that Stéphane Grappelli was not alone in Europe.

From Copenhagen it was a short haul to Stockholm, where my friend Nils Hellstrom, editor of *Estrad*, introduced me to some promising Swedish sounds. To wind up my vacation I wanted to relax at a seaside resort. Nils suggested Hälsingborg, Sweden. 'It's a lovely place directly across a narrow sound from here, so you can go back and forth as much as you like; and I'll give you the names of some musicians who are working there.'

The night after my arrival in Hälsingborg, the newspapers reported the Nazi–Soviet pact. The shock was not easy to shrug off, yet somehow, in the euphoric unreality of that summer, we convinced ourselves that a solution would be reached and Poland saved. All through my travels this feeling had prevailed; Hitler, I kept hearing, could be held off for another year or two.

After a few days' swimming and dining with the friends to whom Hellstrom had steered me, I was awakened at 8 a.m. when my hotel-room telephone rang. A party of us had been to a late movie the night before; I was surprised to be awakened so early.

It was a Swedish musician who had been at the movie.

'That was fun last night.'

'Sure was,' I agreed.

'Did you know,' he said, 'it is a war?'

'What?'

'War. *Krig*. It has begun.'

'Who told you?'

'The porter. He just heard it on the radio. What time will you be ready to come to the beach?'

The paradox of his transition from world-shaking news to such mundane matters seemed absurd, but I threw on a robe and hurried downstairs, where fantasy became reality as I looked at a single-sided sheet of newsprint, a local daily with huge black letters across the top: 'Krig!', followed by a belligerent Hitler declamation.

Within hours I learned that the North Sea was cut off; so was all telephone communication outside the country, though I was able to contact my parents by cable. What were my options, assuming I had any? Possibly I could be stranded in Sweden indefinitely. I had a chequebook, precious few clothes, no job here, no place to turn. Moreover, this was a country whose language I did not speak.

The next week was a nightmare of indecision, of inquiries at a travel agency, of hasty consultations by phone with Nils who, hearing I had trouble getting a cheque cashed, promptly sent me enough money to tide me over for a while. Then word came that one ship was due to sail, from Gothenburg – the *Drottningholm*, leaving 12 September for New York. I managed to secure passage and a train ticket north.

The journey to Gothenburg, and the ten-day crossing, constituted an interim of strangely mixed emotions: anxiety, guilt, fear, uncertainty and a sense of anticipation. The anxiety was compounded of concern for my family and personal fear, since there were rumours that the ocean might be mined. Guilt, obviously, since I was not returning to a country now at war. Later it was reported in a couple of publications that I 'left England when the war broke out'. They could have checked the facts, but presumably did not take the trouble. On the other hand, since so few people had known about my plans (the editors at *Down Beat*, Adrian De Haas and Coleman Hawkins), they could hardly be blamed for assuming that the move to the States was not a two-year-old project but an immediate result of the outbreak of hostilities.

Complicating the situation during the early days was the so-called 'phony war'. When I was at last able to find a British radio report, it appeared that Poland had lost just as many lives as if England and France had not declared war; it was seemingly a shadow war on the part of the Allies, and when Germany and Russia had ground Poland underfoot, Hitler might well talk about peace, Chamberlain might capitulate and it could be over in a couple of weeks. Most of England's activities seemed to have consisted of dropping millions of leaflets on the German people. Some of my Swedish friends shared this belief, but the atmosphere of uncertainty prevailed, both in Sweden and aboard the *Drottningholm*.

The crossing was like nothing I had experienced. The first day out, my twenty-fifth birthday, was 13 September; this was my thirteenth crossing of the Atlantic, and during lifeboat drill I was assigned to Station No. 13. The ship was crowded to double capacity. News bulletins were few and confusing. The only good news was that we encountered no mines. During those ten days I thought often about my mother, father, sister, relatives, about all the bonds of friendship with so many people in England; where and when would I see them again?

If the 'phony war' turned out to be real, how soon would America be involved, and how soon would I be called up for service? (As it turned out, when the time came for my physical in New York, I flunked it.) What would happen to the music world under wartime

conditions? To George Chisholm, Dave Wilkins and my other
musician friends? The questions were endless.

When we docked in New York at 5.30 p.m. on Friday 22
September, I was able, by picking up the tabloid *Daily News*, to
flesh out my information on a world with which I had been almost
totally out of touch.

During the days and weeks that followed I tried to concentrate on
the mundane matters of everyday life in New York, rather than
brood about events in England and Poland. Trivial though it
seemed to concern myself about who was playing where on 52nd
Street, it served no purpose to think or act as if I had any control
over the apocalyptic events thousands of miles away.

Some items of my agenda were urgent. I had arrived with a light
suit, summer underclothes, a bathing-robe, sandals and six white
shirts. It would soon be a freezing New York winter. The
immediate needs were food, clothes and shelter.

I went directly from the pier to the apartment of my arranger
friend Adrian De Haas. He could not have looked more startled if
the ghost of Bix Beiderbecke had walked in. Like Coleman
Hawkins and my friends at *Down Beat*, he had assumed that my
plans had been postponed indefinitely instead of being precipitated
by the events of early September.

Benny and Inez Carter dropped in at Adrian's to hear the story of
my arrival and the travels that had led up to it. A sense of relief
washed over me; after ten very lonely days I was once again among
friends.

The next day I went over to Coleman's home. 'Man, I didn't
expect you this soon!' he said. Coleman told me his news: he was
organizing a nine-piece band to open at Kelly's Stable on 51st
Street, and would record it for RCA's Bluebird label. He invited me
to the session; I found it a little disappointing, since the charts did
not set him off to full advantage. One number was devoted mainly
to the singer.

During this tune I left, only to find out later that at the end of the
date, caught short for material, he had ad libbed two choruses of
'Body and Soul'. Not until months later would the full significance
of this casual session-filler make its impact.

Meanwhile, Coleman offered to let me help line up a smaller, less
formal group for his next date. Among the participants were three
of our mutual friends whom we had seen not long ago in London:
Benny Carter on trumpet, Danny Polo on clarinet and Gene

Rodgers, who had played the 'Body and Soul' date, on piano. Unaware of the full meaning to his career of that exquisite ballad performance, Hawkins on this date recorded only medium- and up-tempo standards and one swinging original.

My first moves after arriving in New York had been very tentative. I found a one-room apartment available in the building at 59 West 90th Street where Adrian De Haas lived; the rent was $5 a week, and I was invited to dine nightly with the De Haases. Not surprisingly, it turned out that *Down Beat* was not quite ready for me. I made a series of stops at magazine offices, record companies and music publishers' headquarters. Everyone was friendly, but the last word was usually 'Come back next week' or 'We'll call you.'

The most genuine assistance came from John Hammond, who made several helpful phone calls and loaned me an urgently needed typewriter. At the offices of *Swing* magazine, where I met the new editor, a bright and hospitable young college graduate named Barry Ulanov, I was invited to do whatever writing I cared to, in exchange for copies of the magazine and free records.

Irving Mills came through again, offering me space at his office in the Brill Building, which was virtually Tin Pan Alley. I was free to use the phone, write songs to be published by him, and use my small room as headquarters.

Although my transplantation had come about prematurely and under undreamed-of circumstances, I had long since felt that I was less and less a product of my background, but rather of my American experiences over the last four years. All my closest friends were Americans; adapting to their attitudes and beliefs had already become a half-conscious ambition.

Because my accent set me apart among some Americans who found it a curious and perhaps amusing novelty, I lost no time in discarding it. This was not a matter of deliberately assuming the speech patterns of a New Yorker, but rather of simply falling into them as naturally as one would into an armchair.

The economic challenge of plunging into a new career was similarly less daunting than I had feared. Life in Manhattan in those days, particularly with the entrees I already had into most of the places I wanted to visit, was hardly a financial burden. A breakfast at Nedick's – orange juice, two doughnuts and coffee – cost a dime. On 52nd Street, next door to one of the jazz clubs, I found a restaurant that offered a reasonably decent steak lunch for fifty-five cents. For a nickel you could buy both the *Daily News* and the *Daily Mirror* and still have a penny left over for a stick of gum or candy.

Gradually I worked my way into some sort of schedule, spending my days at the Mills office or at *Swing*, enjoying evenings as a dinner guest at the homes of John Hammond, Billie Holiday, Edgar Sampson or Al Brackman. One evening, after a particularly pleasant dinner in the company of Benny Carter, I accompanied him to the Savoy Ballroom, where he was leading a flawless orchestra. At last I could hear him in person surrounded by a company of his peers: Bill Coleman in the trumpet section, Vic Dickenson, Jimmy Archey and Tyree Glenn on trombones, Eddie Heywood at the piano, Benny in peak form on both alto and trumpet.

During the first intermission I found Benny in conversation with a tall, slender girl. He turned to me and said: 'Have you met Louise McCarroll?' After the introduction had been made, Benny returned to the bandstand, leaving this animated, articulate young beauty in my company.

That was one occasion when Carter's orchestra became unexpectedly relegated to the role of background music. As we shared wine and found out more about one another, I learned that Louise had been a singer with Don Redman's orchestra a couple of years earlier, was an accomplished pianist and violinist, but was presently out of work and at a loose end.

After the final set ended at 2.30 a.m. I walked her along the snow-covered Lenox Avenue to the Ninth Avenue El. It turned out that she lived only a few blocks away from me just off Columbus Avenue.

Benny had inadvertently set in motion a relationship that lasted for half of the next year, one on which Louise and I looked back with nothing but pleasure, although it ended when, frustrated by the lack of work and offered a tour, she left town and we drifted apart. During the time we spent together, I learned what it was to be young, romantically attached to someone and within reach of the best music this city had to offer, whether downtown at the Onyx, Kelly's, the Hickory House, or uptown at the Savoy, the Apollo and, most particularly, the Golden Gate Ballroom.

In fact, New York in 1940 was a jazz mill the like of which I had never encountered before and never would again. The Golden Gate, on Lenox, just two blocks north of the Savoy and launched in competition with it, triggered a rivalry that brought almost every one of the great orchestras to one ballroom or the other.

One week, in an attempt to knock the Savoy out of the ring, the Golden Gate brought in a staggering line-up of five groups – I believe they were the big bands of Les Hite, Harlan Leonard, Teddy Wilson, Claude Hopkins and the Milt Herth Trio. On another evening, when the Savoy booked Duke Ellington, the Gate countered with Jimmie Lunceford. Louise and I found time to catch both, then repaired to the Brittwood, an upstairs bar next to the Savoy, where the plump and cheerful alto saxophonist Pete Brown led a lightly jumping combo.

One of the most remarkable nights we shared was the opening, at the Center Theatre in the Radio City area, of *Swingin' the Dream*, a swing version of *A Midsummer Night's Dream*, with Louis Armstrong as Bottom, Maxine Sullivan as Titania, Butterfly McQueen, Bill Bailey (Pearl's dancer brother) and a phenomenal cast of black actors and singers.

On either side of the stage, in mezzanine boxes, were two jazz groups that supplemented the Don Voorhees pit orchestra. One was the Benny Goodman Sextet with Charlie Christian, Lionel Hampton, Fletcher Henderson, Arthur Bernstein and Nick Fatool. The other was Bud Freeman's Summa Cum Laude group, with Eddie Condon, Max Kaminsky, Pee Wee Russell, Dave Bowman, Mort Stuhlmaker and Zutty Singleton.

This unique and delightful show received generally negative reviews and closed after thirteen performances in eleven days. All that remains of it is a song that still survives as a jazz standard, 'Darn that Dream'.

Bud Freeman, when I talked to him in 1986 as he neared his eightieth birthday, recalled a curious post mortem: 'There was one number for which everyone in the show wore anklets, a sort of African tribal thing with bare feet and the anklets ringing. When Voorhees's orchestra played, they drowned out this gentle sound; but on the band's night off, Benny's sextet accompanied the number. Everyone heard this unique effect of the bare feet and anklets, and there was a three-minute standing ovation. If they'd kept it that way, it could have made the show.'

During those first few months as a resident New Yorker, I was able to move to a slightly larger room on West 92nd Street, even though my rent went up from $5 to $8 a week. The *Down Beat* deal finally came through; on 9 February I presented Count Basie with a trophy on the magazine's behalf at the Golden Gate. Earlier that

week the Charlie Barnet and Coleman Hawkins bands also worked
at the Gate.

Only a few of us are still around to recall how musical and how
inspiring that big Hawkins band was. Formed on the strength of his
success with 'Body and Soul', with Coleman himself as one of the
principal arrangers, this sixteen-piece ensemble played an original
called 'Passing It Around' that might, when Bean was in the mood,
go on for ten or fifteen minutes. With its simple, gospel-flavoured
theme and with Hawkins' powerful tenor playing lead, it exemplified the kind of music that could never be captured on records in
the days of the three-minute 78-rpm disc.

The Teddy Wilson orchestra was another shortlived venture that
deserved a better fate. With arrangements by Wilson and by Buster
Harding (who also played second piano), this band was another
frequent Golden Gate visitor, its soloists (Wilson, Harold Baker,
Ben Webster, Doc Cheatham) as strong as the charts. But Teddy's
personality was too withdrawn; he simply did not have the qualities
that established Lionel Hampton so firmly and permanently.

Downtown was mainly small-combo territory; Louise and I
occasionally dropped in at Nick's in the Village to check the
two-beat action, or at the 52nd Street joints to catch the Spirits of
Rhythm or John Kirby. During all the months of our peregrinations, there was only one unpleasant incident. Woody Herman was
playing at the Famous Door, but the door was abruptly closed in
our faces. Although interracial couples were rare, as a rule they
were by now accepted, albeit sometimes reluctantly.

During this period my radio career took off again, thanks to a
good friend, Bob Bach, who moved between the worlds of jazz
journalism and radio. Under his guidance we began a weekly series
on WNEW known as 'Platterbrains', a variation on the programmes I had initiated over Radio Normandy. Listeners were asked to
send in questions about jazz records in an attempt to stump the
panel of experts. Segments of the records were played until one
panelist attempted an answer. Though the premise was frothy, it
provided a great deal of innocent entertainment while enabling us
to put on the air a great deal of music that would not otherwise have
been heard, as well as according useful exposure to our guest
panelists.

Milt Gabler and I were regulars; Bob Bach was the host. In the
first few weeks our guests included Gene Krupa, Fats Waller,
Glenn Miller, Jack Teagarden, Hazel Scott, Teddy Wilson and Red

Norvo. During our second year Count Basie recorded a Tab Smith original, which he titled 'Platterbrains', for us to use as our theme.

The show lasted for several years on local New York stations; later Bob Bach and I revived it on a more widespread scale when it went on the ABC radio network, in early 1953, lasting until late 1957. By the time 'Platterbrains' went off the air for the last time we had been hosts to almost every major living name in jazz.

There have been few periods in my adult life when I have not been on the air regularly with one programme or another. It is a medium I always found easy to handle, and a good channel of communication with a substantial audience. For some two and a half recent years, on KCRW in Santa Monica, I had a show devoted exclusively to Ellingtonia, a subject on which I was never at a loss for records or words. Presently, on the same station, I am playing a diversified programme. Of all the projects I have ever undertaken, broadcasting has always seemed least like work.

DUKE

If I were under oath and summoned to name the most cheerfully rewarding times of my career, the various periods of employment by Duke Ellington, starting in 1942, would come immediately to mind. As I told Duke many years later, it was as if I had been sent to heaven and immediately appointed special assistant to God.

The association was almost too pleasant to qualify as work. It entailed the perquisites of becoming a part of the Ellington entourage, of drawing closer to Billy 'Swee' Pea' Strayhorn, to Duke's effervescent sister Ruth and her then husband Dan James, who himself was involved with many of the Ellington activities; to Dr Arthur Logan, whose close ties of friendship with the Ellingtons transcended his official role as Duke's physician; to Mercer Ellington, with whom my association would grow even stronger in later years; and to Bea Ellis, the tall, fey, elegant woman who for the last thirty-five years of Duke's life was known as Evie Ellington, though in fact Duke and his only wife, Edna Ellington, were never divorced.

I had known Duke for a year or two before he and Evie met. Our first real encounter took place in 1936, backstage at Loew's State Theatre in New York, where I found him amiable and perspicacious, with a natural conversational ease. At that time a *cause célèbre* among jazz fans was his 'Reminiscing in Tempo', his long work that took up four sides (two 78s). Duke assured me that he attached no enormous importance to the piece, which he said was written entirely on a train during a few hurried days of one-night stands.

He was resigned to playing a certain percentage of popular songs for the Broadway crowd, and he told me, 'They think they know all about show business. If you want to make a living you have to play pop songs or whatever else may suit their requirements, because

Broadway represents the publishers, the bookers, the theatre owners, everyone who is involved in keeping the band working. And there aren't that many theatres left now that can afford to pay us our $5,500 a week.'

We talked about Duke's sixteen-year-old son Mercer, who was with us during part of the conversation. 'He plays the saxophone,' Duke said, 'but I've sent him to study at an institute of aerial technology. Mathematics and engineering are his strong subjects. I let him play, but that's just a hobby.' (Three years later Mercer, who had switched to trumpet, led his own first band.)

Another of our early meetings, at one of Duke's recording sessions, brought a tangible dividend. After the date was finished Duke was kidding around at the piano, singing a novelty song he had written called 'I Want to be a Rug Cutter'. With the brazen bravado of youth, I asked him if he would make a special copy of it for me to take home to England. Duke agreed without hesitation, asked the engineer to set up an acetate, and proceeded to sing and play his way through the number. As an added bonus, Cootie Williams, who was still in the studio and who for some reason was playing a trombone, did so for the other side of the record. As a result, on the back of 'Rug Cutter' I had the only known example of Cootie on trombone, playing the blues, with Duke at the piano.

The autographed copy of these two numbers is still the only one in existence and remains in my possession after a half-century.

By the time Duke asked me to go to work for him I had made the acquaintance of his family and everyone else close to him. Duke was the vortex around whom dozens of us moved at this crucial time in his life. The orchestra, and the music he and Strayhorn were composing for it, had reached a creative peak many of us felt was never surpassed. Even a recording ban that had kept the band out of the studios since 1 August did not seem to diminish the prevalent enthusiasm.

I had visited the orchestra in Chicago when it recorded a few sides just under the wire. Duke was playing at the Sherman Hotel. One evening, after the last set, as the men were walking off the stand, I saw Ben Webster burst into tears. He had just learned of the death at twenty-three, hours earlier in California, of Jimmy Blanton, who had been closer to him than to anyone else in the orchestra.

Despite this melancholy news there was jubilation not long afterwards in the Ellington ranks. The excitement began when

William Morris Jr, a booking agent whose concern for Ellington went beyond grosses and commissions, told him: 'I want you to write a long work, and let's do it in Carnegie Hall.'

Duke had been talking for years about an elaborate Afro-American suite, but now that Morris had thrown down the gauntlet, talk had to give way to work. A date was set, 23 January 1943, and Carnegie Hall, where only Benny Goodman had presented a recital by a genuine jazz orchestra, was made available because it was arranged to stage the concert as a benefit for Russian War Relief. (The Soviet Union was our ally and Senator Joseph McCarthy was not yet looming on the horizon.)

As a small cog in Duke's organizational wheel, I was like an overgrown kid in a candy store, with free samples available in the form of trips to Baltimore and Philadelphia to discuss plans, dream up public-relations ideas, and compile a list of distinguished Americans whose names would appear on a plaque to be presented in the intermission.

The actual premiere of 'Black, Brown and Beige' took place not at Carnegie but at Rye High School in the suburbs, where the head of the music department, Dr J. T. H. Mize, was one of those then very rare musicologists aware of the significance of Ellington's music.

Hearing it in full for the first time, we were all stunned by the brilliance of Duke's 'tone parallel to the history of the American Negro', as he subtitled it. Most of us had just one reservation: towards the end of the 'Beige' movement, Duke had written a lyric, pompously delivered by Jimmy Britton, declaring that: 'We're black, brown and beige but we're red, white and blue.' Such simplistic flag-waving seemed redundant, but I had already found out that Duke was stubborn about clinging to his convictions. Only after Bill Morris, Dr Mize, Dan James and I had expressed our feelings strongly was it agreed that Duke did not need to wear his Americanism on his sleeve. The lyrics were eliminated and 'B, B & B' ran forty-eight instead of fifty minutes the next night.

Duke was both depressed and angry that his masterwork received mixed reviews. Doug Watt, in the *Daily News*, snidely observed that 'the concert, if that's what you call it, showed that such a form of composition is entirely out of Ellington's ken'. John Briggs in the *New York Post*: 'Mr Ellington had set himself a lofty goal, and with the best of intentions he did not achieve it.' Paul Bowles in the *Herald Tribune*: 'The whole attempt to fuse jazz as a form with art music should be discouraged.' Even John Hammond expressed negative views that led to a three-year rupture in our friendship.

Still, *Metronome, Down Beat, PM, Time,* Dr Mize in *Orchestra World* and several others understood the intent of Duke's masterpiece and what it symbolized.

After the recording ban ended, Duke was allowed to preserve only certain segments of his *magnum opus* on RCA. The work did not appear in its entirety until three years after his death, when a recording taped live at the concert was released in a three-LP set on Prestige.

Soon after the concert, my next assignment was the ghost-writing, in collaboration with Billy Strayhorn, of a booklet that appeared under Duke's byline, *Duke Ellington Piano Method for Blues.* Only forty-four pages long, selling for $1.50, it included a succinct history of the origins of the blues, technical analyses of its form, harmonic and rhythmic structure, examples of rhythmic figures, of boogie-woogie, and finally a series of piano solos, most of which we had to extract directly from Duke's records.

Strayhorn transcribed all the more difficult solos. Although the process of transferring music from a record to manuscript paper was new to both of us, it was a stimulating challenge to figure out just what gave the keyboard passages on 'Mr J. B. Blues', 'Across the Tracks Blues', 'Sepia Panorama' and others their singular character.

In typical Strayhorn style, this project was completed during casual, easy-going sessions, at my 71st Street apartment. During the couple of months it took us to finish the job, Swee' Pea became an enthusiastic and regular volunteer panelist on 'Platterbrains', sometimes along with Duke.

On 1 April the Ellington orchestra opened at the Hurricane, 49th and Broadway, for the kind of engagement that existed only in the golden years of swing: the band stayed there, with liberal airtime, for six months. Although by the end of that run our official ties were broken, we kept in close touch through his annual returns to Carnegie, the *Esquire* concerts, frequent social encounters (often over dinner at the Hickory House, Duke's nocturnal *pied à terre*), and later through our collaboration on his disc-jockey show in 1948.

Then came disaster. One evening in November 1949, my second wife Jane and I were on our way to dinner at Pete Rugolo's when, crossing 96th Street, we were hit by a driverless car that had been parked up the hill and had somehow been shaken loose. For a week I was intermittently unconscious in hospital, hovering between life and death; my father flew over and stayed until he was sure I was out of danger. My main injuries were two broken legs and a shattered right arm; Jane suffered a fractured pelvis and severe concussion.

After two months Jane was released from the hospital; I stayed another month, then was bedridden at home, wearing three casts, later graduating to a wheelchair, then crutches, a cane and, after a year, the ability to walk unaided and use my right arm for its normal purposes. Visits by Billie Holiday, Charlie Parker, Buddy De Franco, the Shearings, the Hammonds, the Gingriches, the Palmiers, Barry Ulanov, Oscar Pettiford and others helped take my mind off the pain.

One night I was carried bodily down the winding staircase that led from our penthouse at 1 Sheridan Square to the elevator on the eighth floor. From there I was manipulated down to the basement, which was Cafe Society Downtown. How could I not be there? It was opening night for both Charlie Parker and Art Tatum.

A few weeks later, in July, Duke and Evie dropped by our apartment. He could not have been more sympathetic, and was aware that along with my limbs, my career had been broken. 'We have to get something going for you,' he said. 'As soon as you can get around, come up to Tempo Music.'

Tempo was the company through which Ruth Ellington James channelled all her brother's music. I was put in nominal charge of working up some ideas to activate this priceless catalogue. The only accomplishment I can remember is that after finding a copy of 'Perdido' and discovering that it had lyrics, I determined to arrange for a vocal version; soon after I had sent a copy to Columbia Records, Sarah Vaughan recorded it.

I was not cut out for the music-publishing business and soon became restless, but Duke had other plans in mind: he wanted Mercer and me to start our own record company, with Strayhorn and Duke as silent partners. Duke's involvement was, I assumed, in technical violation of his Columbia contract, though he never recorded the full band for our Mercer label.

The Mercer sessions generally involved members or alumni of the orchestra. We got off to a fine start when Oscar Pettiford, who had been practising jazz cello, taped our first session. It was my thirty-sixth birthday, as good a day as any to produce the closest thing we would ever have to a hit: Oscar's 78 of 'Perdido'. Throughout the date Duke played piano and even acted at times like a sideman.

A week later we were back in the studio with three singers: Chubby Kemp, who made an early version of what eventually became a hit for B. B. King, 'How Blue Can You Get?'; Sarah Ford, who sang Mercer's 'Set 'em Up', and Al Hibbler in a typically sonorous 'White Christmas'. All three vocalists were backed by the Ellingtonians: Duke or Strayhorn, Johnny Hodges, Harry Carney, Wendell Marshall, Pettiford on cello, and two unlikely modernists, Red Rodney and Max Roach.

The arrangements for occasions like this were usually by Swee' Pea and invariably were brought in at the last minute or even finished in the studio. On one date Mercer himself, who had been working in his father's brass section for a few months, played mellophone behind Hibbler. My favourite Hibbler session was made a year later, after the upheaval that had brought Willie Smith, Juan Tizol and Louis Bellson into the band: on that occasion he sang 'Slow Boat to China', for which his mocking, pseudo-Cockney accent somehow seemed perfectly suited.

Both for Mercer and me the most auspicious event was the teaming of Duke and Strayhorn for a set of two-piano duets. I had recorded them in 'Tonk' on a single keyboard at the *Esquire* date for RCA, but the new, two-piano version set this delightful collaboration in full and fascinating perspective.

The rest of the tunes were the antithesis of 'Tonk', mostly unplanned versions of several blues, and of Strayhorn's 'Johnny Come Lately' and Ted Grouya's 'Flamingo'. The empathy was amazing; it was hard to tell when one pianist was turning over the lead part to the other, and often they interacted for a miraculous simultaneously ad libbed effect.

The eight duets (four with Wendell Marshall on bass, the others with Joe Shulman) have been reissued often. There could have been four more, but Duke insisted that we begin the first date by using the pianos to back his not very inspired vocal protégé, Jimmy McPhail, in four songs. They were never released; the masters, along with everything else we made for Mercer, were destroyed in a fire, though fortunately most survived because spare copies of the tapes had been sent overseas.

It was not the fire that put a coda to Mercer Records, but rather our distribution through Prestige Records, which invariably gave precedence to the selling of its own product; aside from this, we were caught in the cracks between the demise of 78s and the onset of LPs. Some of our sessions did come out on ten-inch albums, but despite some great reviews the records simply did not recoup Duke's investment. Reluctantly I pulled out, and Mercer soon afterwards brought the short but happy life of our company to a close.

The Mercer interlude provided my most frequent opportunities to spend time with Duke in a one-to-one situation. It has been repeated endlessly that he was a very private man whose suave, love-you-madly façade nobody could pierce. This was true up to a point, though I found that when the two of us were alone in his Brill Building office or hotel room, uninterrupted by phone calls or hangers-on, the veil would be lifted a little and some of his true feelings might emerge, many of them quite negative.

One night in 1955, taping his foreword for my first *Encyclopedia of Jazz*, he discussed Jelly Roll Morton and broke his own rule about never speaking ill of another musician. Some years earlier, during a blindfold test for *Metronome*, he was no less vigorous in his reaction to a Babs Gonzales record ('desperately unadult').

During the 1968 election campaign, Duke amazed me by bursting into a tirade of invective against Senator George McGovern, a decent, liberal man who was running against Richard M. Nixon. Duke was at once a musical progressive and a political conservative. Three months after Nixon took office, Duke's support was richly rewarded when he received the Congressional Medal of Freedom at the White House on his seventieth birthday.

Certainly the most unsettling experience was one I could not write about in my long essay on Duke that appeared in the book *From Satchmo to Miles*. To have mentioned it during Duke's lifetime would have ruptured our relationship for ever.

We were at the 1965 Monterey Jazz Festival, where the Ellington orchestra was to play Saturday evening. That afternoon, to everyone's surprise, Evie showed up. For years it had not been Duke's custom to take or invite her anywhere except for an occasional dinner in New York.

According to Evie, her greeting from Duke was: 'What the hell are you doing here?' followed by a campaign of near-silence. Evie, not a cheerful personality at the best of times, was mortified. That evening she told Jane: 'I'm so depressed I don't know what to do.'

Jane, compassionate as always, said, 'After the festival why don't you come down to LA and spend a few days with us? Maybe that'll cheer you up.'

Little did we know what we were letting ourselves in for. Evie stayed ten days. I took her to Shelly's Manne Hole, accompanied her to a Kenton concert, invited Benny Carter and other friends over to meet her. Under those conditions her company was pleasant; but for the rest of the time – morning, noon and night – it seemed that all she could talk about was the innumerable wrongs Ellington had done to her.

The number and diversity of her complaints were limitless and by the second or third night had become embarrassing. Did Evie have some idea in mind for an exposé book? I would of course have rejected any such suggestion. (Among the minor details about Duke's duplicity, she swore that he had really been born in 1898, not 1899.)

Though we sympathized with her, it seemed to us that Evie might have been better off accepting Duke's need for total freedom, to write his music without being disturbed, to conduct his overlapping affairs without complaints from her.

Alternatively, as Jane and I asked ourselves time and again, if she can't stand the heat, why doesn't she get out of the kitchen?

A few weeks later, in town for a record date with Ella Fitzgerald, Duke said, 'Thank you for being so nice to Evie.' Jane and I often wondered whether he had any inkling of what had gone on during those ten very stressful days.

Evie never got out of the kitchen. When Duke lay dying, she also had cancer and was confined to a hospital. Duke kept in close touch with her by telephone. A few months after his passing we received a short, affectionate note; Evie told us she was undergoing more treatments and hoped they would work this time. She survived Duke by barely a year and was buried beside him.

Duke's attitude towards those close to him was hard to assess. Certainly his love for his sister Ruth was deep and abiding. He and Mercer, as Mercer's book later made clear, had a strange, blow-hot-blow-cold relationship. Basically he did not seem to want another musical Ellington competing with him.

Too much time and newsprint have been devoted to Ellington's flaws, as if we ought to expect every genius to be a perfect human being. What I remember best about him will never change: the geniality with which he 'adopted' me as a member of the Ellington entourage; the matchless nights at Carnegie Hall, at the Met, at the

White House, at concerts and festivals and Disneyland dances; and most of all I remember when he and Evie presented themselves at our door and helped to bring me back from one of the lowest ebbs in my life.

PRESS

After having spent many years directly involved in jazz – writing about it, writing and playing it, lecturing, producing records and concerts by some of the acknowledged leaders of the art form – I found it frustrating that many of my adversaries refused to let me forget that for a brief period during that very long span of time I was obliged to work as a publicity agent.

This phase lasted only from 1941 until 1943, by which time, having returned decisively to journalism as a writer for *Metronome* and *Esquire*, I gave up my only two remaining accounts, Duke Ellington and Lionel Hampton, and never again worked as a press agent for anyone or anything. The term 'publicist', sometimes not even preceded by 'former', haunted me for many years afterwards.

Fortunately the artists with whom I had direct associations were those whom I would gladly have publicized regardless of any official connection. For a long time I had been a frequent visitor to Cafe Society, where I found both the music and the social ambience more agreeable than at any other night spot in New York. I came to know the owner, Barney Josephson, whose gentle personality and liberal social attitudes were totally at odds with those of the typical club owners I had known. I also became a friend of Ivan Black, the club's publicist.

By early 1941 my career was at a new low. I had lost my job at *Down Beat* after imprudently suggesting that $40 a month was not an adequate stipend, and was now without any regular paying outlet for my writing. Although the sale of a few arrangements and the recording of a session now and then encouraged me, the rewards, contrary to general belief among my critical peers, were small. It was therefore a pleasant surprise when Ivan Black offered to hire me as his assistant at a salary of $15 a week to be supplemented by a commission on any accounts I brought in. Ivan's office by then was in the building that housed Cafe Society Uptown, on the midtown East Side near Lexington Avenue.

Ivan's offer was a dual godsend, for it meant that I had regular access, without payment, to two clubs where I could hear Lena Horne, Hazel Scott, Teddy Wilson's band and others of their calibre. Cafe Society was his main client.

Just before I accepted the job, coincidentally, I was involved with Cafe Society on a very different level. Bobby Burnet, the excellent trumpeter who had just left Charlie Barnet's orchestra, wanted to start his own group. I suggested hiring such sidemen as Charlie Holmes on alto and Albert Nicholas on clarinet, both Armstrong alumni. We then put together a rhythm section with a promising eighteen-year-old pianist, Sammy Benskin; the bassist Hayes Alvis (ex-Ellington and Carter) and Manzie Johnson, the superb drummer whom I had heard often with Don Redman's band.

This made Burnet the first white leader in history to organize an all-black group; it also made front-page news in *Down Beat*, with an encouraging story headlined, 'Barnet Horn Man Fronts Colored Band' and displaying a picture of Burnet captioned, 'He's Leading a Sepia Band'.

In an interview for a new magazine, *Music and Rhythm*, headlined 'Can a White Man Successfully Lead a Negro Band?', Burnet was quoted as saying, 'I never learned a thing from white musicians. Every white musician can learn something from a Negro musician.' This was somehow considered more newsworthy since Burnet, who had studied at a private school in Switzerland, was a member of a socially prominent Chicago family.

Our first requirement, of course, was a library. Burnet was a first-class arranger, and since the instrumentation was that of the John Kirby sextet, I had little difficulty writing several charts to round out the repertoire. Functioning as arranger, publicist and de facto booker without pay, I persuaded Barney Josephson to put the group in Cafe Society Uptown.

The two-week engagement at the club, during which time I began officially with Ivan Black, was well received, but Barney Josephson already had John Kirby booked in to follow, and very soon the Burnet group was out of a job. I could do no more than recommend Bobby for a few gigs at the Famous Door and a series of off-nights (Mondays) at Nick's. The band never secured a record date; within a couple of months it was defunct, leaving only a very satisfying memory for those of us who heard it. Burnet rejoined Barnet briefly, then faded from the scene, eventually moving to Mexico, where he died some years ago.

Working for Cafe Society was, at least by the standards of press agentry, an ideal job. I was able to dream up such ideas as a convention of Fletcher Henderson alumni, which Fletcher himself attended, and which gathered considerable space in the music press and the black papers; and a similar evening honouring W. C. Handy.

With my new strictly relative financial security, I made two other bold moves: taking a three-room apartment at 140 West 71st Street, and becoming engaged to Carol Roberts, a blonde teenager from Brooklyn whom I had been seeing off and on for several months.

Carol played piano, sang a little, had worked under two or three different names, and loved jazz; by my standards in 1941 we were destined for each other, and because we could spend so much time at Cafe Society and other clubs, I met her requirements. Ivan helped to find a judge who would marry us, and we deliberately took the step on a Friday the thirteenth (both of us had also been born on the thirteenth). Out of this came a song, 'Born on a Friday', which we wrote together, and a marriage that became shaky after less than a year. Carol later had a brief fling at a Hollywood movie career.

We were back in each other's company in time to attend the first *Esquire* concert together, and continued to see one another during most of 1944, before agreeing that our lifestyles were incompatible and that it would be best to bring the marriage to an amicable end. We remained in touch off and on over the years until not long before she died in 1977.

There was another side to the publicity business to which I soon became exposed, an ugly undercurrent that affected my work with Ivan. Cafe Society, with its interracial policy for both artists and customers, acquired a radical image, and indeed was a gathering place for many far-leftists. As a result, it was rendered suspect by the right-wing press and, as I soon found out, the right wing had tentacles almost everywhere. There were eight daily newspapers in New York, of which only two, the *Post* and *PM*, could be classified as liberal. The others were populated by the likes of Walter Winchell, Westbrook Pegler, Hedda Hopper and a variety of others who often made it difficult, sometimes impossible, for Ivan to plant an item in a column. Even landing a photo of Hazel Scott or any other black performer on a front page was considered an exceptional achievement.

Still, Ivan persevered; he was even able to arrange for me to do a few byline pieces in the *New York Times* about such subjects as the history of boogie-woogie piano, jazz in the concert hall or Louis Armstrong's twenty-fifth anniversary in jazz. Since most daily papers then, even the *Times*, paid little or no attention to jazz, these were considered by Ivan and me to be great coups.

Two months after my marriage I made what seemed like a step upwards, joining a publicity office run by Hal Davis and Les Lieber, both of whom, of course, were jazz fans and had clients mainly in that area. My salary was now $20 a week plus possible commissions. I was still friendly with Ivan and Barney; when Count Basie opened at the Uptown Cafe, Carol and I were frequent visitors.

My radio show, 'Platterbrains', was still heard weekly, now on WMCA; often the guest panelists would be musicians who were working at the Cafes, Kelly's or the Savoy. Sometimes our nights would run very late, as when Fats Waller, after his show at the Apollo, dropped by and sat up with us, listening to records, drinking, playing our small upright piano, until about 5 a.m., somewhat to the consternation of at least one neighbour.

One essential aspect of engendering publicity for an artist was the necessity to avoid controversy. I found this out the hard way when, following a common practice, I sent out a letter to the editor under the byline of a client. The trouble was that the letter took sides in some touchy political issue, and Lionel Hampton's name was attached to it.

Joe Glaser, who had hired me to work for Lionel, was understandably furious, and hell had no fury like Glaser's. Running into me at the Three Deuces, he cursed me so loudly that I suspect everyone in the club knew I was fired. (He rehired me two months later, probably at Lionel's suggestion.)

For the most part, working in publicity, despite its advantages of bringing me into contact with so many musicians I respected, was an unpleasant business, because it meant catering to so many sleazy gossip columnists and remaining at their mercy. The power they exercised was frightening. It was a happy day when I was able to give it up for ever.

Even during the couple of years in publicity I had been fortunate enough to continue such side ventures as the odd record session here and there, the radio show and one other undertaking that calls for separate discussion. In fact, it seems in retrospect that a turning point in my whole career was a meeting, and subsequent collaboration, with a Belgian jazz fan named Robert Goffin.

GOFFIN, *ESQUIRE* AND THE MOLDY FIGS

Robert Goffin, passed over briefly or ignored in most analyses of jazz historiography, deserves to be remembered for his several auspicious contributions to jazz.

Born in 1898 near Waterloo, Belgium, he wore so many hats in his long life (he died in 1984) that *Down Beat* once called him 'the world's most versatile jitterbug'. He was one of his country's foremost criminal lawyers, a draughts champion, author of books on legal finance, gastronomy, poems, rats, spiders, eels, history and jazz, and a former vice-president of the Brussels Ice Hockey Club.

Around 1927 he took over direction of *Music*, the Belgian counterpart to *Metronome*, and liberalized its policy towards jazz. He wrote a subjective, somewhat melodramatic book, *Aux Frontières du Jazz*, published in 1932 but never translated into English. It showed a reasonably sensitive understanding at a time when most critics, particularly in America, equated jazz with Paul Whiteman (Goffin's *bête blanche*) and Bing Crosby.

In the vanguard of Belgium's anti-fascists, he had to leave hurriedly when his country was invaded, saying goodbye to his 3,000 78s, his Renoirs and Gauguins and Modiglianis. Escaping to France and Spain, he sailed from Portugal and arrived in New York in July 1940.

Goffin was an imposing figure, over six feet tall and weighing more than 250 pounds. His big, beaming smile, zestful love of life and down-to-earth manner seemed, to some, at odds with his serious record of cultural achievements. His only frustration was a failure to master the English language.

We met just days after his arrival in New York and became good friends, making the rounds together often to visit the Savoy,

Kelly's Stable and the Apollo. One night, after attending a screening of the movie *Blues in the Night*, then catching the Basie band at the Famous Door, Goffin told me about a plan on which he had been working: he wanted to give a full, officially sponsored course on the history of jazz at the New School for Social Research in the Village, on West 12th Street. Because he still spoke a somewhat hilarious fractured English (friends imitated his standard greeting, 'Ow you feel?'), and because of my fluency in French, he suggested that I collaborate with him, translating his scripts and giving separate lectures.

Aside from a few isolated lectures by visiting bandleaders, there had never been any attempt to offer a serious history and analysis of the music, as part of a regular curriculum. Goffin's initiative would set an important precedent. I agreed eagerly to take part.

The lectures, fifteen in all, were set to begin 4 February 1942. We agreed on a series of topics: the blues, ragtime, Louis Armstrong, Duke Ellington, boogie-woogie, Chicago style and so on. In addition to using records, we planned to persuade musicians to help us with live performances. Because of the unique nature of the project we had no trouble in attracting them: at the first lecture our guest speaker-performers were Louis Armstrong, Benny Goodman and Benny Carter. For a New Orleans session we had Red Allen and Sidney Bechet; to illustrate the blues, our live vocalist was Helen Humes. The African Student Group from Columbia University arranged to send Liberian musicians to demonstrate the origins of rhythmic concepts that were said to have laid the foundations for jazz. Other guests were Pete Brown, Mel Powell and Bobby Hackett.

One of our main problems in assembling the series was that there was virtually no literature on jazz. Even Goffin's own book and Panassié's *Le Jazz Hot*, published in 1934, were already somewhat outdated. The only other books of any consequence were the very superficial ghost-written autobiography of Louis Armstrong, a somewhat better Benny Goodman autobiography, *The Kingdom of Swing*, written by Irving Kolodin, and Charles Edward Smith's *Jazzmen*, which dealt almost exclusively with the New Orleans aspect of jazz origins. *The Jazz Record Book*, of which Smith was co-editor, was more recent and a little broader in scope.

We were obliged to depend mainly not on books but on our own knowledge and first-hand experience. Occasionally I would illustrate a point at the piano; often we would rely on our fairly

THE NEW SCHOOL
FOR SOCIAL RESEARCH
66 W TWELFTH ST   NEW YORK

SWING MUSIC

15 weeks. Tuesdays, 8:20-10 P.M. $12.50.   **Robert Goffin** and **Leonard Feather**

Beginning September 29. The course deals with the background and development of jazz, musically and historically. The lectures are illustrated by recordings and by musical demonstrations in the form of weekly "jam sessions," featuring outstanding white and Negro musicians from the leading swing bands.

Sept. 29   Before jazz in New Orleans
Oct.   6   Ragtime and the pioneers
Oct. 13   First period of Negro jazz
Oct. 20   From New Orleans to Chicago—King Oliver
Oct. 27   Jazz from America to Europe
Nov.   3   Original Dixieland
Nov. 10   White pioneers
Nov. 17   Louis Armstrong
Nov. 24   From Fletcher Henderson to Duke Ellington
Dec.   1   Chicago style
Dec.   8   Big white bands
Dec. 15   Benny Goodman
Dec. 22   Outdated and small Negro bands
Jan.   5   Big Negro bands
Jan. 12   From spiritual to boogie-woogie

The series: $12.50

Each lecture: $1.10

ROBERT GOFFIN. Docteur en Droit, Brussels. Editor, La Voix de France; formerly editor, Alerte, anti-Nazi weekly, Brussels; Music, first jazz magazine. Secretary, P.E.N. Club; former president, association for jazz studies in Europe. Author, Jazz Band; Aux Frontières du jazz; Empress Carlotta; Rimbaud vivant; other books.

LEONARD FEATHER. Conductor of WMCA jazz quizz program, Platterbrains; writer of lyrics, music and arrangements for Count Basie, Duke Ellington and other band leaders. Formerly director, Rhythm Club, London; BBC jazz programs; special recording bands for Decca, Columbia and Victor recording companies in London and New York. Public relations counsel for Louis Armstrong, Lionel Hampton, et al. Contributor to New York Times, Down Beat, Music and Rhythm, and leading music publications; to Melody Maker, and Radio Times, official BBC journal, London.

substantial collections of 78s for demonstrations. (By now some of my own collection had been shipped over from England.)

The course was successful, attracting close to 100 evidently serious students; we repeated it in the autumn. In a sense we had given birth to jazz education, but this accomplishment was not enough for Goffin, who had even more ambitious ideas. One night in 1943 we sat in the Hurricane, listening to the music of Duke Ellington's orchestra. With us was Arnold Gingrich, the editor of *Esquire*. As the evening progressed, Goffin's unquenchable enthusiasm was directed towards a new and daring end. Because he knew of Gingrich's intense interest in jazz, he sensed that the moment was right.

'Jazz has never had any continuous, serious exposure in any national American magazine,' he said. 'Why can't you have a jazz poll, print the results in your magazine, and run a series of articles?'

Gradually a plan crystallized. We did not want our poll to wind up like those conducted in *Down Beat* or *Metronome*, in which, typically, Charlie Barnet or Tex Beneke would be the leaders on 'hot tenor', followed by Coleman Hawkins and Ben Webster; Ziggy Elman would win for 'hot trumpet' and Alvino Rey for guitar; Helen O'Connell or Dinah Shore would be elected No. 1 female jazz singer while Billie Holiday went unhonoured.

'The only way out,' I said, 'is to put together a panel of experts, rather than rely on the readers.'

'Right,' Goffin said, 'and we know who the real experts are.'

That Gingrich agreed enthusiastically did not surprise me for, like Goffin, he had long counted jazz among his seemingly endless range of intellectual concerns. He had helped to found the magazine in 1933, establishing it as a publication of the kind that did not feel the need to translate any French or Latin references in its pages. Ernest Hemingway, an early contributor, led Gingrich to John Dos Passos, Ring Lardner and scores of others. (Gingrich had published 'The Snows of Kilimanjaro' in *Esquire*, paying Hemingway $1,000 – twice his regular fee.)

Sitting in Arnold's office, as I occasionally did during the next thirty years, I was never surprised when a discussion we were having about the relative merits of Roy Eldridge and Red Allen would be interrupted by a phone call from Tennessee Williams, Truman Capote or Hemingway. He would then pick up the conversation exactly where we had left it.

Balding and thin-faced, with a heavy moustache, Arnold smoked powerful and repulsive French cigarettes, which I refused regularly, and drank Irish whiskey, which I accepted willingly.

He attracted a seemingly limitless circle of friends and took joy in his every interest, from jazz, about which he wrote occasionally with authority and passion, to fishing, which was his abiding love. He was considered one of the world's greatest fly fishermen.

When Gingrich told David Smart, then *Esquire*'s publisher, about our ideas for a jazz adventure, Smart not only agreed, but took it one step further. 'Let's not just announce the winners,' he said. 'Let's get them all together and put on a concert – the *Esquire* All Americans.'

In assembling our board, Goffin and I ensured that it was racially integrated. At one time or another while the polls were held, our panelists included E. Simms Campbell, the black *Esquire* cartoonist and author of a couple of articles on jazz; Dan Burley, the writer for Associated Negro Press and a competent jazz pianist; and Inez Cavanaugh, a singer and writer who had contributed to *Metronome* and *The Crisis*.

Our first panel, voting in late 1943, comprised George Avakian, Campbell, Goffin, Feather, Abel Green of *Variety* (included, against my wishes, for political reasons, and dropped the following year); Elliott Grennard of *Billboard*; John Hammond; Roger Kay, an Egyptian critic then writing for *Orchestra World*; Harry Lim, from what was then known as Java, conductor of jam sessions; Paul Eduard Miller, the Chicago-based writer who, along with me, became a regular contributor to *Esquire*; Bucklin Moon, author of *The Darker Brother*; Timme Rosenkrantz, who had edited a swing magazine in Copenhagen; Charles Edward Smith; Frank Stacy, then the New York editor of *Down Beat*; Bob Thiele, editor of *Jazz Magazine*, and Barry Ulanov, editor of *Metronome*.

A patriotic motive was involved; plans were set up to present the evening as a benefit for the Navy League. Additionally, our concert coincided with the opening of the government's fourth War Loan Drive; seats were sold for war bonds, with the house scaled from $25 to $100. Station WJZ set up a bond booth in its building to sell tickets. With the help of large donations from several very wealthy fans, we were proud to be able to announce afterwards that $600,000 worth of bonds were sold.

Because the power of *Esquire* and the importance attached to the venture enabled Smart and Gingrich to pull some strings, the winners were set to appear in the first jazz concert ever given at the

Metropolitan Opera House. As for the poll results, they reaffirmed our faith in the voters and our preference for this method over the system of drawing on the public's relatively limited knowledge.

The winners were: First Choice (Gold Award): Louis Armstrong, trumpet; Jack Teagarden, trombone; Benny Goodman, clarinet; Coleman Hawkins, saxophone; Art Tatum, piano; Al Casey, guitar; Oscar Pettiford, bass; Sid Catlett, drums; Red Norvo and Lionel Hampton, tied for miscellaneous instrument; Louis Armstrong, male vocal; Billie Holiday, female vocal; Artie Shaw, best musician in the Armed Forces.

Second Choice (Silver Award): Cootie Williams, Lawrence Brown, Barney Bigard, Johnny Hodges, Earl Hines, Oscar Moore, Milt Hinton (tied with Al Morgan), Cozy Cole, Leo Watson, Mildred Bailey; Willie Smith (the saxophonist) and Dave Tough tied for Armed Forces.

Soon after the votes were tabulated, I set about organizing a record session with a group of the winners. The entire Gold Award rhythm section was available (Tatum, Casey, Catlett, Pettiford), as were Coleman Hawkins, Cootie Williams and, on clarinet, the third place winner, Edmond Hall.

All were eager to participate, even though only union scale was to be paid and, in Tatum's case, it meant working as a sideman for the first time since he had arrived in New York many years before as Adelaide Hall's accompanist.

Bob Thiele, of Signature Records, had agreed to produce the session, but after all the musicians had been booked a crisis arose: Thiele could not be reached on the phone and had not signed the contract. Desperate, I called Milt Gabler to ask if he would be willing to take over the session for his Commodore label. His affirmative decision was one he never regretted, since the four tunes we made on 4 December 1943 turned out to be, with the possible exception of Billie Holiday's 'Strange Fruit', the most successful records ever to appear on the label, and have been reissued several times.

As soon as *Esquire* sent out a press release announcing the winners' names, the Negro press gave our undertaking massive support. A four-column streamer headline in the New York *Amsterdam News* read: '20 of 26 Winning Musicians in *Esquire* Band Poll are Negroes; Winners at Met Opera House January 18.' The Pittsburgh *Courier* announced: ' "Ace" Negro Musicians Sweep *Esquire* Mag's Jazz Band Poll. All American Jazz Band Top Heavy with Race Stars; Set for Historic Debut in Sacred Confines of Famous Metropolitan Opera House.'

This enthusiasm was not unanimous. A small magazine called the *Jazz Record*, edited by the pianist Art Hodes and by Dale Curran, published a savage attack under the byline of Jake Trussell Jr, who called the results a 'foul and dismal smirch' on our reputations as critics. Breaking the votes down by race, he found that 'only one [critic] awarded the white musicians higher than 42.9% of the total votes: this was George Avakian'. He concluded that, 'This Avakian proved himself a really big man amongst jazz critics.' Next highest, he declared, was Charles Edward Smith, 'who gave the whites fifteen out of a possible thirty-five points . . . Feather, Harry Lim and Timme Rosenkrantz were low men, with all awarding less than seven points . . . to white players. If this isn't inverted Jim Crow, what on earth is?'

Trussell made his stance clearer by avowing that: 'The top men for small hot-jazz-band work today are predominantly white men!' He went on to single out his own dream band, with such members as Yank Lawson, Georg Brunis, Pee Wee Russell. But the most memorable statement was Trussell's complaint that Jess Stacy, Joe Sullivan and Art Hodes received only four, three and two votes respectively. 'These men,' he wrote, 'are the three greatest small-band piano men on contemporary wax. *To mention Art Tatum in the same gasp with them is blasphemous!*' (my italics).

Such was the state of jazz criticism, at least in the *Jazz Record* and other small publications, in 1944.

Not all the objections to *Esquire*'s efforts had such a flagrantly racial basis. What bothered the offended critics most often was their equation of 'the real jazz' with the older New Orleans musicians, principally Bunk Johnson and George Lewis, *vis à vis* the artists they dismissed as 'swing musicians' while categorically denying that swing music was jazz. In an article titled 'Featherbed Ball' in the *Record Changer*, Ralph J. Gleason took this position in an impassioned attack on what he called 'the Feather–Miller–Goffin–Ulanov axis', branding us as 'the exponents of big-band jazz, or the small bands like Norvo and Wilson'.

Gleason praised the independent record labels through which 'you and I get more George Lewis and Bunk and James P., and we can skip the Norvo and the Basie'. He pointed out the necessity 'to make firms like Decca agree to record Bunk Johnson instead of King Cole', and suggested that 'the way to combat the nonsense

spewed out by the Goffin–Feather–Ulanov axis and its satellites is
not to get mad and talk to the boys and write letters to each other,
but to get mad and write articles for *Down Beat* . . . and *Esky* . . .
there is no answer but to usurp the fountainheads of information
ourselves and attempt, by using the word jazz to mean the music of
Bunk and Oliver, to erase, in time, the damage already done by
Feather–Miller–Goffin–Ulanov and their ilk.'

In the same publication one Jazzbo Brown suggested that 'the
so-called experts of *Esquire*, by keeping good jazz safely hidden
from the public while forcing upon them the Eldridges, the Tatums
and the Pettifords, have created in the minds of intelligent music
followers a totally false impression of real American jazz music'.

The first *Esquire* concert was held 18 January 1944 in an
atmosphere of extraordinary excitement. It was as if, after so many
years underground, jazz was about to be apotheosized. Gold and
Silver 'Esky' statuettes were awarded to the winners. Never did I
observe, backstage, any sense of rivalry or jealousy among the
musicians. Louis Armstrong and Roy Eldridge worked side by
side; Billie Holiday and Mildred Bailey took their turns, as did
Lionel Hampton and Red Norvo, who also played a vibes duet on a
single instrument when Hampton's broke down. With Teagarden,
Bigard, Hawkins and the gold-star rhythm team rounding out the
personnel, it was a night not merely to remember, but to
commemorate, logically, in an album.

Recordings of the concert were, in fact, released on V Discs, for
use only by the Armed Forces. Over the years I tried persistently,
through Joe Glaser (who managed many of the artists) and Milt
Gabler at Decca Records, to arrange for the release of a live album.
As the artists died off the matter of obtaining clearances from the
estates became more complicated and the idea, though never
actually shelved, went on the back burner. Inevitably, many years
later, the entire concert showed up mysteriously on an album
pressed in Japan; I had to send to Tokyo to obtain a copy.

Aside from the poll and the concert, jazz enjoyed ancillary
benefits. Paul Eduard Miller edited *Esquire*'s *1944 Jazz Book*, a
230-page volume with a knowledgeable introduction by Gingrich,
bio-discographies of anyone who had received any votes in the poll,
articles by Miller, Smith, Campbell, Goffin, George Hoefer and me
among others, and numerous illustrations.

In the magazine itself, Goffin contributed a 'desert island discs'
feature that appeared in September of 1943, listing a dozen records

chosen to accompany various musicians and critics in the event of involuntary isolation. Starting in the June 1944 issue, Miller and I began what was known as 'The Rhythm Section', in which we would alternate in conducting a jazz symposium and contributing features and record reviews.

Despite (or possibly because of) the initiative taken by *Esquire*, no other national magazine gave jazz regular coverage. I had been able to secure a few bylines in the *New York Times* starting in 1941, and several writers, notably Hammond and George Frazier, continued to find outlets, but *Esquire* essentially remained an oasis.

For our second annual celebration the concert was transferred to Los Angeles, where many of the winners gathered at the Philharmonic Auditorium. Again the concert was a benefit, this time for the Volunteer Army Canteen Service. Hollywood celebrity flourishes were added: Lionel Barrymore presented Duke Ellington with his Esky; Lena Horne, in one of the evening's most touching moments, paid tribute to her friend Billy Strayhorn and gave him his award. Billie Holiday was particularly moved to receive her Esky from Jerome Kern (it was one of Kern's last public appearances; he died later that year), and Judy Garland made the presentation to Anita O'Day. Danny Kaye was the master of ceremonies.

A new dimension this year was a three-way radio hookup, with segments from New Orleans, Los Angeles and New York. Under the auspices of the National Jazz Foundation in New Orleans, Louis Armstrong was presented, leading an all-star group. Nesuhi Ertegun, editor of the *Record Changer*, had scarcely a good word to say even about this segment ('Higginbotham playing horribly, Armstrong playing badly and Bechet playing superbly'), though the rhythm section with James P. Johnson, Richard Alexis and Paul Barbarin came in for a little faint praise. Leon Prima's band, despite the presence of Irving Fazola on clarinet, drew almost none.

The New York segment presented Benny Goodman. From Los Angeles were heard the Duke Ellington orchestra (giving Ertegun a chance to observe: 'I have never heard the Ellington band sound as bad as when they played a composition by Leonard Feather'), Art Tatum and Anita O'Day backed by some Ellington men and Sid Catlett. For a finale the three cities merged for a collective Armstrong–Ellington–Goodman blues, a live experiment comparable to the overdubbing that would later be a common practice in the recording studios.

There was a bonus for me in this California visit: I fell in love. Invited to dinner by Peggy Lee, I met Jane Leslie Larrabee, a singer I had heard but not known on 52nd Street. Jane had all the right qualities for me: she was attractive, affable, sweet-natured and glad to keep me company as we went, the following evening, to hear Gerald Wilson's new band at Shepp's Playhouse. I proposed that night. A few weeks later, after thinking it over, Jane came to New York, and soon after that I remember calling Red Norvo: 'Have you got a dark suit? OK, put it on; I want you to be the best man at my wedding.' Over forty years later, Jane and I are still married, proud of our daughter and son-in-law, and glad that I had acted somewhat impulsively in 1945.

During my Los Angeles visit in January for the concert, I made several radio appearances to promote the event and talk about this year's poll. The board of voters had been expanded to twenty-two, and the number of winning categories slightly increased.

The Gold Award winners were Cootie Williams, J. C. Higginbotham (Ertegun's 'horrible' trombonist), Johnny Hodges, Coleman Hawkins, Benny Goodman, Teddy Wilson, Al Casey, Oscar Pettiford, Big Sid Catlett, Red Norvo, Louis Armstrong and Mildred Bailey (vocal), Ellington (arranger and band), Buck Clayton, Armed Forces. Silver winners were Roy Eldridge, Lawrence Brown, Benny Carter, Lester Young, Edmond Hall, Art Tatum, Oscar Moore, Slam Stewart, Dave Tough, Harry Carney (miscellaneous instrument), Joe Turner and Billie Holiday, Billy Strayhorn, Count Basie and Willie Smith (Armed Forces).

Added this year was a New Stars division, for which bronze Eskies were given to Dizzy Gillespie, Bill Harris, Herbie Fields, Flip Phillips, Aaron Sachs, Eddie Heywood, Remo Palmier, Chubby Jackson, Specs Powell, Ray Nance (violin), Eddie Cleanhead Vinson, Anita O'Day, Johnny Thompson (arranger), Lionel Hampton (band) and Mel Powell for Armed Forces.

Once again *Esquire*'s efforts were lauded by musicians, by the public, by everyone but the traditionalist critics. Along with Ertegun, Rudi Blesh of the *New York Herald Tribune* found fault with almost everything. Reviewing the first thirty minutes in the ninety-minute broadcast, he complained that Bunk Johnson, 'this perennially great player', was lost and inaudible in the noise of inappropriate swing. 'Thus ended thirty minutes which presented only a travesty of the original and still vital jazz which was to have been presented.'

The New York portion gave Blesh a chance to take a swipe at Benny Goodman (whose 'flashy virtuosity has fooled so many into thinking him a great player and a creative personality; in spite of great commercial and popular success he is, of course, neither') and to insult Mildred Bailey, 'the white woman who imitated the wrong Negro singers'.

During the final portion: 'Duke Ellington played a puerile, moronic riff tune, composed – if that is the term – by one of *Esquire*'s jazz critics. The effect was that of waterlogged saxophones snoring in a welter of sound effects.' Later came 'a trite Ellington tune, dished out in successive choruses by the Duke in a turgid turmoil, by Armstrong in a clipped, imaginative, masterful variation, and by a fumbling piece of Goodman embroidery'. Blesh concluded that *Esquire* has 'missed the opportunity and disavowed the responsibility to present true cultural values'.

At the suggestion of Arnold Gingrich, for the third year we placed the New Stars voting in the hands of musicians: specifically, all who had been winners in previous polls, and all those on the board of experts who also were currently active as musicians. Not all the potential voters could be reached; however, a total of forty-one musicians fulfilled their obligations by participating in this New Stars selection.

The 1946 list showed a few changes, three of them prompted by the achievements of Nat King Cole, whose trio included Oscar Moore on guitar. The Gold winners were Cootie Williams, Bill Harris, Benny Carter, Hawkins, Goodman, Cole, Moore, Tough, Jackson, Norvo, Ellington (arranger and band), Armstrong and Ella Fitzgerald/Mildred Bailey (tied). Silver awards went to Charlie Shavers, Vic Dickenson, Hodges, Don Byas, Bigard, Wilson, Palmier, Krupa, Stewart, Stuff Smith, Strayhorn, Herman (band), Cole (vocal), Holiday.

The New Stars, selected by the jury of their peers, were Pete Candoli, J. J. Johnson, Charlie Parker, Charlie Ventura, Jimmy Hamilton, Erroll Garner, Bill De Arango, J. C. Heard, Junior Raglin, Ray Perry (violin), Ralph Burns (arranger), Herman, Eckstine, Frances Wayne.

The celebration this time took the form of an hour-long broadcast on the ABC network, from the Ritz Theatre on West 46th Street, with Orson Welles as narrator and featuring the Ellington and Herman orchestras, along with the King Cole Trio. With Ellington supplying a gentle piano obbligato, Welles delivered a sensitive tribute to jazz. Later I made the Esky presentations, among them one for Welles, honouring his contributions to jazz (he had been involved with a series of broadcasts presenting traditionalist musicians). The finale found Herman's vocalist, Frances Wayne, joining with the Ellington orchestra to sing Duke's 'I'm Checkin' Out, Goombye' (*sic*) and the two bands teaming up for 'C Jam Blues'.

I was delighted to see Woody Herman honoured. I knew of no other bandleader more respected by his sidemen, and none who worked harder to keep his standards high. This was a spectacular year for him: he had his own sponsored radio series on the ABC network, with a segment in which I interviewed a different member of the orchestra each week. In 1986, the year of his fiftieth anniversary as a leader, Herman still had his unique reputation and still fronted a band of brilliant youngsters.

By now it was evident that the *Esquire* undertaking had met with unprecedented approval almost everywhere; but the *Jazz Record* was still on the warpath. An article by Sergeant John Broome in the August 1945 issue was headed 'On the Feather in *Esquire*'s Bonnet' and subheaded 'Cult of Shining Mediocrity Takes All Meaning out of Jazz Criticism and Reduces It to Profitable Trade'. In the November 1946 issue a piece by one Carter Winter informed us that:

> Every single year there's a new crop of phoneys – black and white – trying to pervert or suppress or emasculate jazz. This year it's Diz Gillespie . . . a few years ago it was Cab Calloway . . . before that it was Whiteman and Grofe . . . On the one hand you have the professional vipers – the real mad [*sic*] cats – headed by Diz Gillespie who try to cut the heart out of the real main line jazz and twist it into something like one of Carmen Miranda's hats because they want to be frantic . . . On the other hand you've got those characters who are convinced . . . that jazz is dead or dying . . . Their groove is just as crappy as Gillespie's.

Even in *Esquire* an occasional critical voice would be heard through the letters-to-the-editor department. Typically, one such letter read:

> We have been taken aback by the opinions of your chief critic Leonard Feather, who is, we feel, either completely incompetent

or thoroughly dishonest. We feel that some of his ideas may influence some of your readers . . . to prefer . . . the sentimental, affected honkings of Coleman Hawkins or the shrill 'I-can-blow-higher-and-louder-than-you-can' shriekings of Roy Eldridge to the simple, honest playing of Bud Freeman or the incomparable Muggsy Spanier . . . Nor do we feel that such examples of Mr Feather's type of jazz as his Commodore recordings with the Esquire All Stars are worthy of the name . . . If Mr Feather wants to write of his 'jump boys', let him, but please have someone else around who can write of Dixieland or New Orleans, of the music that is real, that is jazz.

It was in June 1945, in the *Esquire* letters column, that the term 'Moldy Fig' originated. Wrongly attributed to me (and often spelled Mouldy Figge), it was actually coined by Sam Platt, a member of the US Navy whose letter to the editor so characterized the supporters of the older jazz. It was, of course, picked up by me, by Barry Ulanov and eventually by many others on both sides of the schizoid jazz world.

That artists of the calibre of Hawkins and Eldridge, along with Tatum, Ellington and the rest, could be sneeringly dismissed as the 'jump boys' was typical of one aspect of the mid-1940s *Zeitgeist*. (Yet the same issue carried a letter from a GI in Italy who welcomed the Rhythm Section department of the magazine, and who declared that 'Tatum, Casey and Hawkins were never better' than in my 'Esquire Bounce'.)

Beyond doubt, however, the venom flowed in both directions. Take, for instance, this quote from the September 1945 issue of *Metronome*:

Just as the fascists tend to divide group against group and distinguish between Negroes, Jews, Italians and 'real Americans', so do the moldy figs try to categorize New Orleans, Chicago, swing music and 'the real jazz'. Just as the fascists have tried to foist their views on the public through the vermin press of *Social Justice,* the *Broom* and *X-Ray*, so have the Figs yapped their heads off in the *Jazz Record, Jazz Session* and *Record Changer*. The moldy figs are frustrated by their musical illiteracy, just as they are frustrated by their inability to foist their idiotic views on the public, and frustrated by the ever-increasing public acceptance of the critics and musicians they hate.

These mean-spirited, clumsily written words were my own. Having been virtually branded as a musical fascist, a pseudonymous writer for the *Record Changer*, calling himself Bilbo Brown, responded in kind. He took the names of *Metronome*'s editors and altered them to resemble those of prominent Communists: we became William Z. Feather, George Browder Simon and Barry U. Leninov. This was unfair to Simon, who was really not involved in the battle of words, but Barry Ulanov and I continually asked for trouble by assuming that the best defence was attack. If the writers in both camps had moderated their tone and concentrated on trying to advance the cause of the musicians they believed in, without denouncing those they opposed, much of the ill feeling could have been avoided.

In one of the best researched and less hysterical articles attacking me, Hugues Panassié rightly pointed out that my holier-than-thou attitude, and my assumption that as a musician I was *ipso facto* a better critic, were unjustified. Critics who are musicians disagree among themselves just as often as those who have no empirical background. As Panassié also wrote, it is possible, through selective quotation, to pick out opinions that agree with one's own and contradict those of the critics with whom one disagrees. I was certainly vulnerable in this area, having often quoted remarks by musicians whose views coincided with mine. Later, when I began the 'Blindford Test' series in *Metronome*, my conscience was clear, since I never edited the subjects' views regardless of their divergence from mine.

That the pervasive bitterness in the jazz community would lead to trouble of a more consequential nature should not have surprised us, but in 1947 shock waves were felt in our world with the publication of the latest *Esquire Jazz Book*. What happened, or how it came about, was never made entirely clear. Somewhere along the way Arnold Gingrich left *Esquire* and moved to Switzerland and the editing of the *Jazz Book* fell into the hands of Ernest Anderson, a promoter best known for his close association with Eddie Condon, whose very name was anathema to the modernists.

Under Anderson's guidance the book was quite unsubtly transformed into a virtual publicity outlet for Condon and his associates, while the space devoted to the poll and the winners was conspicuously restricted.

If the attempt to capture the book for Condon and his friends had not been so blatantly opportunistic, perhaps the uproar that ensued might have been avoided, but the tone and intent of the book left room for no reaction but anger on the part of the musicians who had been given short shrift, along with the panelists whose votes previously had been the *raison d'être* of both the books and the concerts.

The black press was particularly outraged. 'Musicians Squawk Over Omissions in *Esquire Jazz Book* Results', one headline read in the *Amsterdam News*. It was complained that the book had:

> a bare listing of the winners, with none of the details about the musicians and the scientific tabulation of the voting of the critics as in former issues. The book . . . carries thirty-seven photos of white musicians with only seventeen of Negro musicians and singers. At least twenty of the pictures are of musicians . . . with the Eddie Condon outfit. [The book] carries an article by Eddie Condon's booking agent . . . articles are printed by such close Condon pals as Art Hodes and others. There is a series of about twenty pictures of the Condon group in an eight-page spread and not a single Negro face appears among them. It reeks of 'Dixieland' and 'white supremacy' music . . . While Sarah Vaughan is listed as the award winner for female vocalist, there's nothing in the book about her save her name. On the other hand, however, there is a full-page spread on Lee Wiley, a white singer who has appeared with Condon.

The story went on to complain about the absence of a photo of Art Tatum, the failure to list the specific findings of the critics, failure to include articles by any of the voters, and failure to detail the musicians' own choices for the New Star listings.

These are the musicians whose achievements were downplayed in the book: Gold Award: Armstrong, Harris, Carter, Hawkins, Goodman, Wilson, Moore, Buddy Rich, Jackson, Norvo, Ellington (band and arranger), Armstrong (vocal), Holiday. Silver Awards: Gillespie, Dickenson, Willie Smith, Lester Young, Bigard, Tatum/Cole (tied), Barney Kessel, Tough, Ed Safranski, Carney, George Handy (arranger), Herman, Cole (vocal), Fitzgerald.

The *Esquire* New Stars for 1947 were Miles Davis, Trummy Young, Sonny Stitt, Lucky Thompson, Rudy Rutherford, Dodo Marmarosa, John Collins, Shadow Wilson, Ray Brown, Milt

Jackson, Tadd Dameron, Boyd Raeburn, Al Hibbler, Sarah Vaughan.

What had been meaningful in the *Esquire* adventure was not only that national attention had been brought to the Tatums and Norvos and Holidays, but also that many of the winners, particularly in the New Stars category, had never before been singled out for recognition; in many cases it would be years before they would be similarly acknowledged by *Down Beat* or *Metronome*, and in too many instances, such as Lucky Thompson and John Collins, even Billy Strayhorn, this was the only award they ever won. Consequently, the lack of any special attention given to them in the *1947 Year Book* was doubly deplorable.

Word travelled fast during that disputatious era. The resentment among the *Esquire* winners, past and present, was unanimous. A letter was drawn up and addressed to David Smart. It read as follows:

Dear Sir:

We, a group of musicians who have won awards in the *Esquire* All American Jazz Polls, hereby protest against the treatment given to the poll in *Esquire*'s *1947 Jazz Book*. We wish to know the answers to the following:

1) Why was the book edited by the personal manager of Eddie Condon, who has nothing to do with jazz today, and why did it devote much of its space to publicity stories and pictures of musicians who work for Condon and for the editor?

2) Why were our individual votes (which are widely read by musicians) not printed in the book?

3) Why is there not a single story or picture, anywhere in the book, on any of this year's New Star winners?

4) Why does the list of the year's so-called 'best records' ignore practically every record made by the younger jazz musicians, including the *Esquire* winners, while devoting most of its space to records made by older musicians of the Dixieland clique?

We regard the entire book as an insult to the musical profession and to the jazz musicians who have helped *Esquire* by taking part in its jazz activities.

As long as the present unfair set-up continues, we do not wish to vote in any future polls, and we will refuse to accept any future awards.

The top copy of this letter was not sent to David Smart; instead, he received a duplicate, for a simple reason: the original, still in my possession, is a unique and valuable document. It carries the signatures of Louis Armstrong, Coleman Hawkins, Roy Eldridge, Red Norvo, Buddy Rich, Charlie Shavers, Dizzy Gillespie, Willie Smith, Boyd Raeburn, Charlie Ventura, Miles Davis, Al Casey, Flip Phillips, Pete Candoli, Shadow Wilson, Trummy Young, Tad (*sic*) Dameron, Sarah Vaughan, Aaron Sachs, Billie Holiday, Buck Clayton, Big Sid Catlett, Johnny Hodges, Harry Carney, Oscar Pettiford, Cootie Williams, Teddy Wilson, Ella Fitzgerald, Duke Ellington, Ray Nance, Nat King Cole, Chubby Jackson and J. C. Heard.

That, of course, marked the end of the *Esquire* era. The entire board of twenty, with the exception of Dave Dexter and Charles Edward Smith, served notice on *Esquire* that they were severing all connections with the magazine. It was probably the first and only time in the history of jazz criticism that so many experts, representing such a wide span of opinions, had come so close to unanimity on anything.

Possibly the revolt was inevitable and the poll doomed. The writing had already been visible on the wall: *Esquire* had dropped its regular feature coverage, Gingrich was not around to help us, and as a devastating postscript Robert Goffin sued the magazine, claiming that he had been frozen out of the picture. That I refused to testify on behalf of *Esquire* undoubtedly helped his case. Among the promises he supposedly received in the course of a settlement was that *Esquire* would never again run a jazz poll.

It was a melancholy ending to a glorious four-year ride. What Goffin and Gingrich and I had concocted, that night at the Hurricane with a live soundtrack by Ellington, survives not only in memory, but in the statuettes still proudly displayed by those lucky few who were in the right place, with the right talent, at the right time.

The end of our *Esquire* collaboration did not connote a break with the Gingriches. Jane and I continued to see Arnold and Helen Mary, who was both his first and his third wife (there was a brief second marriage in between). We visited them in Switzerland, met them often after Arnold returned to New York and became editor of the short-lived *Flair* for Fleur Cowles. Soon he rejoined *Esquire* and in 1952 became publisher and a vice president. I wrote for the magazine a few more times, but our friendship long outlasted the

Mr. David Smart   2/14/47
Esquire Magazine
919 N. Michigan Ave.
Chicago, Ill.

Dear Sir:

    We, a group of musicians who have won awards in the
Esquire All-American Jazz Polls, hereby protest against the
treatment given to the poll in Esquire's 1947 Jazz Book. We
wish to know the answers to the following:

1) Why was the book edited by the personal manager of Eddie
Condon, who has nothing to do with jazz today, and why did
it devote much of its space to publicity stories and pictures
of musicians who work for Condon and for the editor?

2) Why were our individual votes (which are widely read by musicians) not printed in the book?

3) Why is there not a single story or picture, anywhere in the
book, on any of this year's New Star winners?

4) Why does the list of the year's so-called "best records" ignore practically every record made by the younger jazz musicians, including the Esquire winners, while devoting most of
its space to records made by older musicians of the Dixieland
clique?

    We regard the entire book as an insult to the musical pro-
fession and to the jazz musicians who have helped Esquire by taking
part in its jazz activities.

    As long as the present unfair set-up continues, we do not
wish to vote in any future polls, and we will refuse to accept
any future awards.

                         SIGNED:

business relationship. After Smart died, Arnold reached the mandatory retirement age of seventy but stayed on as editor-in-chief. Helen Mary died in 1955; later we saw Arnold in the company of his last wife, Jane. Our mutual interests in jazz, social issues and a spectrum of other topics never abated.

The last time I saw him, a few months before his death, he was still following the daily routine: up at 4 a.m., fishing for an hour in the river that flowed behind his New Jersey home, changing clothes and flagging down a bus with a lantern around 5.30 a.m., studying music books en route to New York, practising the violin at the office from 7 to 8 a.m. before starting work.

I doubt that he ever gave up those foul French cigarettes; in July 1976 I picked up a newspaper in Nice and read that he had died of lung cancer. He was seventy-two.

In *Nothing But People*, his book of memoirs recalling the early days at *Esquire*, he wrote: 'Looking back, I suppose I got more personal enjoyment out of the jazz promotions than out of any other single thing the magazine ever did.' Then, typically, he proceeded to disclaim credit: 'This whole jazz hoopla was about one tenth my idea and nine Dave's.' He neglected to point out that since Dave Smart knew and cared nothing about jazz, his suggestion that we stage the concerts would not have come about but for that indispensable one tenth. The starting points, without which the whole enterprise would never have been born, were Arnold Gingrich's lifelong affection for jazz, and Goffin the catalyst standing close by.

LEO

The winner of the Silver Award in the first *Esquire* Jazz Poll was
Leo Watson. This meant that in the opinion of several leading
experts he was the most talented male jazz singer after Louis
Armstrong, who won the Gold Award.

What seemed strange about this victory was that it took a
three-month search to find Leo Watson and present him with his
Esky statuette. When found, he was not earning a living as a
vocalist; he was discovered in a war plant, loading and unloading
trucks, totally forgotten by everyone but the few loyalists who had
voted for him.

In an article about him that appeared in *Esquire,* headlined 'The
James Joyce of Jazz', I pointed out that Watson might also be called
the Gertrude Stein of jazz. Another phrase, coined on his behalf by
George Simon, was 'the man who sings in shorthand'. Elsewhere,
he was known as the world's greatest scat singer, or simply as the
mad genius.

It was certainly appropriate to call Leo Watson *sui generis,* though
if you had told him that, his answer might have been: 'Say what?'
Leo was a man of few words, most of them self-invented and many
of them delivered in a stream-of-consciousness style the like of
which had never before been heard and has not been heard since.

Leo supposedly invented a word that became world-famous in
the early 1940s, the word 'zoot'. He was as astonishing to watch as
to hear. In his novel *Brainstorm,* Carlton Brown described how
Watson used to 'whirl his ukulele around and whack it terrifically
on the back while taking vocal riffs phrased like good trombone
solos'. There was no literature on Leo – my piece may have been
the only full examination ever undertaken. Those of us who had
attempted to follow his career knew him soon after he loomed into

view around 52nd Street with a vocal and instrumental novelty jazz group called the Spirits of Rhythm. Leo usually played the tiple, akin to a small ukulele, but when he sang he would move his right arm up and down as if he were manipulating a trombone slide. His voice did indeed resemble a surrealistic trombone when this squat, dark, huge-mouthed figure let loose his torrents of sound.

Singing was one word for it, though what Leo Watson did could hardly qualify as singing in any accepted sense. It was a combination of words and meaningless syllables fitted to intensely rhythmic phrases, all entirely spontaneous. For example, on a tune called 'She ain't no Saint' his first ad lib passage began: 'Oh when the saints go marching in give 'em a drink of gin all around and round and round she goes around table a round Mabel . . .' On a scat version of 'Honeysuckle Rose' some of his inspirations ran like this: 'Oh honey sock me on the noseyama yama yama yama root de voot de voot . . . oh honey so sock so sock sock sock sock sock cymbal rymbal symbal a nimble nimble nimble . . . so sock me on the nose . . . ose gose goose goose goose moose gavoose bablow your nose . . . hello Rose how's your toes put some papowder on your nose ah Rosetta are you feeling bettah . . . ah rose nose nose rose me lamble damble damble reezy voot mop mop broom broom sweep sweep so honey sock my nose . . .'

Leo was the drawing card with the Spirits of Rhythm, most often at the Onyx Club. He and the other members didn't always see ear to ear; from one week to another one could not be sure whether it would be the Six Spirits of Rhythm, the Four or Five Spirits of Rhythm, or two separate groups working at rival rooms. At one point Leo and his sometime partner, the guitarist Teddy Bunn, merged with the original John Kirby sextet. Leo, though vague about musical theory, took up the trombone during that time and, as I recall, was getting along quite well until a hock shop came between man and horn. He next decided to concentrate on the drums.

Another drummer, Gene Krupa, who had recently formed his own orchestra, came into the Onyx and was captivated by the Watson talent. Krupa hired him as male vocalist with the new band. He lasted, surprisingly, eight months. There are several versions of how he lost the job, but the most plausible was that on a train, somewhere in the South, Leo, perhaps for want of a drum to bang or a horn to blow, was amusing himself by slashing a window shade. When the conductor tried to put a stop to this sabotage, Leo plunged his fist through the windowpane. He was removed from the train and from employment by Gene Krupa.

Leo may not have been easy to handle, but there were those along Broadway who felt it was worth the trouble. The Andrews Sisters, who came into the Onyx regularly to marvel at him, persuaded their manager, Lou Levy, to fix Leo up with a Decca Records contract. He was provided with some odd material, such as 'Utt Da Zay', a pop tune based on a Yiddish folk theme. This immediately suggested to Leo such interpolations as 'buy me a beer Mr Shane' (his variation on 'Bei Mir Bist Du Schoen') and 'utt da zay zaz zu zay uttdazay zazzuzay bah-yeep bah yeep beh yeedle dah de vope . . . matzas pratzas . . .'

One of Leo's pastimes, when he had run out of other ideas, was to holler abstractedly but emphatically the word 'zoot!' This became a virtual password along 52nd Street.

From the Onyx, Leo and some of the Spirits moved downtown to Greenwich Village, where they became the intermission act between spells of Dixieland music at Nick's. George Wettling, the drummer with the two-beat group, told me how insistently Leo demanded to play his drums. 'Leo didn't know any of the orthodox technique, so he'd just beat the hell out of my kit. After he'd broken my foot pedal four times – and you know that's a tough thing to break – I told him he had to lay off.'

Leo's passion for the drums was not easily quenched. He migrated to the West Coast, where local musicians recall his appearing publicly during the notorious zoot-suit riots. Leaving home, snare drum in hand, he took a taxi to the scene of the most violent rioting, jumped out and started marching up and down beating his drum, proclaiming 'Ain't no zoot suiters gonna stop me!' It was as a drummer, not a singer, that he made a brief appearance with Lena Horne in the film *Panama Hattie*.

A little later Leo went to work in a club where the bandstand and most of the room had been decorated with large mirrors. All night long Leo, seized by a Narcissus complex, concentrated on his multiple images, staring and grinning and making a series of weird faces at his mirror images.

One night he began to take a drum solo and it got him in a strong, steady groove; so good, in fact, that he just didn't want to stop, not for anyone. Loud and relentless, the solo went on for fifteen, twenty, thirty minutes, an hour. By this time the customers were more than slightly aroused. All efforts to stop Leo failed. Finally the police were summoned; as Leo was dragged bodily out of the club in the arms of two cops, he still had a small side drum in his grasp, and was beating it steadily as he passed out of sight.

During my visit to Los Angeles for the second *Esquire* concert, I attempted to track down Leo Watson. For a week my efforts were in vain; then someone reported seeing him in a restaurant, reportedly employed as a floor cleaner. Word reached him; he called me, and I booked a studio, rounded up Teddy Bunn and another guitarist, Ulysses Livingston, along with Red Callender on bass, and a drummer named George Vann who also sang the blues. I prepared some material, including special lyrics to 'Coquette' and 'Honeysuckle Rose' which Leo was free to mess up any way he chose. I played piano and tried to keep some sort of order in an inspired but chaotic date. The records came out on Black & White; they have never been on an LP and, as far as I know, have disappeared.

The following year I arranged with Bob Thiele to record Leo for Bob's Signature Records. This time I used Vic Dickenson, whose trombone sounded to me like the closest possible instrumental counterpart to Leo's voice. They traded off superbly, with a rhythm section that included the guitarist Arv Garrison; his wife, Vivien Garry, on bass; Doc West on drums, and me. I played this date under the name of Jelly Roll Lipschitz, which, according to the Jepsen discography, was a pseudonym for Eddie Heywood!

Leo was in magnificent form that day. We did 'Jingle Bells', on which I played tack piano to set the seasonal mood. Leo's stream ran something like this: 'Jingle bells, jingle bells . . . wedding bells . . . bells of the wedding . . . wedding cake . . . cut the cake . . . cake . . . snowflake . . . snowflakes of Chicago . . . Chicago, Chicago, that toddling town . . .'

It occurred to me that the cornier the song, the more fun Leo could have with it, so I suggested 'Sonny Boy', which he sang first as a pseudo-straight ballad before lapsing into the wildest imaginable vocalese, trading off against Vic in some manic fours. To round out the session we did 'The Snake Pit', its title taken from a then popular novel and film about a mental home, and 'Tight and Gay', on the changes of 'Night and Day'.

This session was reissued a few years ago on Thiele's Dr Jazz label. Whitney Balliett wrote about it in the *New Yorker*, but it sank without a trace. So, I'm afraid, did Leo. His profound and unique talent could not counterbalance his affection for pot and other diversions. He was in and out of jail once or twice, and in obscurity for the rest of his short life, dying in Los Angeles in 1950.

Back in 1945, when I was researching my piece on Leo, a musician, listening to one of his records, remarked: 'Fifty years from now, people will dig what Leo is doing.'

It seems unlikely. Leo didn't hold up, and neither did the records; yet who knows? By 1995 those manic sounds may rise again on someone's compact disc.

FROM DIXIELAND TO BEBOP

During the *Esquire* years I became involved with the recording activities of dozens of past, present or future poll winners, and with a fair number of artists whose importance had nothing to do with whether or not they had won critical acceptance. Sarah Vaughan, in fact, did not become a winner until 1947, but I had been following her career since the first day of her professional life, when she opened with Earl Hines at the Apollo. She was then nineteen, and I reported enthusiastically in *Metronome* on the inherent musicianship she displayed during her treatment of 'Body and Soul'. That was in April 1943; the following year, along with Dizzy Gillespie and several other Hines graduates, she joined the Billy Eckstine orchestra. One day I ran into Dizzy, outside the Nola Studio at 52nd and Broadway; he was carrying a demonstration record.

'Come upstairs and listen to this,' he said. What I heard was a single song ('Night in Tunisia', I believe), enough to offer evidence that this was a vital new sound, crying to be recorded. Because she was now working for a male singer, who at that point had recorded only his own vocals, Sarah clearly needed a session of her own. (She did get to cut one tune with the Eckstine band for the shortlived De Luxe label.)

There was no apparent interest in Sarah Vaughan; Savoy and one or two other labels I approached turned her down without even listening to the demo. Finally Donald Gabor at Continental, who also never bothered to hear her, grudgingly said: 'Well, if she's as good as you say, let's try her out. But I can't afford . . .' The rest of his remarks followed what was then a pattern among independent companies: keep the costs at a minimum.

With this in mind, I agreed to work for $12.50 a tune and, in order to save expenses, put myself down as pianist – a mistake, since I had trouble reading the piano part on 'Interlude', Dizzy's vocal version of 'Night in Tunisia', and he had to help me out by doubling at the piano on that number.

A lyricist, Jessyca Russell, had brought me a couple of her potential songs. I had fitted one of them, 'Signing Off', with a harmonically oblique melody to which I knew Sarah, with her keen ear, could do justice.

We recorded late at night on New Year's Eve of 1944; Sarah received $20 for each of the four songs. 'East of the Sun', in particular, displayed her uncanny musicality. 'No Smokes Blues', a trivial piece I had written about the then prevalent cigarette shortage, could better have been replaced by another standard, though Dizzy was in good form in the boppish head arrangement. My own chart for 'Signing Off', voiced for clarinet (Aaron Sachs), tenor (Georgie Auld) and Dizzy, came off well.

Released early in 1945, the two 78s were well enough received to encourage Gabor, who authorized me to line up another date. This time I wanted to use both Dizzy and Bird, an idea that delighted Sarah, who had told me she never had more fun in her life than during the time she spent with them in the Hines band.

I found her very quiet and withdrawn when we sat in her small room at the Braddock, around the corner from the Apollo, talking over plans for the dates. In those days she looked awkward, almost dowdy, with a gap between her front teeth; her glamorization began a couple of years later, when the trumpeter George Treadwell became her husband and her Svengali.

The second date began disastrously: Charlie Parker didn't show up. We were about to go ahead without him when he ambled in very casually an hour late, with an apology but no explanation. We had time for only three tunes, but Bird's solo on 'Mean to Me' made it all worthwhile. Ironically, after I had bowed out of a playing role this time, Nat Jaffe, the pianist, had a little difficulty with the part Tadd Dameron had written on another melody I had set to a Jessyca Russell lyric, 'I'd Rather Have a Memory than a Dream'. Tadd took over on piano, while Bird played some gently understated obbligatos and Flip Phillips rounded out the front line. We had a strong rhythm section with Bill De Arango, Curly Russell and Max Roach. Sarah already was offering proof that ballads were her forte; Peggy Lee's song 'What More Can a Woman Do?' seemed made for her.

BOP CONCERT
CARNEGIE HALL
SUNDAY, FEBRUARY 20 - 8:30 P. M.
COMMENTARY BY SYMPHONY SID OF WMCA

LEONARD FEATHER & MONTE KAY

. . . present . . .

THE KING COLE TRIO

IRVING ASHBY - *GUITAR*   JOE COMFORT - *BASS*
AND AUGMENTED AFRO-CUBAN RHYTHM

WOODY HERMAN

AND HIS ORCHESTRA FEATURING MARY ANN McCALL

THE FABULOUS **"FOUR BROTHERS"**	**BILL HARRIS** *Trombone*	**OSCAR PETTIFORD** *Bass*
SERGE CHALOFF *Baritone Sax*	★ ★ **RED RODNEY** *Trumpet*	★ ★ **TERRY GIBBS** *Vibes*
★ ★ **STAN GETZ** *Tenor Sax*	★ ★ **EARL SWOPE** *Trombone*	★ ★ **ERNIE ROYAL** *Trumpet*
★ ★ **"ZOOT" SIMS** *Tenor Sax*		
★ ★ **AL COHEN** *Tenor Sax*	★ ★ **COUNT LEVY** *Piano*	★ ★ **DON LAMOND** *Drums*

RALPH BURNS conducting "SUMMER SEQUENCE" and "LADY McGOWAN'S DREAM"

<u>ONLY</u> *NEW YORK APPEARANCE THIS SEASON*

TICKETS AT BOX OFFICE AND THE ROYAL ROOST $1.20 TO $3.60 INCL. TAX

A full year elapsed – from May 1945 to May 1946 – before Sarah signed her first regular recording contract, with Musicraft. Then she made 'Body and Soul', 'It's Magic' and a long series of superb performances that sold reasonably well, establishing her firmly as the new vocal jazz star of the decade.

That I was able to record Sarah Vaughan, Dizzy Gillespie and Charlie Parker before any of them had secured a contract with any company was naturally a source of special pleasure to me; so was my series of Carnegie Hall concerts from 1947–9 in which, with the help of the young jazz promoter Monte Kay and the popular bebop disc jockey Symphony Sid Torin, I was able to prove the existence of a substantial audience for the music of Dizzy (and, on the first concert, Bird). A little later, in 1949, my first published book *Inside Bebop* (later somewhat cautiously retitled *Inside Jazz*) set the entire movement in perspective with the story of its evolution, biographies of some ninety musicians and technical analyses of the music.

That such efforts were needed remained all too clear in the light of the continued assault on these artists by the moldy figs. A classic instance was a review of two of Charlie Parker's greatest masterpieces, 'Ornithology' and 'Night in Tunisia', appearing in the *Record Changer* of September 1946 under the byline William Purcell. Among other things, he said:

> Incredibly dull music. If this is a good example of the 'advanced' stuff the so-called progressives are raving about . . . one cannot help wondering what causes the shouting. These compositions are just as cute, as phoney and as unexciting as Raymond Scott's and Alec Wilder's 'innovations' [*sic*] of many years back . . . no one among these men produces truly creative music . . . pseudo-oriental atmosphere in 'Tunisia' makes it rather vulgar. 'Ornithology' ('How High the Moon') follows a watered-down tune pattern similar to Dizzy Gillespie's 'Groovin' High' ('Whispering'). Added to the poverty of the material is the lack of fire in the interpretation . . . the rhythm section is awful and has no beat at all. So there was nothing, nothing whatsoever to hold your interest.

Even as late as 1951, when most of the reactionaries had caved in and some had even taken to producing bop records, an article entitled 'And Whatever Happened to Jazz?' appeared in *Capitol*

News, a throwaway sheet distributed by the record company. Described in a subsequent *Down Beat* editorial as a 'bitter, malicious diatribe', the article, written by Dave Dexter (ironically a former *Down Beat* editor) stated that nothing new was happening in jazz, called the entire bebop movement 'pitifully abortive', and even accused his own employers, Capitol Records, of pulling 'the *faux pas* of the decade' by recording some of the *Metronome* and *Down Beat* winners. 'You give us Tristano, De Franco, Konitz and that crowd? We'll give them back, less handling charges,' he said.

Apparently convinced that there were no good, new singers, Dexter dismissed Sarah Vaughan as a 'tinny, shallow flash in the pan'. Fortunately by the time this tirade appeared in print, Sarah Vaughan was internationally established and had been recording for Columbia; Dizzy Gillespie, in addition to his *Esquire* victories, had won four annual *Metronome* polls and enjoyed global respect. Charlie Parker was winning both *Down Beat* and *Metronome* polls annually, and in 1955 was elected to the *Down Beat* Hall of Fame.

Although Gillespie by the mid-1940s had become more than a cult figure, he was still freelancing on lesser labels that were too often hard to find. But by that time I had established a good relationship with Steve Sholes, the corpulent, friendly and amenable executive at RCA. My insistence that bebop was the music of the future, and that *Bebop* ought to be the title of an RCA album, met with his qualified approval, 'I like the idea, but I'm not sure about that title.'

I went ahead with two sessions, the first a borderline bebop affair billed as 'Coleman Hawkins' 52nd Street All Stars' with Allen Eager, Pete Brown, Mary Osborne, Jimmy Jones, Shelly Manne and Al McKibbon. Again I had a nonpareil ballad in mind as a Hawkins vehicle: 'Say It isn't So' turned out as well as 'My Ideal'.

At that time there were a few songs floating around 52nd Street known to everybody by melody but not always by title. One of these was a Denzil Best line on which, imprudently, I suggested having Hawkins and Eager trade fours. We tried one take, but Bean was clearly uncomfortable, and the concept did not appeal to him; on the take used he let Eager and Pete Brown divide the honours. We called the tune 'Allen's Alley', but later found out that Denzil called it 'Wee'.

A few weeks later Dizzy finally made his major-label debut, heading an all-star group with Don Byas, Milt Jackson (whose vibes at that time sounded more like tuned milk bottles), Al Haig, Bill De

Arango, the nineteen-year-old Ray Brown and J. C. Heard. An instrumental version of 'Tunisia' was clearly called for. I contributed, under another of my countless phony names, an original entitled 'Old Man Rebop'. Again we had an untitled tune to deal with: Dizzy played a riff and said, 'Let's do this thing of Monk's.' We did it, and because we had heard it played regularly as a sign-off by the bop groups along 52nd Street, I suggested, 'Why don't we just call it "52nd Street Theme"?' Apparently Monk had no objection; it has been known by that title ever since.

Despite my enthusiasm, RCA would not go along with the name *Bebop* for the album of four 78s yielded by these two sessions. 'That's a controversial word,' I was told. Sholes suggested the euphemism *New 52nd Street Jazz*, and when it appeared in the shops the music spoke quite vividly for itself. A year or two elapsed before RCA gave in, and a four-disc set labelled as *Bebop: an Album of Modern Jazz* was released, with two numbers each by Dizzy (who by then had signed with RCA on the strength of our testing-the-waters venture), Kenny Clarke's group in two tunes produced in New York by Charles Delaunay (whose predilection for bebop had brought his long friendship with Panassié to a bitter and permanent end), and two each from sessions I had made with Coleman Hawkins (my own 'Jumping for Jane' and Tadd Dameron's 'Half Step Down, Please') and Lucky Thompson.

The story of Lucky Thompson, whose velvet tenor sax won him the *Esquire* New Star award in 1947, was all too typical of the hard-luck tales that separated countless superlative musicians from the recognition due to them. Except for one or two dates on obscure, defunct labels, he had not recorded as a leader. In the group I built around him were Benny Carter, Neal Hefti, a baritone player who read ensemble parts, and a rhythm section that comprised Dodo Marmarosa, Barney Kessel, Lee Young and Red Callender.

Lucky was an admirable ballad player in the Hawkins tradition. My suggestion of 'Just One More Chance' as a ballad vehicle appealed to him; he played it with a sinuous beauty that has established this as perhaps his best ever record. One number was built around Benny Carter, who wrote the tune and chart for 'Boulevard Bounce'. 'Boppin' the Blues' gave everyone a chance to take off, and 'From Dixieland to Bebop' was essentially a bop chart I had scored for the four horns, preceded by a collectively improvised chorus on the same changes, supposedly in traditional jazz style, though it seemed to me that you couldn't take the bebop out of Neal Hefti.

The session should have been lucky for Lucky, but in the years ahead lay nothing but occasional breaks and frequent disappointments. He recorded in many cities at home and abroad, but whatever luck he may ever have had ran out long ago; I have heard nothing of him in about ten years. His last consequential job, in fact, was probably his brief sojourn with Stan Kenton in the late 1950s, mainly in Europe.

Not all my time during the early years of the new jazz was devoted to the preservation of bebop. Some of the most productive encounters were those I had with the long-established giants. Of the four *Esquire* All Star groups I put together (the first for Commodore, the second for Continental) I suppose the third and fourth, both for RCA, were the most rewarding and perhaps the best musically.

Because Duke Ellington and Louis Armstrong were both recording for RCA, a far-fetched idea occurred to me: why not bring them together for a session? They had never worked in tandem. Duke's reaction was, 'Just tell me where you want me, baby,' while Louis's was slightly more cautious, 'If Mr Glaser says it's OK, I'll be there!'

I could hardly believe my good fortune. The two men I admired most, who had played a formative role in my education, were coming together to help me by taking part in an unprecedented gathering that included Johnny Hodges, Charlie Shavers, Jimmy Hamilton, Don Byas and a rhythm section worthy of them.

Duke arrived early, with Billy Strayhorn. To amuse themselves they sat at the piano playing their four-hand version of a delightful piece they had cooked up. Called 'Tonk', it was something they had enjoyed playing for friends at parties. They had never thought of recording it. 'Why don't we get a take while we have time on our hands?' I suggested. They not only obliged, but followed it up with an ad lib 'Drawing Room Blues'. Our session had two brilliant bonuses before we had officially started.

Louis Armstrong and the others filed into the studio to try out the first number, a blues called 'Long Long Journey' which Louis and I had performed together on a radio show. Duke's piano solo midway through this four-minute take (we were recording for twelve-inch records) was his contribution; Louis played and sang his way through most of the number.

On 'Snafu', an instrumental that had turned out well as a vehicle for the trumpeter Shorty Sherock in a date I had produced with him in Los Angeles, we had a slight problem. Louis read his part accurately, but it was too evident that he was reading; the notes came out staccato and self-conscious.

How was I to resolve the situation without seeming brash and tactless? I could imagine the reaction among the musicians and visitors in the studio: 'Who is this English idiot telling a genius how to play?' Then it occurred to me that Neal Hefti, of the Herman band, was here, with his horn.

'Louis,' I said, 'we want to get more of your own feeling into this. Why don't we just let Neal read the part, while you ad lib in the open spots, and then go into your own chorus?'

The idea worked just as I had hoped. Neal, a fluent reader, handled the buoyant phrases of the tune while Louis tossed in a few perfectly spotted ad libs, then blew a masterfully improvised thirty-two-bar solo. The myth that he was set in his ways and had forgotten how to play spontaneously was immediately dispelled. It is sad that the alternate takes were not saved, since he played quite differently from one master to the next.

Louis stepped down and Charlie Shavers took over for an up-tempo romp that seemed right for his bravura personality, 'The One that Got Away'. I had written this for a Slam Stewart date on which Red Norvo played; Red was on hand again as one of several soloists.

By now it was long after midnight and the sense of relative sobriety in which the session had begun seemed to be disappearing, along with the supply of libations. I let Jimmy Hamilton, Red Norvo and Shavers go; the time had come to settle down with an after-hours ballad.

'Gone with the Wind', a tune I had long wanted to record, was agreed upon. Backed by Strayhorn, Remo Palmier, Chubby Jackson and Sonny Greer, the sublimely melodic Don Byas and Johnny Hodges shared the honours on what I felt represented the *beau idéal* of their creative genius.

Eleven months later the final *Esquire* session took place in the same studio. The direction was less traditional, though the solos were divided between swing masters and modernists. With Hawkins on hand it was time for yet another neglected ballad, Victor Herbert's 'Indian Summer'. In boppish contrast I wrote a tune on the 'How High the Moon' changes (by now the most prevalent chord pattern along 52nd Street) and, with J. J. Johnson from Indianapolis featured and 'Indian Summer' set for the flip side, it seemed logical to call it 'Indiana Winter'.

'Buckin' the Blues', which I had originally written as 'Blues at Mary Lou's' for the Continental date, seemed well suited for adaptation to horns; accordingly, I wrote an arrangement highlighting Buck Clayton (for whom it was renamed) and the guitar of a New Star winner, John Collins. Completing the date was 'Blow Me Down', which was not only credited to Billy Moore Jr but also, unlike the numbers for which I had borrowed his name, actually written and arranged by him.

The pseudonym gambit never worked better than on these final *Esquire* pieces. Although the date with Duke and Louis had produced results that were, to my mind, almost impossible to top, the album containing the products of the second date was appraised in *Down Beat* as 'infinitely superior to last year's volume' with a pointed comment that 'none of the tunes was written or arranged by Feather'. Had I used my name on 'Indiana Winter' and 'Buckin' the Blues' and disguised my identity on my originals the previous year, no doubt the verdicts would have been reversed.

Having impressed Steve Sholes with the Ellington–Armstrong summit meeting, I had a free hand to produce almost anything that seemed like a viable suggestion over the next two years. I brought in Mildred Bailey and Ethel Waters for a blues album I had in mind, providing them both with elegant piano-trio backing (Ellis Larkins for Mildred, Herman Chittison for Waters). To complete the album there were blues tracks on dates I made with Armstrong and Jack Teagarden.

Another concept I had on the schedule was a piano album. On four dates, in a total of less than a dozen working hours, I recorded three established giants and a brilliant newcomer. None of them had ever recorded for RCA; in fact, the youngster, a sixteen-year-old named André Previn, had never recorded at all except for a date on Gene Norman's independent label. As happened around the same time with Dizzy Gillespie, this one-shot date led to his being signed to the label exclusively.

I recorded Previn and Erroll Garner in Los Angeles. Previn's date came off quietly and uneventfully. What I recall best about Garner is the spirited, utterly spontaneous mood he sustained. All I had to say would be 'How about "Stairway to the Stars"?' or 'Why don't you just play some blues?' and three minutes later we had it on acetate. Erroll's conversation was confined largely to the exclamation 'Hoochie coochie coo!' which he repeated incessantly. I don't recall making more than one take of anything.

In New York I recorded Lennie Tristano and Art Tatum. I had begun studying with Tristano, traipsing out once a week to his Long Island home, where he tested my ear on recognizing chords, and showed me how to voice harmonic concepts of my own. He was an invaluable teacher. On our date he made only two tunes, but since he recorded so little for the major labels they were valuable documents of a heterodox talent.

Tatum was a breeze. If it had not been contrary to union rules we could easily have made two or three more tunes in the allotted time. Again it was just a matter of proposing ideas for tunes, and on his part the comments were simple ones such as: 'Can you send out for another six-pack of beer?'

Pleased though I was with the piano dates, the several encounters with Louis Armstrong and Jack Teagarden, separately and together, were the most meaningful of my entire RCA Victor association.

I had been urging both Louis and Joe Glaser to consider dropping the big, unwieldy orchestra that had put Satchmo for too long in the position of a greyhound pulling a truck. With his assignment to play an acting role and lead a small combo in the film *New Orleans* the band was at least temporarily discontinued. Louis's so-called 'Dixieland Seven' in the movie put him in the company of several excellent musicians such as Barney Bigard and Red Callender, along with a few old-timers: Kid Ory playing his tailgate trombone, and the banjoist-guitarist Bud Scott.

Visiting Los Angeles for a series of sessions, I cajoled Louis and Glaser into letting me adjust this combo slightly for a more cohesive and less traditionalist sound. We kept Callender, Bigard and the pianist Charlie Beal, but put Vic Dickenson in the trombone role and Allan Reuss on guitar. Zutty Singleton was not the ideal drummer in this company, but as an old friend of Louis he helped establish a congenial atmosphere.

I had written two blues for the occasion, and took over at the piano for both. Louis was in his element throughout, yet during a subsequent correspondence with him concerning the Carnegie Hall debut I planned to set up, he insisted on retaining the big band; however, he suggested bringing in the small combo he had used in the film to open the show. This turned out to be economically impractical, but Louis compromised by agreeing to work with the fine sextet Edmond Hall was leading at Cafe Society.

With my two co-producers, Bob Snyder and Greer Johnson, I arranged to divide the programme into New Orleans, Chicago, New York and Hollywood segments. But show biz, of which Louis never ceased considering himself a part, dominated in this final set, with Louis's male singer delivering the ballads and, contrary to Louis's promise, Velma Middleton, a massive lady, not only singing but also clowning and doing the splits. By way of compensation we introduced Billie Holiday, who had been in the movie and who also had never appeared before at Carnegie Hall. Big Sid Catlett made a guest appearance in the last set. Teagarden being unavailable, Ed Hall's bassist Johnny Williams shared the vocal duet on 'Rockin' Chair'.

Satch soon afterwards recorded what would be the final session with his big band. Two months later, in May 1947, he appeared at Town Hall, with Bobby Hackett, Teagarden and a rhythm section; by now both he and Glaser had seen the light. It was typical of his generous spirit that he told me later: 'They were a nice bunch of cats and I didn't want to see them all out of work. But the trend was changing.'

The small Armstrong combo, also in the spirit of the times, was interracial from the start, with Dick Cary on piano and Teagarden in the original personnel.

A month after Louis's Carnegie debut I had recorded an RCA session with Jack Teagarden's Big Eight, an impeccable group with Max Kaminsky, Peanuts Hucko and Dave Tough among those present. Big T. was a laid-back Texan whose drawl, both speaking and singing, coupled with his burring trombone, always seemed to be of a piece. Then in June, just weeks before the new Armstrong combo was assembled on a permanent basis, I brought my two idols together for the first time since they had teamed for the classic 'Knockin' a Jug' in 1929. With Hackett, Hucko, Johnny Guarnieri and a few others, they breezed through 'Rockin' Chair', Louis sang the ballad called 'Some Day' which he told me had come to him in a dream, and they joined vocally on a piece called 'Fifty Fifty Blues' which I had written for the date, singing in harmony on the last chorus. From that time on, Joe Glaser never again thought of sending Louis on gruelling tours of one-night stands encumbered by eighteen performers. The new format gave him more latitude to work in nightclubs, at concerts and to tour internationally with greatly reduced hotel and transportation costs. This setting, which made musical and economic sense, served Louis well for the rest of his life.

PART THREE

Prejudices

RACE

In 1936, visiting New York as a reluctant ad salesman for the *Melody Maker*, I found myself in the offices of MCA, then a giant talent agency. I had an appointment with Freddie Martin, one of the big pop bandleaders of the day, and his manager.

To give them an idea how their ad might look, I showed them a dummy sheet on which a few artists' names or photographs could be seen. Because Irving Mills had bought a substantial block of space, one of them was a photo of Duke Ellington.

The manager looked at the sample page and turned to me in horror. 'What?' he said, 'you want to put Freddie's ad on the same page with a nigger?'

Also during one of my early New York visits, I was at the home of Red Norvo and Mildred Bailey, enjoying a pleasant social evening, when the phone rang. Mildred picked it up, talked for a couple of minutes, then hung up in disgust. 'Oh, shit,' she said. 'It was Joe Venuti. He was supposed to come over, but he begged off when I told him we expect Teddy Wilson. He doesn't believe in socializing with coloured people.'

Another incident involving Red and Mildred took place at Adrian Rollini's Tap Room, in the basement of the President Hotel. Together with John Hammond, Felix King and Marshall Stearns, then president of the Yale Hot Club, we had come to listen to a quartet led by Red Allen and Buster Bailey. At the end of the set Allen came over to join us for a drink. Only moments later he was approached by an angry-looking representative of the management. 'Hey,' he said, 'we don't want you people sitting with the customers.'

The remark succeeded in alienating musicians and patrons alike: the following evening Allen and Bailey sent in subs.

Because of Louis Prima's apparently swarthy complexion in photographs we had seen, and because of such spoken remarks on his records as: 'What's on your mind, Creole?', it had been widely assumed in England that he was black. When we met, he hastened to reassure me: 'Hell,' he said, 'I've never even *used* any coloured musicians.' From his tone of voice it was clear that he never intended to.

During another visit in the summer of 1936, I arranged a meeting with Nick La Rocca, who at the age of forty-eight was planning to revive his Original Dixieland Jazz Band, which had flourished in the second decade of this century. After a few minutes' conversation with him, I closed my notebook: it was too easy to guess what was coming. Before long he had assured me that every worthwhile jazz musician gained his education from white Dixieland records and not from coloured artists; that no musician ever learned from Louis Armstrong, but rather that Armstrong and King Oliver had learned from the Dixielanders; that if you set up any white band against a coloured band, the latter would have no chance; that Negroes had done little or nothing to further the cause of jazz and that the only men who had copied nobody, and had started something themselves through sheer inspiration from Heaven, were the Dixielanders.

There was an ironic postscript to this encounter. Two years later, in Copenhagen, I ran into Emile Christian, who had played trombone in the Original Dixieland Jazz Band; he was now a bassist with the Leon Abbey orchestra, its only white member. They had been touring together amicably for two or three years.

It struck me as more than coincidental that so many of these incidents involved Italian-Americans: Venuti, Prima, Rollini, La Rocca. In the light of Italy's rape of Abyssinia, the evidence at that time seemed even more compelling; but I was wrong. In fact, it was another Italian-American, a musician I grew to admire both for his artistry and for his attitudes, Joe Marsala, who broke the colour line on 52nd Street.

It was the summer of 1936; to my surprise, on opening night I found Red Allen wearing the regular band uniform in the circular bar of the Hickory House, as a member of the group billed as 'Joe Marsala and Eddie Condon's Chicagoans'. The other members were Mort Stuhlmaker on bass and the nineteen-year-old Joe Bushkin on piano. Red was able to play only the first two nights, as he had a commitment to return to the Mills Blue Rhythm Band;

however, he was replaced by another black trumpeter, Otis Johnson. This happened at a time when there was no other truly integrated jazz orchestra. Jess Stacy was still playing piano with Benny Goodman, who used Teddy Wilson only as a 'special attraction' with the Goodman trio: he had not yet hired Lionel Hampton.

Marsala's initiative was based on his genuine concern for integration. 'When the right time comes,' he told me, 'I want to form a real mixed band. It's a logical development. Why should I have any different attitude toward a musician because of his colour? When I was a kid a lot of my buddies were coloured boys. I used to go to their homes and they came to mine. I've been brought up without any prejudice.'

Unfortunately, the band drew only a handful of people, and Marsala's run at the Hickory House was short, though he played there frequently over the next decade. He never did live to see the realization of his ambition to form a truly integrated orchestra.

It was not long before I found out that the incidents involving Venuti, Prima and the others were isolated examples of a much larger picture, and that American racism was indiscriminately spread through every stratum of white society. Indignities and humiliations, some of them relatively petty, others entailing outright physical violence, were embedded in the black lifestyle.

On the non-violent side was Andy Kirk's visit to my hotel room. I came downstairs to greet him, but as we headed for the passenger elevator, we were shunted aside; the operator insisted that we take the freight elevator.

Fats Waller, coming out of a Harlem club at 5 a.m. with his brother, Edward Lawrence Waller, hailed a taxi. As he was about to enter it, two white girls came up to ask him for his autograph. Immediately, two white men, one a twenty-two-year-old ex-convict named Kehoe, came over to remove the girls, whom they had been escorting. As they cursed and beat the women, Waller's brother protested; Kehoe told him to mind his own business. In the fight that followed, Kehoe drew a gun and fired two shots into Edward Waller's chest and leg. Kehoe was then beaten into unconsciousness by the infuriated Fats, and by a crowd of people from inside the club who rushed out to assist him. Edward Waller and Kehoe were taken into a hospital in critical condition. Waller recovered; Fats never told me what happened to Kehoe.

Two aspects of this story impressed me: if you were Fats Waller's

size and were standing on a snow-covered sidewalk, grappling with
a man who had a smoking gun in his hand, you could consider
yourself reasonably brave. Moreover, although occurrences of this
kind took place daily or nightly from New York to Mississippi and
all over America, it was only when celebrities were involved that we
were likely to hear about them.

It may be argued that these examples of the black experience all
happened several decades ago. The argument doesn't bear close
examination. In 1964 three young civil-rights workers, two of them
white, were murdered in cold blood in Philadelphia, Mississippi. In
November 1985 in Philadelphia, Pennsylvania, white neighbours
rioted, shouted 'nigger' and had to be restrained after a black
couple, and a black man with a white wife, moved into their
neighbourhood. Whether it's Philadelphia, Mississippi in 1964 or
Philadelphia, Pennsylvania in 1985, the struggle goes on.

It would be unrealistic to claim that conditions have not
improved for the black American, and specifically for the black
musician, but the pace has been painfully slow and its impact has
affected only a small minority of Afro-Americans. Miles Davis, Ella
Fitzgerald and a few others have become millionaires and can now
stay in neighbourhoods where for many years, as a result of the
so-called restrictive covenants, they could not live.

What white Americans see, what even most white jazz musicians
see, is a change that has been largely cosmetic. Looking at the
affluent, secure Miles Davis, they ignore the memory of Davis,
blood streaming from his head as a white policeman beat him
repeatedly. His 'crime' was that he had been standing outside
Birdland between sets, and answered tersely when the cop wanted
to know what he was doing there. (His real crime was that he had a
white woman standing beside him.) At the hospital, ten stitches
were put in his head. Miles sued the city for half a million dollars
for illegal arrest. Eventually the suit was dropped and his scars
healed, but the emotional scars ran deep and will never disappear.
They extend back to his childhood, when a white child
ran after him on the streets of East St Louis shouting 'Nigger!
Nigger!'

Not all the millions he can accumulate will erase such incidents
and enable Miles Davis to forget and forgive; this is true of
countless others who suffered as he did. Wealth is no protection; as
it happened, Davis was not raised in poverty. His father was a
well-to-do dental surgeon and landowner. Neither for him nor for

any member of any black family did this ensure security under local or state or federal law.

White Americans look at Miles Davis or Quincy Jones, or at Ella Fitzgerald in her Beverly Hills luxury, and react: 'See? Anyone can make it.' They cannot be blamed entirely for their ignorance, since the history books in America's classrooms, white and black alike, had very little to say about 365 years of Afro-American life; for millions of whites, the television series *Roots* came as a revelation. White Americans growing up saw no blacks in their neighbourhood except delivery boys, no blacks on their local movie screens except the likes of Stepin Fetchit shuffling and saying, 'Feets, don't fail me now!' or two white men, Amos and Andy, in grotesque blackface.

If they were born a little more recently, whites may have seen blacks first on television, though it may have escaped their attention that almost no black artists could have their own sponsored programme; that for many years there was not a single black newscaster, and that the orchestras seen regularly on network programmes were all-white or practised the merest tokenism.

During more than twenty-five years in Southern California, I have seen the situation improve, though at a pace that would make a snail seem like a greyhound. Yes, there have been white men of goodwill who have taken affirmative action to put blacks into the all-white enclaves of the TV studios; Jerry Fielding not only brought Buddy Collette into the band on the Groucho Marx TV show but also played an active role in helping to desegregate what were then two local musicians' unions. Not until 1953 did the all-black Local 767 disappear, merging into the white Local 47.

Jerry Fielding, Milt Holland, George Kast and others were among the whites of goodwill in those days; later Nelson Riddle and the trumpeter John Parker hired blacks when many of their contemporaries still resisted. In more recent years, among Hollywood's jazz-orientated orchestras, only the bands of Bill Berry, the 'Juggernaut' ensemble led by Nat Pierce and Frank Capp and the mainly black unit led by the trumpeter Leslie Drayton have maintained a substantially bi-racial personnel.

Other white musicians, thinking themselves free of prejudice, still make no active attempt to change the status quo. Meeting a Freddie Hubbard or a Wayne Shorter, they will not see in him the great-grandson of a slave who was owned by someone named Hubbard or Shorter, a slave who took his name from his master and who, according to the US Constitution, was officially graded as three fifths of a man and was entitled to none of the rights granted to a slaveholder.

The grandparents of, say, a Milt Hinton or a Gerald Wilson may have lived their entire lives disenfranchised, may have been among the millions who were terrorized, whose jobs were taken away from them, if they dared to register to vote. It is more than likely that Hinton and Wilson, growing up, saw the Klan burning crosses to 'keep the niggers in their place'; that some member of their families was lynched, or had a loved one who was lynched; lynchings at one point early in this century took place about once every three days. Of course, most of the victims were blacks, or occasionally whites who had dared to stand up for the rights of blacks.

All this may seem irrelevant in these supposedly emancipated times, yet it is very relevant indeed. It explains the behaviour of black musicians, who have reacted in various ways. Some have risen above the conditions imposed on them and seemingly are able to live relatively happy, normal lives, working quietly against racism. Others, for reasons having to do with their upbringing or psychological nature, have been unable to cope with the realities of American life. That is why we have, on the one hand, a Benny Carter or a Buddy Collette, and why we had, on the other hand, a Charles Mingus, and still have a Miles Davis and a Max Roach for whom the wounds have not completely healed. ('What happens,' Langston Hughes asked, 'to a dream deferred? Does it dry up, like a raisin in the sun? . . . or does it explode?')

Growing up in England, then spending the last days of my adolescence and almost my entire adult life in the United States, I arrived fairly early at a realization that the jazz world, like any segment of society in which black people played a significant part, was riven by gigantic problems. It took me a while to understand some of the nuances in the bi-racial, too often polarized community to which I was exposed.

The first man I ever heard using the word 'nigger' was Glenn Miller. This seemed remarkable to me at first, though I would soon realize that Miller was a basically decent fellow. He certainly admired the Jimmie Lunceford orchestra, had Lunceford's own Eddie Durham arranging for his band, and, had the social conditions of the day seemed right, he might well have hired Durham to play in his trombone section. Different people hear different overtones in the use of the word. Blacks used it among themselves; tens of millions of whites used it; some, like Glenn Miller, tossed it off apparently innocuously, while others shouted it as they chased a black down the street.

Still, this episode came as such a surprise that it engraved itself permanently in my mind. In fact, I can remember exactly where it happened: at a restaurant on 57th Street near Broadway, where my table was close to Miller's. He and a friend were talking about someone who had just bought a supposedly ostentatious new car; he was acting, Miller said, laughing, 'real nigger-rich'.

In the context of the times, and in retrospect, this was almost meaningless, particularly when I compare it with the way it was used by a famous cornettist who led a series of all-white record sessions in the late 1920s and early 1930s, and who contemptuously dismissed John Hammond as a 'nigger lover'.

There was also the case of Louis Armstrong's road manager. We were in New Orleans at a time when the city was so crowded that I had to share a hotel room with him. Before we turned out the lights, I was subjected to a barrage of anti-black venom the like of which I had never heard before. The niggers were ignorant, they deserved no better than they got, and on and on. Why he had been hired to travel with Louis, and why Louis tolerated him, passed my comprehension.

As I had long since found out, it was the whites who were truly ignorant. Blacks, looking out for their own security and hearing whites talk to their white friends, knew the whites and all their racist foibles. But the whites only thought they 'understood' the Negroes who, more often than not, told whites just what they thought the ofays expected to hear, and behaved in front of whites as they thought the ofays expected them to behave.

Was Louis Armstrong an Uncle Tom? Or was he merely a pragmatist? Do we not all, black or white, often tell people what they prefer to hear, do what we think they want us to do, in the interests of our wellbeing?

Was Stan Kenton a racist? Or was he simply, as Carol Easton suggested in her biography of him, someone raised with the values of the quintessential WASP? 'The data with which he was programmed "in front" simply cannot accommodate an appreciation of the implications of being black in America,' she wrote.

Kenton's posture was observed by a generation of musicians who had seen around them a growing degree of racial integration. Kenton himself had employed several black musicians, though none lasted long with the exception of the singer Jean Turner, who was with him for about a year. He was well liked by all the musicians, white or black, who worked for him. Yet there was in him a hidden defensiveness, an attitude that came to the surface only rarely, reaching a climax when he read the results of the 1956 *Down Beat* Critics' Poll.

Kenton promptly fired off a telegram that read as follows:

Blenheim, Ontario

TO THE EDITOR:
JUST SAW YOUR FOURTH JAZZ CRITICS' POLL. IT'S OBVIOUS THAT THERE IS A NEW MINORITY GROUP, WHITE JAZZ MUSICIANS. THE ONLY THING I GAINED FROM STUDYING THE OPINIONS OF YOUR LITERARY GENIUSES OF JAZZ IS COMPLETE AND TOTAL DISGUST.
                                                    STAN KENTON

Reaction in jazz circles was swift and strong. Four weeks later, in the issue dated 3 October 1956, *Down Beat* published my open letter to Kenton:

Dear Stan:
    Say it isn't so!
    I am writing this letter more in sorrow than in anger. I write as one who, while often disagreeing with your musical aims, always wanted to believe in your basic sincerity and honesty. Unlike many musicians and critics who have discussed you so often among themselves, I have bent over backwards to give you the benefit of the doubt on your racial views.
    There was doubt when, for so many years, of all your hundreds of sidemen, every single one was white except a couple of trumpet players who were light enough to pass.
    There was a graver doubt when, returning from your first European tour, you told Nat Hentoff in a *Down Beat* interview, 'It seems the Kenton band means more in Europe than any other band – more than Basie, Duke, Dizzy . . . It would appear that the reason is that we had taken Negro jazz and put it in European terms. *The harmonic structure of Negro jazz was not enough to satisfy Europeans* . . . We have played music more advanced in melodic and harmonic content than Duke's . . . Our tour proved to Europeans that white musicians can play jazz, too.'

With your telegram to the editor published in the 5 September *Down Beat*, I am afraid all possible doubt was removed . . .

Clearly this wire expressed long-bottled feelings, now un-corked and spilled in a moment of rare candour. Nobody will doubt your sincerity this time, Stan. What you were saying, in effect, was that the critics voted for too many Negroes and too few white musicians, and thus, by implication, that critics make their choices in terms of skin colour rather than talent.

Several musicians have ventured the opinion that your 'complete and total disgust' could possibly have been coloured by the fact that you failed to win the last two *Down Beat* polls (a Readers' Poll *and* a Critics' Poll).

Nobody heard you complain about polls while you were winning. Nobody heard a peep out of you when real prejudice existed, back in the early 1940s when Negro musicians were almost completely excluded from the winning slots. But in this poll your name was right at the bottom of the big-band category with one lone, solitary vote, and now you hate polls and critics and are riding your white charger to defend white supremacy.

Let's get down to cases. Specifically, which of the critics' selections aroused your ire? Were you upset by the victories of Dizzy Gillespie and J. J. Johnson, whose styles are imitated by just about every trumpeter and trombonist you have ever hired?

Do you feel Lester should secede from his Presidency?

Do you feel that first place on piano should have gone to Stan Kenton rather than Art Tatum?

Can you find me one drummer, white or Negro, who was resentful of Jo Jones' triumph?

Tell us more, Stan – *tell us exactly which Negro musicians aroused your complete and total disgust by winning the poll.* Tell us which critics you accuse of voting for pigmentation instead of inspiration. Me? Nat Hentoff? Barry Ulanov? Jack Tracy? Or did the whole bunch of us, except for the one single cat who voted for you, arouse your complete and total disgust?

Of course, you didn't note the fact that the critics did elect Benny Goodman, Tal Farlow, Phil Woods, Bobby Jaspar, Jimmy Giuffre and others. To mention them would have weakened your case. You conveniently ignore the theory, long held among most musicians and jazz authorities all over the world, that almost every major development in jazz history has been the work of Negro musicians and that even the few exceptions such as Bix, Benny Goodman and Tristano admit that they leaned heavily on the inspiration of Negro predecessors.

The fact that most of the winners in this critics' poll happened to be coloured had nothing whatever to do with any racial attitude, conscious or unconscious, on the part of the voters. The sheerest chance change of mind on the part of a few critics about a few arbitrary choices could easily have reversed the proportions.

Believe me, Stan, I would rather think you didn't send the wire; rather admire you than censure you. My statement, in a lengthy analysis of your contributions which I wrote for *Jazz Magazine* in Paris very recently, to the effect that the balance is in your favour and that your recent band was your best ever, and that fans everywhere owe you a debt for the interest you have aroused in jazz, still holds good.

But your telegram was so painful to read, so hard to believe, and has already lost you so many friends among your fans and so much respect among your fellow musicians, that I wish I could believe it was a hoax, sent in viciously by somebody else under your signature to besmirch your name.

Say it isn't so, Stan. Say anything except that you meant all the ugly implications in that wire. For just as it is love that makes the world go 'round, Stan, it is hate that can make the world go square.

Sincerely,
Leonard Feather

That the subject of alleged positive discrimination among the jazz critics remains a sensitive issue can be deduced from a letter sent to the editor of the *Los Angeles Times* in 1980 by Leo Walker, author of *The Wonderful Era of the Great Dance Bands*. Protesting about my review of an event that presented the orchestras of Ray Anthony, Tex Beneke and Mercer Ellington, he objected to my negative reactions to the Anthony and Beneke bands, then added:

He praises the Duke Ellington orchestra, conducted by his son Mercer . . . the audience . . . almost unanimously disagreed with Leonard's appraisal . . . It was a bad band and Duke must be turning over in his grave . . . Leonard is entitled to his opinions but . . . he is unable to give a fair review to the performance of white musicians . . . For years he has appeared to have been conducting a one-man black-superiority crusade, and convinced that its success depended on ignoring or putting down white musicians.

At the risk of sounding defensive, I will name at random just a few of the hundreds of non-black musicians whose talents I have praised over the last fifty years: Benny Goodman, Jack Teagarden, Red Norvo, Artie Shaw, Buddy De Franco, Barney Kessel, Dave Tough, Bill Evans, Gil Evans, Gerry Mulligan, Stan Getz, Zoot Sims, Joe Venuti, Scott LaFaro, Charlie Haden, Emily Remler, Michel Petrucciani . . .

The list is without end, since it is subject at any time to new additions. This may not succeed in convincing those whose minds are already made up; why confuse them with facts?

True, many of us who write about jazz have tried to upgrade the lot of the black musician, and we are happy to observe that in some respects that lot has improved. With the passing of the Civil Rights Act in 1964, blacks could no longer be denied a seat at a lunch counter or a room in a hotel. Unlike South Africa, we had at least eliminated *de jure* segregation. In due course even Las Vegas, where some of the world's most respected artists had been paid huge sums to perform while forbidden to live in the same hotel, at last fell in line. Today blacks are even allowed to lose their money at the crap tables.

On a more personal level, it was heartening to notice that over the years men like Joe Venuti changed their minds; he enjoyed a close friendship and mutual admiration with Milt Hinton and other blacks, made records with Earl Hines, possibly even shared a social drink with Teddy Wilson.

None of this contradicts the inescapable fact that being black in America, even being a successful black musician, still can be hard on the psyche. The Klan still rides, and not only in the south.

As I once wrote in a heavily satirical pseudo-fictional article for *Esquire*, perhaps the only and ultimate solution to racism could be the total merging of the races. (The article was entitled 'Rankin was Right', a sardonic reference to John Rankin, a Southern Congressman who had delivered a thunderous speech predicting that intermarriage would lead to the 'mongrelization' of the races.)

When there is nothing left but a single human race, who will be left to become the object of hatred and violence? Perhaps some day it may be necessary to confront that problem; in the meanwhile a

more sensitive human understanding, the accordance to black
people of the basic dignity, respect and totally equal opportunities
for which they and their ancestors have waited almost four
centuries, would seem to be the only options left to us, in America,
England or South Africa. For those of us in the jazz community this
task should be at least a little less onerous.

Yet even in 1986, the clouds had not left the horizon. On Dr
Martin Luther. King's birthday, the first time this date had ever
been observed as a nationwide holiday, the Ku Klux Klan burned
crosses in Tennessee. The millennium is still around the corner.

UNA TO JUTTA

Although racism in jazz was a self-evident bane, one against which I joined John Hammond and countless others in speaking out during the 1930s (and in trying to match actions to words), it was not long before the existence of another form of prejudice, one against which its victims were equally helpless to effect change, became apparent to me.

The first two women whose recording careers I launched, Una Mae Carlisle in 1938 and Hazel Scott in 1939, both happened to be uncommonly capable pianists and singers. Both were nineteen years old at the time of their initial sessions. Carlisle, in fact, was eighteen when I first heard her, during a hectic weekend in Paris. Playing solos or occasionally piano duets with Garland Wilson, singing novelty songs such as 'Two Old Maids in a Folding Bed', she was an entertainer in the tradition of Fats Waller, whose protegée she had become when he heard her on the radio in Cincinnati.

Una Mae clearly had learned well from her informal teacher. In my first article about her, in the *Melody Maker* in 1937, I invoked a procedure that would become a regular part of my journalistic life almost a decade later: 'How would you like,' I asked, 'to submit to a blindfold test, listen to a typical Fats Waller song, then when the bandage was removed find that seated at the keyboard, instead of the 200 pounds of brown-skinned masculinity you expected, was a light, slim, smiling girl?'

I went on to point out that she had not yet recorded, which 'seems to indicate a ripe opportunity for somebody'. Of course I was the opportunist; in May 1938 I assembled five of the six men who would constitute my own recording band four months later, with Dave Wilkins on trumpet and Bertie King on tenor and clarinet. In under four hours we completed six songs: Gershwin's 'Love Walked In', three standards, a blues and a song of mine written with Fats in mind (in fact, he recorded it three months later when I organized his London date), entitled 'Don't Try Your Jive on Me'. (This bore Edgar Sampson's name as co-writer; I had been his dinner guest one night and Sampson, a brilliant and gentle man, offered to help when I told him I was stuck for a melody on the bridge. The truth is that I was eager to see my name alongside his on a record label.)

Except for two numbers on which she sat in at the Paris session with Danny Polo, those were the only sides I was able to make with Una Mae. After her return to the US she shared a vocal with Waller on one tune, then began a series of her own sessions for RCA Bluebird, two of which, 'Walkin' by the River' and 'I See a Million People', revealed her talent as a songwriter. Perhaps because of a lifestyle as self-indulgent as Fats's own, Una Mae never reached the plateau of fame to which her talent and beauty might have been expected to bring her. She was only thirty-seven when, inactive and forgotten, she died in Ohio, where she was born.

Hazel Scott's was a very different story, one in which great opportunities were grasped but many frustrations encountered. Brought to the US at the age of four by her Trinidad-born mother, who led her own all-woman orchestra, she had begun playing piano and singing professionally at the age of five, had her own radio series at sixteen, and was featured in a Broadway show at eighteen. For a year or so she worked odd jobs around 52nd Street; I saw her first at the Hickory House working the off-night. In the fall of 1939 she opened at Cafe Society and was promptly adopted by its sophisticated clientele; she became Barney Josephson's most valuable protegée and was later transferred to his Cafe Society Uptown.

Soon after her initial success in the Village club, I worked out a somewhat devious way of using Hazel, along with a couple of good friends who had worked on dates with me in London, Danny Polo and the guitarist Albert Harris. Rounding out the group with Pete Brown on alto sax and Arthur Herbert on drums, both of whom were of West Indian descent, and using Pete Barry, a bassist also of British origin, I was able to convince Leonard Joy, then production head at RCA Victor, that the group could reasonably be called the Sextet of the Rhythm Club of London.

Though the premise made no logical sense, it gave Hazel a

chance to be heard on records in good company, playing her somewhat Billy Kyle-like piano in 'Calling All Bars' and putting her deep, throbbing voice to good use in 'Mighty Like the Blues'.

Arranging for Hazel's participation was not easy; her mother was a stern, forbidding woman who looked suspiciously at me when I picked her daughter up for a rehearsal. This was a time in American society when any white man would be assumed to have dishonourable intentions towards a young, nubile black woman. Hazel and I had a platonic friendship that endured long after we were both married and, in fact, ended only with her death.

That Hazel Scott's is not a name to be found in the bulk of jazz literature can be attributed to several factors. Because of her extraordinary beauty, she had a fling in motion pictures, where her work was mainly confined, as was the case with Lena Horne and Dorothy Dandridge, to non-acting parts, or to roles in which the fact of her race could be somehow downplayed. The producers were not interested in a jazz pianist, but rather in a glamorous entertainer.

Her marriage was another impediment: married in 1945 to the Rev Adam Clayton Powell, a flamboyant and increasingly powerful Congressman, she devoted less time to her career. Her recordings were either vocals with pretentious orchestral backings or piano sessions that seemed to be searching for a commercial gimmick.

That she had a genuine talent was recognized by such musicians as Charles Mingus, who in 1955 recorded her, with Max Roach and himself, for Mingus's Debut label. But by now Hazel was more interested in listening to others – mainly Art Tatum and Bud Powell – than in advancing her own artistry. She became an expatriate in Paris, broke up with Rev Powell, then lived for two years in Los Angeles, where I tried to persuade her to work more often, but by then she was intent on writing her autobiography, which was still unpublished when she died in 1981. Hazel was a double victim, of racism and sexism, one of her time's genuine might-have-beens.

Although the sessions with Una Mae Carlisle and Hazel could have given the impression that these were attempts to campaign for women in jazz, it was not until a few years later that I made a conscious effort to correct what I now realized was a problem affecting women musicians. Only the singers and, to some extent, the pianists were able to overcome fixed attitudes on the part of those who were in a position to employ them: not only the producers, but often the male musicians.

During a visit to Chicago in connection with the *Esquire* project, I came across a twenty-two-year-old guitarist named Mary Osborne. Inspired by Charlie Christian, whom she had heard in North Dakota, Osborne had taken up electric guitar and by now was an accomplished soloist.

Arnold Gingrich and I had plans to launch an *Esquire* record label. With this in mind, I booked a studio in Chicago and produced a session with the Stuff Smith trio, a hard-driving unit with Jimmy Jones on piano and John Levy on bass. For the occasion I added Mary Obsborne. The four tunes recorded that day were not to constitute her public record debut, since the *Esquire* project never materialized (other sessions with Eddie South and Joe Marsala, the latter a spendid date with Pete Brown and Charlie Shavers, were either unissued or found limited bootleg exposure). But Mary was encouraged and, the following year, after her move to New York, I hired her for a variety of sessions: with Mercer Ellington and Wynonie Harris and her own trio on Aladdin, with Ethel Waters on Continental, with Coleman Hawkins on RCA and as part of the all-female groups I built around Mary Lou Williams and Beryl Booker.

I had first heard Mary Lou Williams when, during a road tour as Louis Armstrong's guest in the relentlessly hot summer of 1936, I visited Fairyland Park in Kansas City, where she was working as pianist and arranger with Andy Kirk's orchestra. Since leaving Kirk she had led her own group for a while with the trumpeter Harold Baker, who was then her husband; but they had not recorded the combo, and Mary had been heard mainly in a series of sessions with various small groups for Asch Records.

Asked whether she might be interested in recording with an all-female group, she told me: 'If we can get the right people it would be fine; but where are they?'

I reminded her of Margie Hyams, a vibraphonist whom we had heard with Woody Herman, and told her about Mary Osborne. We had heard about a drummer named Bridget O'Flynn, who had studied with Lee Young and was a good friend of Buddy Rich; and a fine bassist, June Rotenberg, who had been with the St Louis Symphony.

The instrumentation – vibes, guitar, piano, bass and drums – was one I had employed successfully for a series of Slam Stewart dates in 1945 on Continental. (Later it would prove even more valuable, with Margie Hyams again on hand, as the original format of the George Shearing Quintet.)

At the last minute we were confronted with a problem: June Rotenberg had a conflicting date. Neither Mary Lou nor I knew of another competent female bassist then in town and available.

'Listen,' I said, 'you know Billy Taylor, who used to play bass with Duke? Why don't we just use him and call him Bea Taylor?'

No photographers and, needless to say, no potential reviewers were invited to the date, which was for Continental. The secret was so well kept that thirty-five years later, when the records were reissued on Onyx, Dan Morgenstern observed in his liner notes: 'The Misses Taylor and O'Flynn, on whom I have no biographical data, do nicely.'

This was not my first supposedly all-female date. Exactly a year earlier I had used Margie Hyams and her sister-in-law, a fluent tenor saxophonist named L'Ana Hyams, along with the trumpeter Jean Starr and a rhythm section composed of Vicki Zimmer, then well known along 52nd Street; the guitarist Marion Gange, whose credits went back to the Ina Ray Hutton band of the 1930s; Cecilia Zirl on bass and Rose Gottesman on drums. This group, billed as the Hip Chicks, cut six numbers for Black & White Records with somewhat uneven results. One tune had a vocal by Vivien Garry, for whom I had other plans in mind, since she was an excellent bassist and was married to a brilliant guitarist, Arvin Garrison.

The Hip Chicks date is forgotten, and perhaps it is just as well, but the Mary Lou Williams session was successful enough to suggest a broader canvas: why not a series of recordings, an entire album of 78s with nothing but women musicians? They had been all but excluded from the discographical annals.

It was because of Steve Sholes' willingness to take chances with almost anything I suggested at RCA that a large number of great musicians were recorded between 1945 and the second record ban in 1948. (He later achieved some sort of immortality as the man who brought Elvis Presley to RCA.) Sholes took to the idea of what we planned to call the *Girls in Jazz* album. Women might have been uneasy about being called girls, but nobody was sensitive enough (or brave enough) to voice any objection.

Given the green light, between July and October I completed five sessions: two with Mary Lou, one with the Beryl Booker Trio, one with the Vivien Garry Quintet, and one with the International Sweethearts of Rhythm. With the exception of the Sweethearts, these were all specially assembled recording groups.

Both Mary Lou and I were delighted with her first date, for which we no longer needed 'Bea Taylor'. Instead, we had June Rotenberg, along with Osborne, Hyams and Gottesman, playing two of my originals, two of Mary's, and a standard ('It Must be True') sung by Mary Osborne.

The second session was played by a trio, with Rotenberg and Bridget O'Flynn. For this occasion, remembering my experiences with 'Waltzing the Blues' and 'Jamming the Waltz', I asked Mary whether she had any objection to writing a waltz.

'Why not?' she said, and brought 'Waltz Boogie' to the date. It was a charming piece and has occasionally been revived by other pianists.

Vivien Garry's group (recorded on the West Coast) introduced to records two artists whose reputations never quite caught up with their ability, the violinist Ginger Smock and the trumpeter Edna Williams, who at one time was a member of the Sweethearts and who died young. With them were a good Los Angeles pianist, Wini Beatty, and the drummer Dody Jeshke. One original I wrote for the occasion, a blues entitled 'A Woman's Place is in the Groove', could have made a logical title track for the album. Two days after this session I used Vivien again, along with her guitarist husband, on a wild Leo Watson date.

Vivien Garry and her quintet date created some valid music; Smock's solo on 'Body and Soul' displayed an exceptional, legato style, and Edna Williams distinguished herself.

Of all the small-group dates for this album, the one that turned out most unexpectedly well was led by Beryl Booker.

A self-taught musician from Philadelphia who had never learned to read music, Beryl came to town as a member of the Slam Stewart Trio, and remained with Slam off and on for five years. Because of the quality of her work, and perhaps also because we shared a sense of humour and an affinity for bad puns, we became lifelong friends; I produced all but two of her seven record sessions.

John Collins, the other member of Slam's trio, has fond recollections. 'We met in Philadelphia. Billy Taylor, Slam's pianist, wanted a leave of absence for his honeymoon, and Beryl came in to sub for him, later replacing him permanently.

'I was impressed with her chordal style,' says Collins, 'and with her total devotion to playing. After our regular job I would follow her around to all these after-hours spots just to hear her, and she would play all night long.

'Art Tatum loved to hear her; in Chicago, he was at a club down the street, and he'd come by between sets to listen to Beryl. That's how inventive and inspiring she was.'

Attempting to find for Beryl Booker the recognition and security she deserved became almost a pilgrimage for me during the next few years. After the session for RCA, with Mary Osborne and June Rotenberg, there was a lull of a year or two until I found that my enthusiasm was shared by Bob Shad.

A knowledgeable producer who in his lifetime racked up an amazing list of credits ranging from classical music to R & B to jazz to pop, Shad had his own label for a while, known as Sittin' In With. After recording Beryl for this shortlived company, with John Collins and Slam Stewart, he joined Mercury Records, and during his first year there allowed me to assemble a group for another Booker date.

We tried to reach a wider audience by having Beryl sing, using a rather weird echo-chamber effect on her voice for 'You'd Better Go Now'. Musically it was intriguing, but commercially it failed; the next year, Shad let me produce a date with Beryl, Collins and Oscar Pettiford for his new Mercury subsidiary, EmArcy Records. Still there was no rush to the record stores, but at least Beryl was honestly represented on records as a creative artist.

Somewhere during this time Beryl called up one day and announced: 'I'm getting married and I'd like to have the ceremony at your place. Will that be all right?'

A few days later Beryl showed up with her bridegroom, whose last name I can't recall, though I believe his first name was Felix. She also brought the minister and Slam Stewart, who was best man. After the ceremony we talked for a while, drank to the health of the couple and said goodbye. I never saw or heard of Felix again.

What would it take to draw more attention to Beryl? A brainstorm struck me: why not the first all-female in-person modern-jazz combo?

'That's fine with me if we can find the right people,' Beryl said. This took less time than we exptected. Bonnie Wetzel, a bassist, had worked in the Tommy Dorsey orchestra along with her late husband, the trumpeter Ray Wetzel, until his death. She had a full sound and a supple touch that would be in keeping with our concept for the trio.

Elaine Leighton, whose schoolmates had included Shorty Rogers and Stan Getz, went on to play drums with Jackie Cain and Roy Kral, and with a later edition of the Sweethearts of Rhythm. At the first rehearsal with Beryl and Bonnie we all knew that this chemistry would be right. The three women worked out routines on 'Thou Swell', 'Symphony' and some of Beryl's originals.

After a few more rehearsals I was able to set them for a Discovery Records date, which I produced in October 1953. All the trio needed now was a suitable in-person opportunity.

Around this time I began to assemble, with the help of Joe Glaser and the Swedish promoter Nils Hellstrom, a show to accompany Billie Holiday on her first European tour. We had lined up the Red Norvo Trio and Buddy De Franco's quartet; there was still room for an opening act. Why not Beryl, Bonnie and Elaine?

'Ah,' Glaser growled, 'that ain't gonna mean shit. Who wants to come and hear three broads playing jazz?'

I pointed out that the audiences would be attracted primarily by Billie Holiday, secondarily by De Franco and Norvo; the Booker trio would be a suitable warm-up opening act and quite possibly would come as a pleasant surprise to the audiences.

This prediction proved accurate. When the three unknown women took to the stage on opening night in Stockholm, there was a burst of applause before they had even made their way through the first up-tempo chorus of 'Thou Swell'. It went the same way every night for the next three weeks.

I was able to arrange for the trio to record again as soon as we arrived in Paris. After five numbers by the trio we added a distinguished local resident, Don Byas, to bring his glowing tenor to three tunes, one called 'Beryl Booker's Byased Blues'.

Back in New York, the group struggled to stay together, but the odds were insuperable: the absence of a hit record, coupled with suspicion concerning the validity of an all-female group, counteracted the unquestionably favourable reaction to the trio in the few clubs they played. The project was reluctantly abandoned that summer; Beryl went back to odd jobs, working occasionally with Slam, and later rejoining Dinah Washington, whom she had accompanied some years earlier.

After my move to California, Beryl and I kept in touch through an occasional letter and phone call. She was back in Philadelphia, apparently resigned to failure, though not without a trace of bitterness.

Finally, a letter told me: 'At last! I'm going to move out to San

Francisco. At least I can be with my daughter, and maybe there'll be some work.'

I made a mental note to call her, but waited a couple of weeks. One day, I dropped in on Dave Dexter at the offices of *Billboard*. 'Hey,' he said, 'we got a report that Beryl Booker died. Wasn't she a friend of yours?'

Beryl had suffered a stroke shortly after moving West. My procrastination had prevented me from talking to her at least once more. Yet again, as has happened too often in jazz as in all the arts, an unhealthy brew of bad luck and lack of guidance had aborted a potentially brilliant career.

During the European tour with Billie Holiday, Beryl and I had been much impressed by a young woman we heard at a club in Duisborg. Jutta Hipp had fled from her native Leipzig when the Russians occupied the city, and had worked in Munich, then led her own trio in Frankfurt.

Jutta showed what appeared to be a Lennie Tristano influence, coupled with an individuality that seemed powerful enough to justify greater prominence than she could find in a small German nightclub. After I had corresponded with her for several months, she began to express interest in coming to America.

There was a long period of indecision. When she finally arrived in November 1955, Jane and I invited her to stay with us, which she did for the first couple of months. There were union problems to be straightened out before she could go to work; meanwhile we became aware of her other talent.

Jutta had studied painting at the Academy of Arts in Leipzig. Much of her spare time in New York was spent doing black-and-white sketches in a style I found somewhat frightening: all the faces, even those of friends we knew to be cheerful and perhaps handsome people, somehow looked gross, menacing and ugly.

Because of their shared origins and language, I introduced Jutta to Alfred Lion. Although Blue Note at that time was dedicated almost exclusively to hard bop played by black groups, Lion recorded Jutta, first with a trio, then on a second album with Zoot Sims. Meanwhile she had begun to make a slight name for herself, working at the Hickory House, but her style was undergoing a change that I found disturbing; she had come under the influence of Horace Silver, and much as I admired Horace, this seemed to have the effect of destroying Jutta's individuality.

Her personality was a major problem. Extraordinarily withdrawn and totally without self-confidence, she was very near-sighted but refused to wear glasses. Later I realized that some of her emotional problems must have had to do with the trauma of leaving home during the Russian occupation.

The Jutta Hipp story, in so far as her career in music was concerned, came to a swift conclusion. By 1958 we had lost touch with her; word reached us that she had taken a day job at a tailor's shop. Since then a few friends have run into her occasionally. She seems to have no regrets about having deserted music. The brief time she spent in the public eye apparently left her frustrated and scared. The end of her story differed from Beryl Booker's in that her departure was voluntary, yet in another respect it was comparable, since it meant the loss to jazz of a potentially significant talent.

It took only a glance at those sketches she drew to convince me that something was amiss. Seldom have I met two more antithetical personalities: Jutta discouraged and depressed, drifting away from music; Beryl, despite all her reverses, cheerful and upbeat to the end.

SWEETHEARTS

After completing the sessions with Mary Lou Williams, Vivien Garry and Beryl Booker, I wound up the *Girls in Jazz* album by bringing to the studio the only big band that seemed worthy of inclusion in this project, the International Sweethearts of Rhythm.

The Sweethearts symbolized all the handicaps that could restrict a career in music. They were black; they were female; they were poor (most of the original members were orphans) and they were systematically, painfully exploited by commercial interests that took advantage of their youth and innocence.

I first heard the Sweethearts early in 1944 at the Apollo, and again at that theatre several times during the next few years. Gradually, as I talked with some of the members backstage and with Rae Lee Jones, who described herself as their chaperone and manager, the pieces of their almost incredible hard-luck story fell into place.

The band was born at the Country Life School in Piney Woods, Mississippi. Dr Laurence C. Jones (not related to Rae Lee) had started the band in 1937, inspired by the success of white female orchestras such as Ina Ray Hutton's. After touring to raise money for the school, they made their first big-time professional appearance at the Howard in Washington in 1940. Edna Williams, whom I had recorded with Vivien Garry, was their original musical director.

It was outside Washington, at a ten-room house they occupied in Arlington, that the girls, all teenagers when they first went on the road, came under the tutelage of Eddie Durham, the composer and trombonist who had played with Basie and Lunceford and had contributed arrangements to the bands of Glenn Miller and Ina Ray Hutton. By now they had severed all connections with the school;

in fact, when they quit in 1941, police chased their band bus, following a complaint by Dr Jones that eight members had yet to graduate.

At first, some of the Sweethearts told me, they could do little more than hold long notes and could barely read music. With Durham's help, they began reading more fluently, their performances achieved a thoroughly professional level and they became a potent commercial attraction in black theatres and at dances. They were directed by Anna Mae Winburn, a stunning young woman in slinky gowns who had not been to the school; she was hired mainly as a figurehead, to conduct and do a little singing. (Previously she had led an all-male band that included the guitarist Charlie Christian.)

Pauline Braddy, the drummer, recalled the early days: 'Boy, did we ever have rules and regulations! If you broke them, you were out. Young ladies don't smoke, and young ladies don't sit at the bar, and young ladies always carry their gloves and wear their hats, and young ladies never dance with fellas who aren't wearing ties and jackets – and Mrs Jones had everybody paid off, so that if you broke a rule she'd find out.'

As the band flourished, the young women took to the bus life. Because it was hard to find accommodation in those Jim Crow days, especially for a more or less 'mixed' band (the personnel included a few Puerto Ricans, Mexicans, Asians and later two or three whites), the band slept in bunks aboard the bus. The pianist Johnnie Rice recalled, in an interview many years later: 'We practically lived on the bus, using it for rehearsals and regular school classes, arithmetic and everything.'

After Eddie Durham left (he later led his own all-female orchestra), Jesse Stone took over, beefing up the personnel with musicians whose level of professionalism enabled him to write some of the most challenging arrangements the band had dealt with. Stone married the band's vocalist, Evelyn McGhee. Next came Maurice King, under whose direction the Sweethearts were working when I recorded them for the RCA project.

The more I learned about these young women, the more profoundly my pleasure was mixed with pity. The original members were receiving $1 a day for food plus $1 a week allowance, a grand total of $8 a week. 'That went on for years,' the saxophonist Willie Mae Wong told me many years later, 'until we got a substantial raise – to $15 a week. By the time we broke up we were making $15 a night, three nights a week.'

They were told that the rest of whatever money they were entitled to was used to pay off the mortgage on the house they would own in Arlington. The truth was that their alleged participation in the ownership was illusory. 'Nobody knew what Mrs Jones was getting out of it,' Wong said, 'but I do remember that if the bus blew a tyre, we had to donate back out of our salary to replace it. Some of the real pros who joined up later made as much as $100 a week, $150 a week; the originals made nothing.' Mrs Jones' side of the story will never be known; she died in 1948, around the time the Sweethearts quietly expired.

For several years Anna Mae Winburn kept the Sweethearts' name alive, using groups of various sizes; but the great years, musically, were the early and middle 1940s.

'We had so many types in the band,' she recalled when we met, for the first time in almost thirty-five years, after Carol Comer and Dianne Gregg, organizers of the Women's Jazz Festival in Kansas City, had managed to track down nine original Sweethearts as well as six subsequent members for a sentimental reunion. 'Down South they couldn't tell white from black. The white girls had to put on dark make-up; but of course we couldn't paint their blue eyes!

'In Memphis we played for a black audience; then they emptied the theatre and the cops let the whites come in. One cop said, "You have white girls in this band." My husband, who was the band manager then, said, "You pick out the white ones and arrest them." Well, the only one the cop picked out was a mulatto.'

'We white girls,' Roz Cron said, 'were supposed to say, "My mother was black and my father was white," because that was the way it was in the South. Well, I swore to the sheriff in El Paso, Texas, that that's what I was. But he went through my wallet, and there was a photo of my mother and father sitting before our little house in New England with the picket fence, and it just didn't jell. So I spent my night in jail.

'But it was a ball, and all those gals were my sisters,' said Cron, the gentle Jewish woman from Boston who now worked as a secretary in Los Angeles, taking an occasional gig on saxophone. 'I loved every minute of it, and this reunion . . . this is truly like coming home.'

Cron had not joined the band, which had no white members when I recorded the RCA date. Two of the four numbers, both Maurice King originals, were included in the album: 'Vi Vigor', a showcase for the ebullient tenor saxophonist Vi Burnside, and 'Don't Get It Twisted', with solos by Burnside, the trumpeter Johnnie Mae (Tex) Stansbery, a college graduate from Texas, and Jackie King on piano.

Except for one date for a small independent label, that was the sum total of the Sweethearts' recording career. Nobody under fifty is likely to remember this collection of brave, beleaguered young women who played at the Million Dollar Theatre in Los Angeles and who possibly earned millions for others. Only black GIs who were overseas during World War II may have seen them during their triumphant six-month tour of Europe in 1945.

Most of them inevitably retired from music; by the time of the 1980 reunion only a few still worked occasionally. Some still treasure worn-out copies of their old 78s – the only remaining audible proof that this hardy group existed, fighting the good fight against three concurrent evils: sexism, racism and greed.

It was precisely the absence of these prejudices in the mind of Steve Sholes that enabled me to put the Sweethearts, and all the other participants in these female sessions, on records for the 'Girls in Jazz' project. A few months after I had completed these assignments, the album was issued on RCA; in accordance with the technical necessities of the time, it took the form of a set of four ten-inch 78 discs. Though it sold moderately well and was favourably reviewed, it failed to mark a turning point in any of the careers involved.

The Sweethearts continued on their weary grind of one-night stands and black-theatre dates, never breaking through into the more lucrative world of white bookings at downtown clubs. Except for Mary Lou Williams and Mary Osborne, none of the women succeeded in tearing down the sexist barrier. Only Beryl Booker went on to form a new all-female combo.

Barbara Carroll was more fortunate. The first woman pianist to embrace the bebop piano style, she was heard along 52nd Street with Chuck Wayne and others; she was the only woman instrumentalist whose picture I included in the book *Inside Bebop*.

I had first hired Carroll for a live, all-star bebop session heard over WMGM in 1948 from the Royal Roost on Broadway. She was in fast company: the others present were Benny Harris, J.J. Johnson, Cecil Payne, Buddy De Franco, Budd Johnson, Chuck Wayne, Max Roach, Nelson Boyd and, alternating with her, Bud Powell.

She made such a striking impression that evening with her incisive boppish lines that the following March she was included in a group I assembled for a date led by the multi-instrumentalist Eddie Shu, on Rainbow Records (later reissued on a Mercer LP). Later that year Carroll made dates of her own for Discovery; by 1953 she had enjoyed an acting and playing role in a Broadway musical, *Me and Juliet*, and had signed with RCA Victor, recording a long series of sessions that proved less and less interesting, perhaps because she was working regularly at chic clubs on the East Side and felt the need to modify her style. Married to a successful agent, she was in semi-retirement, then came back, playing in a watered-down style redolent of cocktail piano. Hers was a career that fell apart for reasons of musical preference rather than sexual prejudice.

In 1954, when the Beryl Booker Trio was still active, I included all three members in the female half of the *Cats Vs. Chicks* album for MGM. Predicated, like its predecessors *Hot Vs. Cool* and *Dixieland Vs. Birdland*, on the idea that any undertaking offering a chance to display a series of superior talents was an end that justified the artificial means, this consisted of a male and a female group, each playing the same three tunes: 'Cat Meets Chick', 'Mamblues' and 'The Man I Love'. For a finale, both groups were combined in an arrangement I wrote on Irving Berlin's 'Anything You Can Do'; chase choruses by the two trumpeters, the two guitarists and so on.

The male group was under the leadership of Clark Terry, who had never before made a session as a leader despite his long-established reputation with Barnet, Basie and four years with Ellington. Urbie Green and Lucky Thompson completed a strong and sympathetic front line; Horace Silver, in a very rare appearance away from Blue Note Records, spearheaded an admirable rhythm section with Tal Farlow, Percy Heath and Kenny Clarke.

Leading the women was Terry Pollard. Then in the middle of a four-year stint with Terry Gibbs (playing piano and doubling on vibes for duets with him), Pollard was an intense and compelling performer on both instruments. For this occasion she played vibes, but replaced Beryl Booker at the piano for the finale.

The other women were Norma Carson on trumpet, Corky Hale on harp, Mary Osborne, Beryl Booker, Elaine Leighton and Bonnie Wetzel. Though Carson idolized Clifford Brown and Miles Davis, and despite the extent to which her work on this date proved it, this was her first and last recording. Except for a feature in my 'Girls in Jazz' series in *Down Beat,* she was never recognized or publicized; it was her conviction that working in commercial all-female bands such as Ada Leonard's was a musical and economic detriment; she was exploited, underpaid, and forced to play inferior music with players who did not take their careers seriously. Eventually she went along a stereotypical route, marrying, raising a family and trying to forget about her early ambitions.

Mary Osborne was more fortunate: she spent almost all the 1950s on an early-morning daily radio show hosted by Jack Sterling, in a group that included the trombonist Tyree Glenn. She and her husband later moved to Bakersfield, California, where she has played locally, but there have been occasional outside gigs, among them the Women's Jazz Festival and a record date with Marian McPartland.

Corky Hale was an exception to the rule that has held back most women. Her charmed life has been due partly to circumstances in her background that were advantageous from the start. Born to a well-to-do family, she attended Chicago Conservatory, the University of Missouri, and along the way picked up enough expertise to earn her jobs singing and playing the harp, piano, organ, flute, piccolo and cello. Living on the West Coast in the 1950s and 1960s, she owned a dress shop on Sunset Boulevard, freelanced extensively, and worked briefly with the Ina Ray Hutton and Ada Leonard bands. After living in Rome and London, she settled down in New York as the wife of a wealthy and celebrated songwriter, Mike Stoller. She has since concentrated mainly on studio work as a harpist and occasional nightclub jobs on piano. Though not famous and mentioned in few jazz books, Hale has been successful and has had security in a curiously diversified musical life.

The ten-inch *Cats Vs. Chicks* album was far better musically than might have been inferred from the adversary spirit implied by the title. (I was even foolish enough to ask 'referees' their opinions: 'Judge Barry Ulanov' gave all four rounds to the men, while Nat Hentoff and I found for the women on two tunes, the men on a third, and rated a fourth even.) Though MGM has not reissued it, one or two cuts turned up in the 'Women in Jazz' series on Stash Records.

My faith in Terry Pollard was so strong that three months later I invested some of my savings in a session leading her own quartet, hoping that MGM would take over the masters and combine them with the female portion of *Cats Vs. Chicks* to make up a twelve-inch LP. This failed to happen; my money and, to the best of my knowledge, the masters were lost for ever.

LADY

Eleanora Fagan McKay, remembered by the world as Billie
Holiday, the lady with the gardenia whom Lester Young nick-
named Lady Day, would have been seventy-one years old on 7
April 1986.

At noon on that day, at the corner of Vine Street and Selma
Avenue in Hollywood, a star carrying her name was implanted in
the sidewalk. Almost twenty-seven years after she died in a New
York hospital bed at the age of forty-four, Billie had at last made
Tinseltown's Walk of Fame.

It was a moment for tortured emotions. On the one hand it was
gratifying to see that the event had attracted one of the biggest
crowds ever to attend a ceremony of this kind: close to a thousand
people were jammed into the area on and around the sidewalks.
Carmen McRae, who knew her well and loved her deeply, made a
touching speech. Annie Ross, whom I remembered having seen at
Billie's last birthday party, said: 'Every girl singer should get down
on her knees and thank God there was a Billie Holiday.' Jon
Hendricks spoke. Rosemary Clooney recalled her friendship with
Lady Day; a city councilman offered a scroll. Lorraine Feather, my
daughter and Billie's goddaughter, joined with Charlotte Crossley,
her partner in the vocal trio Full Swing, to sing 'Your Mother's
Son-in-Law', the first song Billie ever recorded. Finally I added a
few words about my own recollections.

The star was unveiled, the battery of cameras and TV equipment
began to wind up its affairs, and the crowd dispersed – some of us a
few doors up the street to the Vine Street Bar & Grill, whose owner,
Ron Berinstein, had joined me in persuading the Hollywood
Chamber of Commerce to allocate a star for Billie, subject to the
customary payment of $3,000 (which we raised by staging a

fund-raiser at the club). Surrounded by old friends of Lady's, and others who knew her only from records, I found my thoughts drifting back to the years when I had known her, and particularly to a letter on lined, prison stationery, handwritten, datelined 19 July 1947, the address reading Box A, Alderson, West Virginia:

Dear Leonard,

Yours received and what a pleasant surprise letters mean so much. How is Jane I am so glad she liked the picture *New Orleans*. Joe Glaser was supposed to have it sent here but I haven't heard from him lately oh yes I know he's a busy man but he has my money and I wrote three letters asking for some. I can only spend ten dollars a month but I can use that green stuff even here.

Leonard if it's not asking too much before you leave please call Joe Glaser and see what he intends to do about some good publicity for me I've had so much bad stuff written and I do think he should do something so that people don't forget me after all a year is a long time for one's public to wait. But I do have you and Jane (smile) and Bobby Tucker has been so faithful he writes every week.

Well dear there is not much else to write only I am getting fat isn't that awful write soon.

As ever,
Billie Holiday

Of course, they didn't forget her. At the time of the letter Billie had been in prison only a few weeks, but she was released a few months before her year was up, and soon afterwards gave a triumphant welcome-back concert at Carnegie Hall. She did not look fat; only filled-out and healthier.

At the risk of sounding, as so many observers have in writing about Billie, like an amateur psychiatrist, I must confess that her frequent statements to interviewers that her main desire was to have a home, a happy marriage and all the normal appurtenances of the good life, were grounded in the truth. Circumstances – her background and environment, the men she chose to associate with, the fair-weather friends – combined to make this dream impossible.

Having known her since my visits to two of her early recording dates, and having crossed paths with her on a number of happy occasions (the *Esquire* concerts, my own Louis Armstrong concert at Carnegie in which she was a guest soloist, and various less formal encounters) I had come to think of Billie as a good friend; this despite my total lack of interest in sharing any of her less desirable social habits.

During those early years she looked young and beautiful and even innocent – as Buck Clayton once put it, 'A healthy, robust girl, the kind I grew up with when I was a boy in Kansas.' Young or mature, plump or thin, innocent or wasted, Billie Holiday never looked less than beautiful until not long before the end.

I suppose that when I spent an evening at her home (shortly after her stint with the Count Basie band, when she was temporarily between jobs), it was the first time she had ever been interviewed. Her mother, a huge, short woman with a kindly manner, was as unaware as I of Billie's private indulgences; they were part of a life she lived away from home.

I found her friendly and communicative; she had no idea that as a young visitor from England who had idolized her from thousands of miles away, I was utterly in awe of her. To me this occasion was not unlike an audience with the Queen.

Not long afterwards, when she joined Artie Shaw, becoming the first black singer with a white orchestra, this was a unique event, the start of which I was unwilling to miss; I took a train from New York to Boston for her opening night. There they sat, at opposite ends of the bandstand, Billie and Helen Forrest, the white 'protection' vocalist who sang on most of the band's records (Billie was under contract to another company). Her relationship with Helen Forrest was friendly; Shaw, Tony Pastor and the others in the band were all very solicitous, but at that period in America's history there was only so much one could do – particularly when (as happened not long afterwards) the band travelled South.

One characteristic incident occurred during a Southern date. A typical cracker, attempting in his own clumsy manner to demonstrate his appreciation of Billie's first number, shouted 'The nigger wench! Bring back the nigger wench and have her sing another song!' To him, of course, 'nigger wench' as a term for a black woman seemed as natural as it was to refer to any black man, of any age, as a boy.

Billie, hearing the request, began to mutter, under her breath but audibly, 'Motherfucker . . .' As Shaw recalls it, she was promptly removed from the premises before any serious trouble could erupt.

Ironically, the last insult struck her up North. The band was playing the Lincoln Hotel and the manager wanted it known that Billie might offend fewer patrons if she used the back entrance. 'That was the last straw,' Billie told me. 'What a hell of a thing to happen in a hotel named after Abraham Lincoln! So I told Artie I couldn't take it any more, and I quit.'

The golden years for Lady Day began with her long tenure at Cafe Society. It was there that I heard her introduce some of her own songs – 'God Bless the Child', with its clearly autobiographical overtones, and the blues 'Fine and Mellow'. It was there, too, in 1939, that she introduced 'Strange Fruit', which brought tears not only to her audience's eyes, but often to her own.

The 1940s saw a steady upturn in her career and creative evolution. Milt Gabler signed her to Decca Records and asked her to record a new song, 'Lover Man'. 'I want to do it with strings,' Billie insisted. She got her way, and this became one of a long line of songs indelibly associated with her. One was her own 'Don't Explain', inspired by an incident involving her husband, Jimmie Monroe. Like 'God Bless the Child' it was written in collaboration with Arthur Herzog.

Along with the advances in her professional fortunes, of course, Billie sank deeper into a morass that inevitably led to her arrest. By the early 1950s she seemed to have recovered whatever ground had been lost during the enforced absence, although to my amazement she had still never played outside the United States. It was then that I assembled the 'Jazz Club USA' concert package, named after my 'Voice of America' radio series, with Billie as the headliner.

The tour opened disastrously. Red Norvo's guitarist, who had crossed the Atlantic ahead of us by boat, was ill in London; a Swedish musician had to pinch hit for the first three shows. Buddy De Franco's bassist and drummer, Gene Wright and Bobby White, had to work on borrowed equipment because their instruments were snowbound in New York. Billie, after a long series of hassles about who should accompany her, had no time to rehearse with Carl Drinkard, Red Mitchell and Elaine Leighton (Beryl Booker's drummer), because all of us had been dumped off the plane in Copenhagen, as the Stockholm airport was snowed under. We straggled in by train a few hours before the first show, which, not surprisingly, was panned by the critics.

Within a few nights, everything had picked up; in fact, from the second night on, Billie was thrilling everyone, looking more attractive and singing better than she had in years. The reception was even stronger when she began to close with 'Strange Fruit', which many of the spectators knew from the record; but no matter how great the reaction, she would never return for an encore, as the song was too much of an emotional drain on her.

The constant aura of applause, bouquets, photographers and autograph-hunters was invaluable to Billie's morale. Though there were a few nights when it was apparent that she had been drinking too much, for the most part she performed impeccably. Even under pressure she didn't buckle.

After missing a band bus in Brussels, Billie and her man, Louis McKay, and the promoter Nils Hellstrom and I had to devote most of the day to two long taxi rides, one to the German border and then across Germany to Düsseldorf, where it turned out that we had just missed the last plane to our destination, Frankfurt. Hellstrom rented an open four-seater plane; McKay had to be left behind to make the trip by train. We managed to get to Frankfurt just around showtime, and to everyone's surprise, possibly including her own, Lady performed splendidly.

Back home after that encouraging tour, Billie found that very little had changed. She was subjected to the same pressures, the same peddlers, the same taxing lifestyle. Her autobiography, *Lady Sings the Blues*, ghosted for her by William Dufty, appeared in 1956. A selective, sometimes wishful recollection of her life, it was favourably received by many who did not know her well enough to perceive its many errors of omission and commission. John Hammond and I, among others, found it wanting on many levels.

Long since divorced from Jimmie Monroe, Billie married Louis McKay a couple of years after the European tour, but by 1958 they were separated. While McKay was living in California, Billie took a small part in two concerts I had organized with a history of jazz format. Her regular pianist, Mal Waldron, was on hand, along with a few other familiar faces: Buck Clayton from the old Basie orchestra, and George Auld from the Shaw band. Those nights were among the few during that period when her failing voice seemed to recapture some of its pristine confidence and security.

I am sure there were times when Billie was off drugs. At one point, she surprised Jane by asking for tea rather than a drink, explaining that she had cirrhosis of the liver. The abstinence probably lasted a few weeks, but I remember that when I dropped by her apartment to take her to Lester Young's funeral, she took along a small flask of gin as protection. In the taxi on the way

K.B.-HALLEN mandag den 18. januar 1954 kl. 19 og kl. 21^{30}

Richard Stangerup og Wilhelm Hansen, Musik-Forlag præsenterer:

Program

Leonard Feather — konferencier

BERYL BOOKER TRIO

Thou Swell	Symphony
Calypso Mambo Blues	The Man I Love
Bags Groove	Satin Doll

It's Almost Like Being In Love

RED NORVO TRIO

Move	Dancing On The Ceiling
Tenderly	Just One Of Those Things
Swedish Pastry	Lover Come Back To Me

BUDDY DE FRANCO QUARTET

Now Is The Time	April In Paris
Show Eyes	Tenderly
Melody Swings	Sweet Georgia Brown

Lady Be Good

BILLIE HOLIDAY

Ved flygelet: Carl Drinkard

I Cover The Waterfront	Them There Eyes
Willow Weep For Me	Too Marvelous For Words
My Man	Lover Man
Lover Come Back To Me	Fine And Mellow
Tenderly	Billie's Blues

FINALE

Flygel: **HINDSBERG**

Ret til ændringer i programmet forbeholdes

downtown she was sunk in gloom, predicting that she would be the next one to go.

She was. Two months later, there was a pitiful final appearance in a benefit at a downtown theatre for which Steve Allen and I were MCs. She struggled through two songs, looking so emaciated and sounding so pathetic that in the morning I called Joe Glaser, her manager. We met at her apartment. Glaser begged her to put herself in the hospital. 'No, I'll be all right; the doctor gave me some shots and I'm sure that'll do it. I've got to open in Montreal on Monday.'

That was seven days away. The following Saturday she collapsed and was carried first to one hospital and then another. As if she had not gone through enough already, the law stepped in and busted her on her deathbed, posting officers outside her room. On admission to the hospital she had some money strapped to her leg and almost nothing in her bank account.

She died on 17 July 1959. A dozen years later, her tall, full-bodied, statuesque, dignified image was dubiously reincarnated by the tiny Diana Ross in *Lady Sings the Blues*, a movie so flawed by inaccuracies and melodramatic clichés that Carmen McRae walked out of a screening before it was half finished.

The movie did have the effect of generating a renaissance for Billie on records; a couple of her albums were reissued and sold moderately well, but it was Diana Ross, with her soundtrack album and her attempts to assimilate Lady's style, who was the real seller and remained for a long time on the charts.

Of course, Diana Ross was immortalized with a star on Hollywood's Walk of Fame. Since no such honour had been accorded Billie, I wrote an open letter, published in the *Los Angeles Times*, addressed to Miss Ross, suggesting that it would be an appropriate gesture if she could come up with the relatively small payment necessary for similar recognition to be accorded to Billie. There was no reaction to the open letter.

Reluctant to give up, in 1985 I approached Ron Berinstein at the Vine Street Bar & Grill. A fund-raiser was arranged for late January; in the course of two capacity shows dozens of singers and instrumentalists, many of whom had either worked with Billie or were conscious of her contribution, offered their services. Even Artie Shaw showed up to reminisce at length about Billie's experiences during her stint with the band.

And so, on the seventy-first anniversary of her birth, Eleanora

Fagan McKay earned a small symbol of recognition that should have been hers in her lifetime. As we prepared to leave the area, I noticed that someone had placed a few flowers on Billie's star. I looked again. They were gardenias. Later I learned that they had been put there by Charlotte Crossley. She was too young ever to have seen Lady Day in person, and several years younger than Diana Ross; but unlike Diana Ross, she was sensitive enough to understand.

TOSHIKO

'Wow! Japanese woman winning American poll! That's really something!'

It was December 1978. I had called Toshiko Akiyoshi with the news that the orchestra she was co-leading with Lew Tabackin, her husband, had placed first in the annual *Down Beat* Readers' Poll.

The news was almost as exciting to me as to Toshiko. Though I had known her since shortly after her arrival in the US in 1956, we had become very close after she and Lew moved to California in 1972 and settled in a North Hollywood house just five minutes from where Jane and I lived. I had followed the progress of the orchestra ever since its formation, less than a year after they settled here, and was gratified that within five years she and Lew had brought this unique ensemble from obscurity to international acceptance.

The poll victory was one of dozens she and Lew would win during the next eight years. By the end of 1982 Toshiko could claim a triple victory: she was elected (again with Lew) leader of the No.1 big band and, on her own, No.1 jazz composer and No.1 arranger, while Lew Tabackin reached the top slot in the flute category.

Such victories are often belittled as a reflection of the jazz public's fickle tastes, but all the evidence made it clear that in these instances they were the result of incomparable musicianship and an indomitable spirit that had defied all the odds. Toshiko was not merely the first woman, or the first Asian, to write an entire library of original music, organize an orchestra to interpret it, and reach the highest peak in her profession; she was the first musician, regardless of sex or origin, ever to register such an accomplishment. (Even Duke Ellington's library included popular songs and arrangements from other sources; Toshiko's was 100% her own.)

Toshiko and I met a few weeks after her arrival in the US to study at the Berklee College of Music in Boston. When George Wein brought her to my apartment in New York, I knew of her only through a few recordings, made in Tokyo at the recommendation of Oscar Peterson. To most observers then, she was one of the better Bud Powell-inspired pianists; nobody had given her serious consideration as a composer.

She seemed shy and lacking in the confidence that would become evident over the years. A few weeks later, in March 1956, I attended her opening at the Hickory House, where she worked off and on between study periods in Boston.

During the next couple of years our paths crossed only occasionally. In June 1958 I assembled an international group under her leadership for an album on MetroJazz, which I called *United Notions*. Though there was some first-rate piano by Toshiko, as well as solos by the Belgians René Thomas on guitar and Bobby Jaspar on reeds, with the Americans Doc Severinsen and Nat Adderley alternating on horns, the album failed to come off as well as it could have if I had asked Toshiko to compose all the music. She wrote only the title tune; the others were standards and a couple of originals by Bob Freeman, an ex-teacher at Berklee.

In the autumn of 1958 Toshiko made a guest appearance on 'The Subject is Jazz', an educational television series on NBC for which Dr Marshall Stearns and I served as consultants. She wore a kimono, in keeping with the curiosity-value image then deemed desirable. The gimmickry, which struck me as counter-productive, was abandoned not long afterwards.

About a year later I was in Chicago, where I ran into Charlie Mariano, who had just finished playing a concert with Stan Kenton's orchestra. With him was Toshiko, who said, 'Guess what – we just got married!' Mariano was an admirable saxophonist but perhaps less than an ideal husband; the marriage fell apart after a few years, but during that time Toshiko gave birth to Michiru (also known as Monday), an exquisite child whom I have seen grow into a beautiful and talented woman.

Toshiko and Mariano were both on the faculty of a campus 'Summer Jazz Clinic' where she taught piano and arranging, and I taught harmony. By then, 1965, she was trying to establish herself as a composer but found it difficult, mainly for economic reasons.

'Living in New York,' she told me later, 'I had no real chance to write, because I couldn't put a band together. Finally in 1967 I organized an orchestra, wrote some arrangements, and put on my own concert at Town Hall. But it didn't lead to anything permanent; the rental for a rehearsal studio once a week would have cost me $1,000 a year, and I just couldn't afford it.'

Her horizons began to brighten when she met Lew Tabackin, began working with him and benefited from his encouragement. They were married in 1969; three years later Tabackin, who was a member of the house band on the 'Tonight' TV show, moved with it to Los Angeles. He and Toshiko stayed with Jane and me for a week or two before they found the North Hollywood house.

'I think we can really get something going out here,' Toshiko told me. 'We can rehearse at the Musicians Union and it will cost us almost nothing.'

Seven months later, Toshiko and Lew began organizing their orchestra. Though Tabackin's tenor sax and flute were the centrepiece, the original personnel was heavy with first-class studio musicians, all of them capable jazz soloists.

Systematically, slowly, the Tabackins built their creation from nonentity to significant entity, first on a local level. Their public debut took place inauspiciously at a rather obscure room called the Ice House in Pasadena. Reviewing the concert for the *Los Angeles Times*, I observed that the standard big-band devices were expanded through 'colourful voicings that recall . . . the incandescence of a Gil Evans score'. I praised Toshiko for leaving the writing 'free of all rock encumbrances', and observed that in addition to the singular skill and vitality of Tabackin there were valuable contributions by Gary Barone and Bobby Shew on trumpets, Britt Woodman on trombone, Dick Spencer on alto sax and John B. Williams on bass. I closed by wondering 'why Disneyland digs back into ancient history for most of its big-band presentations while new, fresh groups like this are crying for a chance to be heard'.

Keeping an orchestra together in the 1970s was an all but impossible task. Helped by a contract with Japanese RCA (recordings in Hollywood or Tokyo were paid for by the Japanese company and were sometimes released, though without much promotional help, by the American affiliate), the band played gigs in and around Los Angeles, a festival now and then, a tour of Japan every year or two.

The team spirit was unique; everyone in the band wanted to see Toshiko and Lew succeed, and the determination of the leaders defied all obstacles.

The band's first album, *Kogun,* was a surprise hit in Japan,

selling extraordinarily well by jazz standards. In its infinite
wisdom, American RCA executives decided it was too uncommercial for release here; instead, the band's second LP, *Long Yellow
Road*, became its first US release.

Issue of the albums in countries other than Japan and the US
took place so slowly that the band had difficulty mounting more
than a brief token European tour. Nevertheless, somehow the word
got around. In January 1980 Toshiko and Lew took part, and I was
the MC, in a jazz festival in Sydney that included Dave Brubeck,
Les McCann, Herbie Mann and a number of Australian musicians.
Because of the economic impracticality of bringing their own
orchestra, they fronted a specially assembled ensemble of some of
Sydney's best instrumentalists. It was a tribute to Toshiko's charts,
and to the professionalism with which the local players tackled
them, that the performance brought out the idiosyncratic essence of
her writing. The Australian audience was one of the most wildly
enthusiastic I had seen in more than six years of watching the
Tabackins at concerts, festivals and clubs.

That the Akiyoshi–Tabackin orchestra was unique was due not
simply to the fact that she composed and arranged all of its music,
but to other factors such as the subtle mingling, in certain pieces, of
American and Asian cultural characteristics. 'Spiritually, my main
influence has been Ellington,' she told me, 'and Duke's music was
deeply rooted in his race, in which he took great pride; that
encouraged me to draw from my own background, my own
experiences.

'I have used some Japanese instruments, but that's a very
obvious infusion. If people listen more closely they'll find more
indirect infusions. Often I'll have the trumpets voiced very close
together. From first to second trumpet, I'll move a whole step; then
a minor third down to the third trumpet, from third to fourth
trumpet a whole tone down. It's not done much in Western writing,
and it's sometimes very effective.'

The variety of textures in her arrangements is nowhere more
striking than in her use of the wind section, which may employ
from one to five flutes, or various combinations of flute, piccolo,
saxes, clarinet, bass clarinet, distributed among the five
musicians.

She credits Lew with inspiring her: 'He is such a great flutist, so
he gets to play the lead and we have a very rich woodwind section.
Lew knows what I want; it's very good to have someone who

understands the writer well enough to gather musicians who are best suited for the work.'

Once, during a chat over dinner at her house, I asked whether she believed she had lost jobs to male musicians. 'I'm not quite sure,' she said, 'because so many male players, and arrangers, don't have jobs either. Sometimes I think jazz is perceived as very masculine music; men don't like to see the female being too masculine – or aggressive. And jazz is precisely an aggressive music; it has always been that way.'

During the decade Toshiko and Lew spent in North Hollywood it was fascinating to observe how many balls she could juggle as composer, arranger, leader, pianist, housewife, mother, cook and chauffeur. Throughout this entire period Tabackin never learned how to drive, perhaps as a subconscious protest against the Los Angeles lifestyle, to which he never adjusted. The move back to New York in 1982 was undoubtedly his idea; Toshiko, saying 'I can be happy wherever I am,' went along with the move in what seemed to be dutiful Japanese passivity.

Nevertheless, she is a strong individual; her musicians have always respected her just as they would a male conductor. ('In Japan they did not like woman to be successful over man.') She could probably have been successful at almost any other pursuit; this was illustrated by an incident that took place one night during a party at our house.

We were running short of mineral water. 'Don't go out,' said Toshiko, 'I'll walk up the street to the store and bring some back.' She left for a nearby gourmet shop, Trader Joe's, which specializes in wines and cheeses. She was gone so long that we became a little worried. Finally she returned, explaining: 'I started looking at the wines, and the man there told me the history of some of them. It was fascinating! I have to go back there and stock up on wines.'

This was the beginning of her hobby as a wine collector and connoisseur; from that night on, every time we visited the Tabackins a larger portion of the kitchen would be taken up by her collection of wines, which now numbers in the hundreds.

The personalities of the Tabackins are a perfect example of the attraction of opposites. His mild-mannered, pipe-smoking style, dry humour and firm but quietly stated convictions about matters musical or political contrast strongly with her restlessness and actively inquisitive manner. Despite her convictions regarding the supposedly 'male' character of jazz, it is she who displays this quality in her lifestyle.

In a typical day in the Los Angeles years she might drive Michiru to school, come home, do a little writing, drive Lew to the union, drive home, go shopping, pick out some more wines, prepare and cook dinner, deal with innumerable incoming and outgoing phone calls, supervise Michiru's homework and flute practice (a firm, strict mother, she insisted that her child speak Japanese every day in order not to lose touch with her heritage), sit down to dinner with Lew and perhaps a few friends, then retire to do copying work on the chart at hand.

A few months after the move back to New York they organized a Local 802 band, which George Wein authorized me to present, in collaboration with Kiyoshi Koyama (a former *Swing Journal* editor who now produces records and concerts) at Carnegie Hall during the Kool Jazz Festival. The Tabackins felt that the new orchestra was superior to its California counterpart and that the reed section, enhanced by the presence of Frank Wess on alto sax and flute, was the best anywhere in the world. My own feeling was that both bands had immense strengths and neither had perceptible weaknesses. Nevertheless, the New York band has worked very little more frequently than its West Coast counterpart, for the same reasons.

In the swing years it was possible to assemble a unit of capable musicians who were willing to go on the road for a reasonable salary, travel by bus or train, find dance halls or colleges at which to play seven nights a week – all locations that are now scattered too far apart to make a cross-country tour workable. The bands could make records that were assured of regular air play when radio was the all-powerful medium; they could even broadcast live every night if they settled into a hotel job for an extended run. Meals and hotel rooms were available at prices that are unbelievable by today's yardstick. Today rooms, meals and plane fares are prohibitive; most jazz musicians would rather scuffle in New York than face life on the road.

Still, Toshiko carries on. Today the orchestra bears her name as sole leader, with Lew billed as featured soloist, but the division of responsibilities has remained the same.

She looks back philosophically on her career up to this point. 'In Japan basically I had to deal with a sexual prejudice. Over here I found myself dealing with two kinds, sexual and racial, because Orientals were not associated with jazz. I got some publicity based on people's amazement that I could play jazz; being Japanese and being a female I was a novelty. Moreover, I didn't meet one first-generation Japanese-American who liked jazz, and very few second-generation either – they associated it with black people and found it undesirable in terms of their search for status.

'Back home I have overcome the prejudice, because I have been acknowledged by the world, so they consider me a pioneer. At first there was every kind of resentment. In America there are still barriers to overcome, but I'm very proud of what I have accomplished.

'I don't want to sound arrogant, but I do feel that everything I've achieved, I earned it. I always had to fight for everything, and I'm just going to keep on fighting.'

MELBA TO STACY

One of the undisputed giants among jazzwomen is Melba Doretta Liston. I had followed her career closely ever since 1945, when I first heard her at Shepp's Playhouse, a Los Angeles club where the then new and stimulating orchestra of Gerald Wilson was breaking in. During the next decade she was the only female horn player (doubling as a composer and arranger of the first rank) who clung successfully to a series of jobs in a male-dominated world, working with Dizzy Gillespie and Count Basie, touring with Billie Holiday and then, in 1956–7, with Gillespie's newly formed band under State Department auspices in the Middle East and Latin America.

Despite all these credits, Melba had never been offered a record date of her own. Having been producing albums for almost a decade at MGM, I was able to rectify this omission, and late in 1958 the album *Melba Liston and Her 'Bones* enabled her to play with and write for a number of her peers. On the first session the other trombonists were Benny Green, Al Grey and Benny Powell; two days later we used Jimmy Cleveland, Frank Rehak and Slide Hampton. If it had offered nothing except her own beguiling 'Melba Blues', this MetroJazz LP would have been justified.

Melba Liston has charmed everyone who has known her. She was a vital asset to the Quincy Jones orchestra when she took a playing and acting part in the Harold Arlen–Johnny Mercer musical *Free and Easy*, presented in Paris in 1959–60. Over the years Melba racked up her fair share of credits as writer, player and teacher, collaborating often with her old friend Randy Weston; she also spent five years (1975–80) in the West Indies, teaching at the Jamaica School of Music, then returned to New York. A year or so after my 1960 move to Los Angeles, an old friend of Melba Liston's came into my life, both as an object of admiration and as a close friend. It began one evening when the drummer Dave Bailey asked me: 'Have you ever heard Vi Goldberg?' I had never even heard of Vi Goldberg, but went along gladly to the Red Carpet, a small club where I was introduced to the powerful, Bird-inspired alto saxophone of Elvira Redd. She was also a moving, gospel-tinged singer.

Vi represents the third step in a four-generation musical family. Her great-aunt, Mrs Alma Hightower, was a celebrated music teacher among whose students were Vi herself and Melba Liston. Vi's father was Alton Redd, the New Orleans drummer whom I had heard in Johnny St Cyr's traditional band on the Disneyland riverboat. Vi had two sons, who have grown up to enjoy some success as a bassist and a drummer.

Married at that time to the drummer Richie Goldberg, Vi had only recently returned to jazz after the exertion of too many negative forces on her life in music. She had spent three years as a county social worker, was now playing one night a week at the Red Carpet, and later earned a few gigs at Shelly's Manne Hole.

Art Blakey, hearing her during a Los Angeles visit, called a New York record executive to sing her praises. Typically, he was told: 'Yeah, but she's a girl . . . Only two girls in jazz have ever really made it, Mary Lou Williams and Shirley Scott.' Instead of being considered seriously on her merits, Vi Redd again was being judged as a novelty.

Today, a quarter-century after our first meeting, Vi Redd looks back on a career marked by sporadic moments of luck: the Monterey Jazz Festival in 1966; my own Beverly Hills Jazz Festival in 1967 (the only artist to appear both nights, she sang spirituals and blues at the traditional concert, playing her alto in the modern programme); a European tour in 1967 that took in a record-breaking ten-week run at Ronnie Scott's club, and another tour of Europe, as a featured attraction (but not a member of the reed section) with Count Basie; Birdland with Earl Hines.

She still has to her credit only two albums as a leader, both of which I produced: one, *Bird Call* for United Artists in May 1962 (later reissued on Solid State), the second, *Lady Soul*, for Atlantic's Atco label. For the United Artists date I wrote 'I Remember Bird', which she was the first to record and which led to many other versions. Her ballad singing, warm and sensuous, was heard to best advantage on 'If I Should Lose You' in the first LP and 'We'll be Together Again' in the second. The latter was recorded partly in

New York with a group that included Dave Bailey, who had introduced me to her, and Dick Hyman on organ.

Despite these well received (but now unavailable) albums, and a couple of dates for other leaders (Al Grey, Marian McPartland), Vi Redd has seen success pass her by and has been obliged repeatedly to return to her basic job as a school teacher. She talks, with surprisingly little rancour, of having been resented as a female, of being passed up for jobs, of seeing men walk off the bandstand as soon as she walked on. Yet she seems at peace with the world. She knows how many black men, as well as black women, have been forced to make sacrifices, have lost opportunities for which they waited too long.

Why did none of those apparent breaks amount to anything? The dates with Basie, the airplay for the albums, the unprecedented Ronnie Scott engagement? She was born in 1928; is it too late for a groundswell of acceptance? Perhaps it is too late even to conclude that time will tell, yet Vi Redd continues to wait, hope, pray and practise.

Clora Bryant, a contemporary of Vi Redd, raised in Texas but a Los Angeles resident for forty years, has had a similarly discouraging career. She has tried the all-female band circuit, from the Prairie View College Co-Eds to the Sweethearts and even the Darlings of Rhythm. She tried R & B with Johnny Otis. She has been an entertainer, doing her Armstrong vocal imitation as part of Scatman Crothers' show. She has still not established herself in the area that is logically hers, as a Gillespie-inspired trumpeter in a small-band setting.

Male bands have accepted her now and then: there were gigs with Bill Berry and Teddy Edwards. About five years ago she told me: 'I may not be very aggressive, but I am determined.' That determination sent her back to school, after a thirty-two-year absence, when she was able, through the government-backed Comprehensive Employment and Training Act (CETA) to return to UCLA and go for her BA in music. But Reaganomics struck, CETA was killed, and she was forced to drop out in 1982, only sixteen credits short of graduation.

Clora Bryant has long been admired by, as much as she is an admirer of, Dizzy Gillespie, who has recommended her for various jobs. Once Charlie Parker sat in with her during a Sunday matinee at a Hermosa Beach club. But not even Gillespie's and Parker's respect and recommendations eased the path.

In 1983 I was putting together a group for Linda Hopkins, who was recording an album consisting mainly of my blues compositions. Sweets Edison, whom I wanted, was out of town. Who else could play in the style of that era, with that particular warmth and blues feeling? Suddenly I thought of Clora Bryant.

When she accepted the job, Clora told me that this was the first record session she had made since 1957, when her trumpet and voice had been heard on *The Gal with the Horn* for the long-forgotten Mode label. Why no other calls in twenty-six years? Ask the male musicians. It is doubtful that any of them can offer a convincing answer.

A trumpeter who represents a much younger generation, but whose experiences have been scarcely less frustrating, is Stacy Rowles, the daughter of the eminent pianist Jimmy Rowles. She had just turned eighteen and had graduated from high school when she and her father played together at the Monterey Jazz Festival. Even at that early stage her sound and conception were impressive.

Rowles learned the scale from her father on his old army trumpet, then studied improvisation and reading with Charlie Shoemake and several other teachers. Her career has been erratic. In 1975 she played in an all-female band led by Clark Terry; three years later there was a tour of Mexico with a predominantly male orchestra. For five months she worked reluctantly with an uninspiring Top 40 lounge band.

What seemed like a breakthrough came in the form of a new all-female local band, subsequently known as Maiden Voyage and led by the saxophonist Ann Patterson. Rowles was heard with this group at the 1980 Women's Jazz Festival in Kansas City. Two years later she returned there, this time with a Canadian Dixieland band, the Swing Sisters.

Rowles' first inspiration was Freddie Hubbard; she has listened to the records of Clifford Brown and Fats Navarro, and has heard Dizzy Gillespie, Chuck Mangione and others often in person. As her efficient reading of difficult charts with Maiden Voyage has made clear, Stacy Rowles is well equipped for any studio assignment, yet she is never called. This may not be due to any conscious sexism on the part of contractors, but it seems odd that so many of the ensembles seen in studios and nightclubs alike are overwhelmingly male and white.

'I know there's a lot of work out there that I'm capable of doing,' she told me, 'but it's a vicious circle. They don't let me get the experience, then they'll say they can't hire me because I'm not experienced.'

Stacy Rowles, who now plays flugelhorn exclusively, has spent much of her time during the last few years in a day job at a Glendale record shop, but has taken time out for occasional jobs with her father, with Maiden Voyage, and with another female group called Alive! Convinced that she needed exposure on records, I arranged to produce a date with her for Concord Jazz. The album, though well received (the personnel included Jimmy Rowles, Herman Riley, Donald Bailey and Chuck Berghofer), did little to broaden the horizons for Stacy Rowles, who in 1985 was doing just about as little in music as had been her lot two years earlier.

The Rowles session was made in Hollywood almost forty-six years after my first Una Mae Carlisle date in London. During that time I saw very little progress for women musicians, despite all the 'focus on females' festivals and the earnest panel discussions about the role of women in jazz.

In fact, it reflects shame on the music world and on recording executives and male musicians, rather than credit on me, that during the 1940s and 1950s most of the recordings led by female instrumentalists were instigated and produced by me, and that of the all-female sessions I was responsible for very nearly 100%. Under my byline there were two series of features on women musicians, the first for *Down Beat* in the 1950s, another for the *Los Angeles Times* from 1981 until 1984.

Kimberley McCord, in her perceptive analysis of the history of women in jazz (for the *Jazz Educators' Journal*, January 1986), pointed out that the Musicians Union has always used the term 'sideman' on its contracts rather than 'musician', and that women often have been required by contractors, booking a club date, to submit 8 × 10 inch photos along with resumés for playing jobs, and details about their age, figure, wardrobe, and marital status.

McCord also recalls the conditions for women on the road with a male band, 'constantly having to cope with the never-ending flow of sexual overtones made by band members and fans. Even though women in the bands had to be tough and dedicated, they were most commonly thought of as gimmicks or viewed as a decoration . . .'

Male critics have sometimes helped to aggravate this attitude, sometimes with unintentionally funny results. McCord quotes a review by George T. Simon of Mary Lou Williams: 'One of the most brilliant jazz pianists of all time, serious-looking, with long hair, a shy smile, and surprisingly attractive buck teeth.'

Whitney Balliett, in the *New Yorker*, helped to stress some popular myths: 'Most women lack the physical equipment – to say nothing of the poise – for blowing trumpets and trombones, slapping bass fiddles, or beating drums . . . Female instrumentalists . . . in the past thirty or forty years . . . in the main . . . have dropped quickly out of sight.'

The trumpeters Stacy Rowles, Clora Bryant, Ellen Seeling, Louise Baptist, Betty O'Hara, the saxophonists Jane Ira Bloom, Ann Patterson, Mary Fettig and Vi Redd, the trombonists Janice Robinson and Melba Liston, the pianists Marian McPartland and dozens more, the bassists Carol Kaye and Carline Ray, the guitarists Emily Remler and Mary Osborne, the drummers Judith Chilnick, Terrilyne Carrington, Jeanette Wrate, Sue Evans and the United Kingdom's Guest Stars and Gail Thompson have not dropped out of sight and will not be intimidated into doing so by such discouraging words.

With the passage of the Civil Rights Act, blacks and women alike became more conscious of the movement to give them stature equal to that of white males when their talents justified it. The strengthening of the feminist movement has played a central part in raising male consciousness. Perhaps the day is not far off when a male contractor, hearing a woman's name suggested for an assignment, will not raise his eyebrows and react: 'What, a chick?'

Women have become an ever more important force in American society, demanding and winning independence in every area. They are gaining an ever-increasing share of the job-market. Female enrolment at college level in the seventies and early eighties rose to the point where women outnumbered men in college; among graduate students, forty-five per cent were female.

These statistics will certainly be reflected in all the arts, and inevitably in jazz. It is encouraging to be able to point out such figures, but with the reservation (and here again the parallel with the situation of blacks is clear) that it should never have been necessary to compile them in the first place.

PART FOUR

Business and Pleasures

BUSINESS

During the early years in New York I learned, albeit too slowly, about the business end of music as it affected the interacting worlds of pop and jazz, and about the confusion that existed, particularly in the minds of business people, concerning the overlapping roles of improvisation, composition and arrangement.

The subtle differences separating the songwriter, the composer, the arranger and the improviser have confused people inside and outside the business community. The Duke Ellington who set pen to paper to produce material such as 'Black, Brown and Beige' or 'Harlem Suite' was a composer/arranger in the purest sense. The Ellington who jotted down a few simple phrases that became known as 'I'm Beginning to See the Light' was a songwriter, even though his orchestration of the tune for his own musicians raised it to a higher level. Such a trifle as 'C Jam Blues', a repeated collection (with slight rhythmic variations) of two notes, is scarcely even a song; an infant could have written it.

That Ellington worked with equal success on these diverse plateaus was a reflection of his versatility and genius. He was to jazz what George Gershwin, also a songwriter/composer/arranger, had been to popular music. Many men of great talent, Fats Waller no more or less than Irving Berlin, were songwriters whose works were arranged by others; they never sat at a score pad to arrange their songs for an orchestra. Even Thelonious Monk was a songwriter rather than a composer/arranger for full ensembles.

The confusion is further confounded by the general use of 'composer' to denote songwriters as well as those versed in the art of composing for an ensemble, and by another subdivision: a popular song or composition that may involve two or more writers, of whom at least one may have written the lyrics. Can the lyricist too be called a composer? When record buyers see beneath the title of 'I'm Beginning to See the Light' the names of Duke Ellington, Johnny Hodges, Harry James and Don George, can they be blamed for wondering how it could have taken so many to create relatively little?

These questions occurred to me very early, and the answers have never become entirely clear. I became aware almost immediately, however, of the business of cutting in, a practice employed not only by music publishers but also by most of the bandleaders and many other artists in a position of power. Even Duke Ellington, who had to share credit with Irving Mills on countless works, was not above using this ploy himself when members of his orchestra, and a few outsiders, brought their original material to him. Like many others of the day, from Chick Webb to Benny Goodman, he felt it his right to participate in the profits from a piece to which he would give widespread exposure. The ethics are still being debated but the practice has never been dropped.

Although, over the years, Irving Mills extended many favours to me and I eventually came to regard him as a friendly and gracious old man, there were moments when the necessity for caution became obvious. One such occasion was the day when I first saw a proof of the copy Mills had sent to the printer of 'Mighty Like the Blues'. The credit line read: 'By Leonard Feather and Irving Mills'. My protests, loud and unsubtle, took immediate effect; no doubt sensing the possibility of repercussions in the press, Mills had his name removed.

Nevertheless, he made twice as much as I out of the composition. The standard song contract called for the publisher to receive 50% of the royalties from all recordings, and the composer or composers to receive or divide the other 50%. But some publishers, when they thought they could get away with it, gave writers a 33⅓% contract, thereby keeping 66⅔% for themselves. For 'Mighty Like the Blues' I had just such a contract. The copyright term at that time was twenty-eight years, with a renewal period of twenty-eight years. Towards the end of the first stage, with the renewal imminent, I asked Mills to change the royalty arrangement to 50%. He agreed. To this day, if someone of his or her own volition records this song (or any of a number of others I assigned to publishers during my innocent youth), half of the income is legally withheld by whoever now owns the publishing rights.

Many of us, unaware of the dog-eat-dog nature of the business, gave our works to publishers even when we had nothing to gain, and anywhere from half to two thirds of our rewards to lose. This happened in numerous cases simply because those of us who were writers did not understand that we could be our own publishers. This realization came to me eventually, but not until I had given up fairly substantial amounts to several publishing companies.

Some awareness of the machinations in the business end of music came to me through my friendship with Billy Moore Jr, a brilliant young arranger who had taken Sy Oliver's place with the Jimmie Lunceford Orchestra. Moore and I shared many experiences; both of us regretted some that we had had with bandleaders and publishers. We both wanted to start our own companies. Billy did so first, opening a midtown office that became my *pied à terre*.

In my case there was the additional problem that any music bearing my name might have trouble getting past an A & R man (Artists and Repertoire – record producer) whom I had offended through some negative review; or, if recorded, might meet with hostility on the part of rival reviewers. For this reason, I began using a variety of pseudonyms, employing this technique more and more often as the attacks of the moldy figs became more vehement.

This worked well, often with results that were helpful to me, since a tune under my own name was certain either to be ignored or derogated, while one under a false name had a normal chance of a good, bad or indifferent review. Several critics unwittingly gave favourable reports on works of which my authorship was unknown. Sometimes, to lend greater authenticity to the pseudonym, I borrowed Billy Moore's name, with results that amused both of us. The best-known of these was 'Baby Get Lost'.

Billy Moore's story tells graphically the difficulties facing those of us who were obliged to deal with the unpleasant commercial realities of the music empire. Not long ago Moore reminisced about it in his Copenhagen home and sent me his thoughts on tape, a resumé of which follows.

BILLY MOORE'S STORY

Leonard and I met through Sy Oliver, who got me the job with Lunceford. Coincidentally, the first song Lunceford had assigned me to arrange was Leonard's 'You Can Fool Some of the People

Some of the Time', which I did as a vocal vehicle for Trummy Young. Sy was very helpful. He really constructed that chart for me. Until then I had only written for an amateur band in Harlem led by the trumpeter Freddie Williams; mostly I transcribed Sy's and Ed Wilcox's arrangements for Lunceford. For five years I had a day job in a butcher shop; then Lunceford signed me for a year at $125 a month.

My troubles with Lunceford began when he put his name on my own tune 'Belgium Stomp'. I was very depressed and told Sy, who exploded: 'Don't let him put his name on anything!' Several years earlier, Lunceford had gotten away with putting his name on Sy's 'Stomp It Off'. So I told Lunceford he couldn't do it to me, and from then on things were kind of cool between us.

I found out from Sy that he had done all those famous masterpieces like 'Margie' for Lunceford at $2.50 an arrangement – and that included the copying! Sy was working out of his heart. Meanwhile Lunceford bought himself a Lincoln Continental, and then his own plane, which he piloted. He and his business manager, Harold Oxley, were coining money, paying the band as little as possible. Meanwhile Cab Calloway was paying his musicians very well, treating them quite differently. Anyhow, that's why Sy became disillusioned, accepted an offer to join Tommy Dorsey as staff arranger, and got me the job with Lunceford.

In my case, the last straw was when Lunceford claimed to be the arranger on my arrangement of Chopin's Prelude No.7. On any public-domain tune, the arranger gets the composer's royalties.

I remember having an argument with Lunceford out on the street one day, with Oxley standing in the background. Anyhow, they didn't renew my contract, so at the end of the year I became a freelance arranger.

Leonard did an article about me in *Down Beat* which I guess a lot of people saw; when I began working for Charlie Barnet the guys in the band seemed to know who I was. Barnet's band really knew how to interpret what I wrote. I worked for him off and on for several years. I did charts on two of Leonard's songs, 'The Heart You Stole from Me' and later, one of the best arrangements I ever made, on a tune of his called 'Lonesome as the Night is Long'. We started recording this, but Lawrence Brown, who had an eight-bar solo, cracked on the high note at the end; he had ten minutes to get back to the Paramount, where he was working with Duke, and he dashed off before a good take could be made. So the record never came out, unfortunately for Leonard and myself.*

In 1944 I made an arrangement for Charlie Barnet on one of his
own tunes. I went to his hotel suite on Park Avenue; typically,
there he was, in bed with a big, beautiful blonde, and he sat up and
said, 'Come in, Bill, here's my song.' He gave me a tune with a
whole bunch of half notes and whole notes. I didn't know what to
do with it, but in desperation I finally put in a countermelody for
the brass. Barnet liked it. Later on I heard that he had switched it
around, putting my melody at the beginning, and then bringing in
his long-note theme played by the reeds. This was 'Skyliner'.

Two or three years later, I suggested we ought to be co-
composers on that. Of course, Charlie demurred. It wasn't until I
got to England that I found out it had been very big over there, and
several bands had recorded it. Whereas ASCAP had refused to
admit me to membership as a composer, the British publisher of
'Skyliner', Jimmy Phillips, got me into the English Performing
Rights Society and I began receiving royalties as arranger of the
tune. During this time I started my own company, Belltone Music,
with two friends of mine. We published some of my things, and a
tune of Leonard's, 'Design for Jiving', which Duke Ellington used
to play on the air. We were both concerned about keeping our tunes
from being taken over by the bandleaders, who almost all had their
own companies. Around this time, too, I agreed to let Leonard use
my name on some of his compositions, because I knew about the
trouble he was having when he used his own name.

I continued to have disagreements with bandleaders. I recall that
Les Brown told me Trummy Young was about to join his band,
which would have been the first time he had integrated his
personnel. So I did some freelance work for Les Brown, and I said,
'When's Trummy coming in? I'm ready to do some things for him.'
'Oh,' he said, 'we've decided against it. Frank Dailey at the
Meadowbrook thought it wouldn't be a good idea, so we just
dropped it.' I got angry and raised hell, so that ended my
association with Les Brown.

Tommy Dorsey would have given me a job when Sy went into
the army, but I heard from Sy about all the trouble he had,
travelling with the band, not being allowed to stay at the same

*This song seemed to be jinxed. Another arrangement of it was written in 1959 by
John Dankworth for a Vic Lewis session in London; this too was never issued, but
in mid-1986 Vic told me he had at last made plans for its release.

hotels; so when Sy proposed the job with Dorsey I turned it down. Some time later, when Charlie Shavers was in the band, I did agree to work for Dorsey for a few months, but by that time I had had my fill of the whole racial situation. I had been through that on the road with Barnet, when night after night Andy Gibson and I had to stay at some inferior hotel, in the black section.

There were so many of these episodes that kept building and building until I didn't see any reason to stay in the US. I wasn't very politically inclined, but the McCarthy era was almost upon us; Lena Horne was called up by the Un-American Activities Committee, and meanwhile I was having difficulty keeping Belltone going, although a couple of times when things were tight Leonard loaned me some money. Anyhow, I finally left the US in 1950.

After living for a while in Paris and London, Billy Moore Jr toured for nine years (1952–61) as musical director and pianist with the Peters Sisters. Settling in Copenhagen, he has since been manager, arranger and pianist for the Delta Rhythm Boys, and manager of the Ben Webster Foundation (he was Webster's personal manager for a while before his death in Amsterdam in 1973).

Moore still has mixed feelings about Lunceford:

He was an inspiring leader, from a distance, and he did mould his men into a most effective orchestra; he kept the men on their toes and maintained a fine public image. But he failed to reward the musicians who were mostly reponsible for his huge success; he didn't realize it was Sy's arrangements the public wanted to hear.

When I first met him, it was pandemonium backstage at the Apollo, with enormous crowds screaming for his autograph. It was sad to see him again, as I did in 1947, when he was at the Apollo again. This time there were no people asking for autographs, and the theatre was one third full. Trummy was gone, Willie Smith was gone; the band didn't sound like anything.

Lunceford said he wanted me to go to work for him again. I told him if he paid me $175 a week I'd write for him.

As I said on the air on Radio Denmark, I don't know whether my demand for $175 a week was a contributing factor, but about four months later, Jimmie Lunceford had a fatal heart attack. It was a very unhappy ending, and I still remember what an exciting orchestra that was to work for during his great days.

Billy Moore's experiences, most of which I had been acutely aware of while they were happening, taught me a lesson, though I was slow in digesting its implications. The music business in the 1940s was totally dominated by three absolute powers: the music publishers, the big-band leaders, and the radio personalities such as Bing Crosby. Today's world is completely different: the power is in the hands of the recording artists, most of whom have their own publishing organizations, and the record producers, many of them independent and more influential than their early counterparts, the A & R men.

Except for certain freak hits that might take off on their own, most of the commercially successful music consisted of songs owned by the solidly established publishers. Even Cole Porter, Duke Ellington and Johnny Mercer left many of their works under the control of companies in which they had no direct financial interest.

Once it was determined that a certain item would be next week's 'plug song', the so-called song pluggers, also known as contact men, employed by the publishers, would ingratiate themselves with bandleaders playing at the leading hotel rooms or dance halls in order to secure priceless 'air time' – usually a remote radio shot from the location, though several of the big white bands had sponsored programmes at a more desirable slot in prime time.

The jazz-orientated leaders, which meant those who led swing bands, were less assiduously courted by pluggers than the 'sweet' maestros such as Guy Lombardo and Sammy Kaye, in part because they allegedly did violence to the songs by not sticking religiously to the melodies. Nevertheless, Benny Goodman at the New Yorker or Charlie Barnet at the Lincoln would be under some pressure from representatives of the million-dollar publishing giants. Most of the black bandleaders, working at the Savoy or Golden Gate Ballroom (where sideman scale for the musicians was $35 a week, but the air time was still valuable) would put up with a degree of influence, though unlike the downtown leaders they tended not to be heavily 'romanced' by the pluggers and not to play golf with them.

In my case, not being an established writer, having no movie or show-tune credentials, and with a conflicting prior image as a critic,

I found it impossible to achieve plug-song stature. Attempts to write material that seemed to me to have commercial potential were therefore not only pointless but, worse, offered captious observers a perfect chance to criticize me, justifiably.

Eventually I decided simply to concentrate on composing instrumentals, vocal blues or ballads of which I could be proud, and to avoid as far as possible any entanglements with publishers. By then, however, at least three bandleaders – Lunceford, Benny Goodman and Woody Herman – had put songs of mine in their companies as a corollary of their recording them. (Count Basie never made any such deal; nor did Benny Carter.)

I could understand how a leader might feel entitled to the publisher's share of the revenue when he had helped me establish a song. Certainly I was never in the same situation as, say, Edgar Sampson, who composed 'Don't be that Way', 'Lullaby in Rhythm', 'If Dreams Come True' and 'Stompin' at the Savoy' while he was in Chick Webb's band in the early 1930s. Later they were recorded by the Benny Goodman orchestra, with Goodman now credited as co-composer. Goodman's income from various composing and publishing deals must have been considerable.

Never having been able to assimilate the thought processes of the typical huckster in the music world, I avoided business involvements in the Tin Pan Alley area as often as possible after the mid-1940s.

Recording royalties were a slight source of income. Another was available in the form of credits for public performances. With that in mind I had joined England's Performing Rights Society in 1938, but it soon seemed advisable to sign up with its US counterpart, the American Society of Composers, Authors and Publishers (ASCAP). In order to join it was then necessary to have two members as sponsors. Deems Taylor, then ASCAP's president, agreed to sponsor me; my other champion, by now a close friend and occasional collaborator, was Fats Waller's perennial partner, Andy Razaf. With their help I joined ASCAP in 1943. Almost forty years later my daughter, Lorraine, followed suit, so that she too could receive due credit for her work, which includes lyrics to Ellington's 'Rockin' in Rhythm' and 'Creole Love Call', Sy Oliver's 'For Dancers Only' and many songs of a more contemporary nature.

I found it ironic that in Jim Godbolt's *A History of Jazz in Britain 1919–50* he described me as, among other things, a manager. Far from managing others, I often felt that I could have used a good manager myself. Thanks to friends like Billy Moore and Andy Razaf, I did finally come to the realization that there is an inherent problem, incapable of resolution, in the reconciliation of jazz (or of valid songwriting) with the business world that still exercises so much control. It's a cold world out there, and you had better wear warm psychological protection.

RECORDINGS: PRE-BAN

The late 1930s, the 1940s and the early 1950s were primarily regarded by the public and jazz historians as the swing era, and to most observers this connoted the years of the big bands. There is a tendency to overlook or at least minimize the importance of that period as an immensely creative one for small combos, for jazz singers and, most particularly, for the blues.

From my point of view as a record producer, composer and lyricist, operating almost exclusively in those areas, these were eventful and creative times. To the extent that my name is known at all, it has always been associated essentially with the roles of critic, historian and journalist. In fact, though, during more than a quarter of a century of my life I was deeply involved in record production and in writing music for my own sessions and others'.

Earlier chapters have dealt with the records produced in England, the first three dates made in New York in 1938 and 1939, and the various sessions featuring women musicians. Additionally, starting in 1940, there were close to 200 sessions for dozens of labels, involving long associations with MGM, RCA and my partnership with Mercer Ellington (his father was a behind-the-scenes associate) in our own company, Mercer Records.

The 1940s happened to be a particularly valuable decade for anyone with a concern for the blues. Of the four sessions I produced between 1940 and the advent in August 1942 of the first Musicians Union recording ban, three were mainly blues-orientated.

Oddly, my first recognition as a blues writer came about through an improbable event. One morning in the autumn of 1940, my phone rang. 'Leonard, this is Dinah Shore. Listen, I'm down here at the RCA Victor studios and they have this blues arrangement they want me to sing on. I know you're a blues expert – can you fix me up some sort of personalized blues lyrics and bring them right down here?'

Seizing a sheet of manuscript paper, I went to work, then looked at the clock and decided to finish the job on my way downtown in the subway. Arriving just in time, I heard Dinah sing my somewhat asinine lyrics – something about her NBC radio programme – and succeeded in satisfying her and whoever was in the control booth, as well as Henry Levine, the trumpeter who then led the house group on the 'Chamber Music Society of Lower Basin Street' show that employed Shore regularly.

'Dinah's Blues' inexplicably was so successful that it remained in the catalogue virtually for ever. A few weeks later I was back at the same studios producing a session of my own in which the blues again played a vital part, but this time on a more meaningful level from the jazz point of view.

Oran 'Hot Lips' Page was a trumpeter and singer from Dallas whom I had first heard at the Reno Club in Kansas City in 1936, where he played not as a regular member of Count Basie's band but as a featured attraction. He had worked alongside Basie in the Original Blue Devils led by his half-brother Walter Page. Both of them then worked in Benny Moten's orchestra.

Joe Glaser, who had been present when I heard Lips Page in Kansas City, had expressed some interest in building a band around him. Arriving in New York under Glaser's aegis, he jobbed around before forming a band that opened in August 1937 at Smalls Paradise in Harlem, where I heard him and commented in the *Melody Maker*: 'His forte is the blues, which he plays and sings almost endlessly.'

His group, too big to sound like a combo but not quite large enough to produce valid orchestral textures, made some records for RCA's 35¢ subsidiary label, Bluebird, as well as a couple of sessions for Decca with a smaller and somewhat better group. But the idiom I had described as Lips' forte had still not been presented on records; worse, in addition to a few of his own vocals on pop songs, he used three other singers at one time or another.

Lips was receptive to my suggestion of a small, intimate blues session; so was Leonard Joy, the head A & R man at RCA Victor. The problem was that of a budget: in a word, Joy had none. We arrived at a compromise of sorts between zero, which was what he said he could afford, and the amount I had requested. The result was the lowest budget combo date I ever produced: the entire undertaking cost exactly $120 – $40 each for Lips and me, $20 (scale) for our two sidemen, the guitarist Teddy Bunn and the bassist Ernest 'Bass' Hill.

Bunn, arriving somewhat late, looked around the studio and said: 'Where is everybody?'

'Teddy,' I said, 'this *is* everybody.'

I was tempted to sit in at the piano, but having not yet joined the Musicians Union I knew that a delegate might walk in to check on us and land everyone in trouble. Luckily the delegate came and left early, enabling me to fulfill a discreet role at the keyboard on two or three tunes.

Lips sang three blues I had written for the occasion, playing trumpet on two and mellophone on a third. Next, having heard Teddy Bunn's amiable vocals with the Spirits of Rhythm, I suggested we let him take over for the last song. Ironically, this was the one that turned out to enjoy by far the longest life, enduring through a sex-change and various lyrical additions and alterations during the next four decades: 'Evil Man Blues', which as 'Evil Gal Blues' would introduce Dinah Washington to records just three years later.

Budget problems seemed to be endemic to the production of small jazz dates. Four months later I put together a group for a shortlived company, General Records, again dispensing with piano and drums, but with a more ambitious front line. Joe Marsala and Pete Brown, who had played on my first two American dates, were on hand again, along with the graceful trumpeter Bill Coleman, whom I knew from his years in Paris. Bill, who had just returned to the US from Egypt, joined Benny Carter's orchestra shortly after this session.

The vocalist on two blues was Dell St John, whom I had heard at the Savoy with Carter. But again it was a vocal ringer on the date who had what turned out to be the most durable song: Bill Coleman sang 'Salty Mama Blues', in another preview of a vehicle destined for success with Dinah Washington.

It was during 1940 that I belatedly began to study arranging. I knew of nobody who gave instruction in the specialized craft of writing for a jazz ensemble, but found a $2 book that showed me the technical basics. Adrian De Haas, my copyist-arranger friend, was helpful in pointing out which trumpet part could be doubled by what saxophone, and in generally editing my first fumbling efforts.

For any neophyte arranger, the transposition of parts is the biggest stumbling block. After continually forgetting that the tenor sax is a B flat instrument, the alto E flat, the trombone in concert and so forth, I decided to write the entire score in concert and do my own transposing later when I copied out each part. This was almost as much of a nightmare as doing it the other way.

I have a vague recollection of taking my first chart, an original called 'Jump It', to Lucky Millinder at the Savoy Ballroom. He was, I think, very polite, but no sale ensued.

Trying a little harder, I embarked on what seemed like a logical endeavour. Count Basie's band had a nonpareil blues singer in Jimmy Rushing; as a consequence Helen Humes was assigned all the pop songs. Why not, I thought, write a blues specifically with her in mind?

Finishing my score for Basie in about the time it would have taken Sy Oliver to write an entire library for Tommy Dorsey, I headed for the Woodside Hotel uptown, where the band lived during its New York visits, and where rehearsals were held in the basement.

The big, smoky room downstairs was crowded with musicians, wives, hangers-on and a line of arrangers who had brought in new material for Bill Basie to try out. I felt like David surrounded by a dozen Goliaths, very humble and very small, in the company of Jimmy Mundy, Don Redman, Buster Harding and others who to me were legends.

After a wait that my wristwatch assured me was only one fourth as long as it seemed, Basie said, 'All right, Leonard, we'll try yours now.'

Buck Clayton played a superb muted blues chorus before the arrangement proper began. Helen Humes was over in a corner; unable to hear her, I could only observe that the band seemed to be having no problem reading my hastily scribbled parts (none of which seemed to have been written in the wrong key).

'OK,' said Basie noncommittally, turning to the next arranger waiting patiently on the sidelines. Well, I said to myself, there goes my career as an arranger.

The next day I had a call from John Hammond. 'Did you know we're recording your arrangement on Tuesday? Basie really likes it.'

It was quite a weekend for me. The rehearsal on Friday; on Saturday my first assignment to write special material for Leonard

Harper's revue at the Apollo (my fee was $5); on Sunday Maxine Sullivan sang my ballad, 'The Heart You Stole from Me', on her weekly radio show, 'Flow Gently Sweet Rhythm', with her husband John Kirby's sextet. Monday I dropped by to see Basie, then spent the evening listening to Jack Teagarden at Nick's. Tuesday at 2.30 p.m. I sat in the booth at the Columbia studio at 799 Seventh Avenue, next to John Hammond, who was producing the Basie date.

I used a pseudonym for the tune, 'My Wandering Man', mainly because it was all too easy to foresee what sort of reception would greet a chart written by a critic some of whose opinions were anathema to my colleagues. Basie and Helen Humes seemed happy; John Hammond was pleased and surprised. The fee for the chart was $50; in view of my non-membership in the union I was lucky to have my work accepted at all, let alone paid for at a rate that was fair enough for 1940.

Early in 1941 I heard Helen Humes sing my number with the band at the Apollo. There and then I determined that if and when the opportunity arose, I would record her as a blues artist. Later that year she left the band to embark on her solo career. I submitted to Decca Records the idea of a session under Pete Brown's name, but with Helen Humes as the centrepiece. Sharing the front line with Pete were Jimmy Hamilton, with whom I had begun studying clarinet, and Dizzy Gillespie; both of them were working in Benny Carter's small band at the Famous Door. (Soon after our session, Helen Humes joined the show at the Door.)

With her high-pitched timbre and high spirits, Helen was a natural for the lighter side of the blues. On our date she did 'Unlucky Woman' (better known later through Cleo Laine's version as 'Born on a Friday') and a traditional blues, 'Gonna Buy Me a Telephone'. 'Mound Bayou' was something very different. Spending a weekend out at Andy Razaf's home in New Jersey, I had noticed a sheet of lyrics lying on the small green-painted upright piano, the one on which Fats Waller had written some of his greatest songs. Andy explained that Mound Bayou was a small town in Mississippi with an all-black population. At his suggestion, and inspired by the idea of using a piano Fats had visited so often, I set 'Mound Bayou' to music. Linda Keene recorded it for RCA with Henry Levine; just a week later Helen made her affectionate version on the Pete Brown session.

I had two regrets about the date: one, that J. Mayo Williams, a

Decca executive, insisted on bringing in another singer, Nora Lee King, to take over on the fourth tune, depriving Helen of a chance to complete a normal four-tune date; second, that I expressly avoided giving Dizzy Gillespie a solo, feeling that much as I admired him, his style would be out of place in a blues situation. (Ironically, a couple of years later Dizzy soloed on a splendid blues session by Albinia Jones, which I did not produce, in her versions of 'Evil Gal Blues' and 'Salty Papa Blues'.) Losing the chance to showcase Dizzy in what could have been his first extended small-combo solos was an example of excessive caution, not one of my customary traits.

Though the Humes–Pete Brown sides were well received, Helen did not record again until December 1944, when I persuaded Herman Lubinsky, a penny-pinching man who was then building a big catalogue for his Savoy Records, to let me put a group together for Helen. The back-up group, billed as Leonard Feather's Hiptet, had an odd front line, with two respected old-timers, Bobby Stark, the trumpeter (whom I had admired in the Chick Webb band, and who died just a year after this session) and Prince Robinson, of McKinney's Cotton Pickers renown, on tenor. Herbie Fields, whose year with Lionel Hampton had established him as the first *Esquire* award-winning white sideman with a major black band, played alto and clarinet. With me in the rhythm section were Chuck Wayne, Oscar Pettiford and Denzil Best. Of that entire group only Chuck and I survive. (Savoy reissued these sides in 1986.)

Helen later had a big R & B hit with 'E-Baba-Le-Ba', which, though it did not represent her at her best, kept her working steadily for many years. We remained close friends and saw one another often in the last years before her death in Santa Monica in 1981. She was a sweet, good-natured, talented woman; we are in Stanley Dance's debt for bringing her out of a long retirement in 1973.

The one pre-ban non-blues date made under my supervision (with Milt Gabler) was a Fletcher Henderson alumni reunion for Commodore. Because Benny Carter, Coleman Hawkins, Sid Catlett and John Kirby had recorded in the 1930s with units billed as the Chocolate Dandies, it was decided to use that name again, though by now its nasty racial overtones should have been evident. (Surprisingly, the name survived until 1946, when Charles De-launay used it for yet another date involving Carter and Catlett.)

Since the date was a tribute to Fletcher Henderson (a tune I wrote for the occasion used Fletcher's nickname, 'Smack', as its title), and because neither Fletcher nor Horace Henderson was available, we went ahead without a piano. This time, awed by the company of men like Carter and Hawkins, I made no attempt to play, but Benny doubled on piano for 'I Surrender Dear', one of two tunes in which the men were allowed to stretch out for a twelve-inch 78 (still only around four minutes).

Roy Eldridge was the third giant on this date; he, Benny and Coleman were in superlative form. These cuts have been reissued time and again; one of Benny's solos was included in the Smithsonian's first anthology of classic jazz. Coleman's solo on a ballad I had written for him, 'Dedication', came off less satisfactorily than it should have, since this was a piece with complex changes that were not too clearly spelled out by Bernard Addison's guitar and John Kirby's always understated bass. Still, it was his first ballad record since 'Body and Soul', and as such attracted some attention.

In general, these four sessions – all that I was to produce before the iron curtain was imposed by James C. Petrillo – turned out well enough to encourage me; I began thinking in terms of what could be done when the ban ended.

For RCA the gap lasted almost two and a half years, depriving us of many Ellington masterworks; Columbia also waited until 1944 before coming to an agreement with the union. But Capitol, Decca and a flock of new independent companies signed up in the autumn of 1943. One was a label called Keynote, run by Eric Bernay, a left-wing intellectual who until then had concentrated on folk music. When I persuaded him to try his hand at a jazz date, it was to have consequences that would play a significant role in his career, in mine, and in that of a teenaged singer named Dinah Washington.

W.C. Handy's Christmas greeting to author, 1935

Benny Carter *(left)* with BBC Dance Orchestra leader Henry Hall, 20 March 1936

Ye Olde English Swynge Band *(l to r)*: LF, Eddie Macaulay, Eddie Freeman, Wally Morris, Al Craig, Archie Craig, Andy McDevitt, Buddy Featherstonhaugh, 4 May 1937

'To Leonard Feather, you "swell" person. Oh! What a change you have made in life. May God bless you and yours days without end. Sincerely, "Fats" Waller'

New York session *(l to r)*: Cozy Cole, Pete Brown, Hayes Alvis, LF, Bobby Hackett *(hidden)*, Joe Marsala, Billy Kyle, Benny Carter, 20 April 1939

Thanksgiving dance at Manhattan Center Ballroom with Jimmie Lunceford *(left)* and LF just behind him, 25 November 1939

Cafe Society Fletcher Henderson alumni reunion *(l to r)*: Jay C. Higginbotham, Kaiser Marshall, Red Allen, Russell Smith, FH, Sid Catlett *(behind FH)*, John Kirby *(rear)*, Lawrence Lucie *(with guitar)*, Buster Bailey *(with clarinet)*, Fernando Arbelo, Benny Carter, LF, 1941

Pete Brown recording session *(l to r)*: PB, Dizzy Gillespie, Ray Nathan, Charlie Drayton, Helen Humes, LF, Jimmy Hamilton, Sammy Price *(seated)*, 9 February 1942

Platterbrains WMCA radio show *(l to r)*: Bob Thiele, Billy Eckstine, Ralph Cooper LF *(rear)*, Earl Hines, Teddy Wilson, c. 1942

Louis Armstrong–Jack Teagarden session *(l to r)*: LF, unknown, LA, Russ Case, Steve Sholes, JT rehearsing '50 50 Blues'

New School *(l to r)*: LF, Earl Hines, Mel Powell, Robert Goffin, Bobby Hackett, Pete Brown, Bill Coleman, Leslie Millington, 1942

Esquire All-Stars session *(l to r)*: Art Tatum, Al Casey, Coleman Hawkins, Sid Catlett, Cootie Williams, Edmond Hall, Oscar Pettiford, LF, 4 December 1943

Apollo session *(l to r)*: Hy White, Charlie Shavers, Ben Webster, Georgie Auld, Coleman Hawkins, LF, Specs Powell *(drums)*, Israel Crosby *(bass)*, 17 May 1944

Barney Bigard session *(l to r)*: Chuck Wayne, Joe Thomas, BB, Georgie Auld, Stan Levey, Les Schreiber *(standing)*, LF, Billy Taylor, *c.* 1944

Esquire All-Stars *(l to r)*: LF, Remo Palmier, Oscar Pettiford, Coleman Hawkins, Specs Powell, Ed Hall, Buck Clayton, 1 December 1944

Esquire awards concert *(l to r)*: Oscar Moore, Johnny Miller, Nat Cole, LF, 1946

Coleman Hawkins's 52nd St All-Stars *(l to r)*: Charlie Shavers, Allen Eager, Shelly Manne *(rear)*, Pete Brown, Mary Osborne, LF, 27 February 1946

Coleman Hawkins's All-Stars RCA Victor session *(l to r)*: CH, Budd Johnson, J.J. Johnson, Fats Navarro, Jack Lesberg, Max Roach and Chuck Wayne *(hidden, rear)*, 1947

Wynonie Harris session for Aladdin *(l to r)*: WH, Bill Doggett, LF, 1947

The first blindfold test: Mary Lou Williams, 1946

Cafe Society Uptown opening for Django Reinhardt *(l to r)*: LF, Roberta Lee, Les Paul, DR, Lionel Hampton, Nat Cole, Illinois Jacquet, 1948

'To my dearest friends and godchild, Jane, Leonard and namesake Billie. Stay happy always, Billie Holiday'

At the Three Deuces (*l to r*): Jane Feather, Duke Ellington, LF, 1946

Sweethearts of Rhythm: Anne Mae Winburn *(conducting)* with Vi Burnside behind her, c. 1946

Mary Lou Williams All-Stars at RCA *(l to r)*: Rose Gottesman, Mary Osborne, June Rotenberg, Margie Hyams, MLW, 1946

Mercer Ellington session for Aladdin (l to r): Lawrence Brown, Bill Pemberton (bass), Harry Carney, Al Sears, ME (trumpet), Heyward Jackson, Jacques Butler, LF, Mary Osborne, 18 March 1946

Billy Strayhorn, Lena Horne, Duke Ellington, c. 1947

Duke, LF, Nat Cole, Johnny Hodges, 1951

Original George Shearing Quintet session *(l to r)*: John Levy *(bass)*, GS, Margie Hyams, Chuck Wayne, Denzil Best, January 1949

Recording 'Hi-Fi Suite' for MGM *(l to r)*: Thad Jones, LF, Frank Wess, 1956

Platterbrains radio quiz show anniversary celebration *(l to r)*: Steve Allen, Gene Krupa, LF, Sammy Davis Jr, Duke Ellington, 1957

Trombonists' convention at Birdland *(l to r)*: Matthew Gee, Trummy Young, Henry Coker, Benny Powell, Al Gray, LF and Melba Liston *(front)*, 12 December 1957

Duke's seventieth birthday party at the White House: LF, Willie the Lion Smith *(derby)*, Duke Ellington, 1969

President Carter with Gil Evans at the White House (Max Roach, Roy Eldridge, Benny Carter, Jo Jones in background), 1978

Billy Moore Jr

Miles Davis, Wayne Shorter, Anamaria Shorter, LF, Greek Theatre Hollywood, 1982

English reunion in Hollywood: *(standing)* Alan Dean, Trixie Shearing, Howard Lucraft, Victor Feldman, Beryl Davis, Cleo Laine, *(seated)* Wendy Shearing, John Dankworth, LF

Israel tour *(l to r)*: Airto, Jon Hendricks, Joe Farrell, Julie Coryell, Larry Coryell, Brian Keane, Judith Hendricks, 1982

Jazz cruise, SS *Norway (l to r)*: Joe Williams, Maxine Sullivan, George Shearing, Clark Terry, Mel Torme, November 1984

DINAH AND THE BLUES
YEARS

This was one of the greatest stage shows ever . . . From beginning to end Lionel and his inspired band at the Apollo put on a driving, jumping performance that eclipsed all but the greatest jazz shows . . . Foremost among the surprises was a new girl singer, one Diana [sic] Washington. Diana sings much like Billie Holiday, in a languorous style, in a relaxed voice and with an authority that is amazing in a girl of nineteen. She did 'The Man I Love' and a series of blues choruses that properly brought down the house.

Barry Ulanov, *Metronome*, March 1943

During that same mid-February week, when Barry Ulanov visited the Apollo, I was also on hand to hear Lionel Hampton introduce this singer, so unknown to Barry that he even had her name wrong.

His enthusiasm was justified, but rather than a Billie Holiday resemblance, I heard in Dinah the boldly beautiful echo of her black church background. As I soon learned, she was from Tuscaloosa, Alabama, but had been raised from the age of three in Chicago, where her mother taught her religious singing and she learned to play piano in St Luke's Baptist Church.

Under her real name, Ruth Lee Jones, she won an amateur contest at the Regal Theatre; the following year, pushing sixteen, she went on the road with the Sallie Martin Gospel Singers. After a transition from sacred to profane, she entered the Chicago nightclub world. While she was working at the Garrick Lounge, according to whose story one believed, she was a ladies' room attendant or a singer in the show, and the name Dinah Washington was conferred on her either by Joe Glaser, who heard her sing there, or by Lionel Hampton, to whom he recommended her.

In any event, it took only one exposure to the tart, take-me-or-leave-me Dinah Washington sound to convince me that as soon as the recording ban was over, this would be my first project.

Fortunately Eric Bernay at Keynote was willing to take my word. Not long after he had signed with the union and resumed activity, a studio was booked for one night during Christmas week, when the Hampton band was due to return to the Apollo.

Lining up musicians was no problem: I simply took six of the principal members of the orchestra, among them Arnett Cobb on tenor, Joe Morris on trumpet, Rudy Rutherford on clarinet and the cheerful protagonist of the 'locked hands' piano style, Milt Buckner.

Fitting Dinah with suitable material was no harder than adding vermouth to gin. 'Evil Man' and 'Salty Papa' underwent revisions as I tailored them to her requirements; to them I added 'I Know How to Do It', a blues Sammy Price had recorded, and concocted a couple of verses for a fourth blues which we called 'Homeward Bound'.

Looking over the material in her hotel room, Dinah grinned and said, 'Shit, you really think you know me, don't you?' All I knew was what I had heard at the Apollo, but it was enough, and after the first take of 'Evil Gal' at that post-midnight date, I was convinced that something of lasting value was happening.

Dinah was short and stout, with an unpredictable disposition. She had eyes that could pierce you with a glance, and fingernails to match. Most of the relationships in her life were stormy. She was married to George Jenkins, Eddie Chamblee, Rusty Mallard, Rafael Compos and one or two others. Her last marriage, to Richard 'Night Train' Lane, was probably the best; it was also one of the shortest, cut off when she died in her Detroit home at thirty-nine.

We were lucky for each other. Of the dozen recordings she made of my songs, four were re-recordings of earlier hits: even though the 'Evil Gal' and 'Salty Papa' masters were taken over by Mercury Records, she made a later, big-band version of 'Salty' for the same company, produced by Quincy Jones in 1961. 'Evil' came out in a second version when Decca released a live concert LP of the Lionel Hampton concert Barry Ulanov and I had presented in 1945 at Carnegie Hall. 'Blowtop Blues', first cut with Lionel, was remade in a Mercury version; there were also two treatments, a few years apart, of 'You're Crying', a lyric I had written to a Quincy Jones melody.

Biggest and best for both Dinah and me was 'Baby Get Lost'. Released in the autumn of 1949, it reached the No.1 position in the *Billboard* R & B chart; Milt Gabler at Decca arranged for Billie Holiday to make a cover version. While Dinah's version was riding high, Jane and I were in the hospital, seriously injured after the car accident.

Soon after the end of my three months in the hospital I called Dinah. 'Thanks, baby – your timing couldn't have been better. "Baby Get Lost" paid for our hospital bills.'

Dinah's reply was typical. 'Fuck the hospital. You didn't break your hand, did you? Just use it to keep on writing them songs.'

That Dinah's solo career on records had taken off as it did was doubly remarkable in view of the almost total lack of interest displayed by Decca, the company for which the Hampton band was recording prior to and after the Keynote session. In fact, Decca did more to hamper Dinah than to help her. In retrospect, the story behind her recording debut has strange overtones of irony.

Lionel was aware of my plans to record her, but it was a surprise to all of us, on that December night in 1943, when he walked into the studio about an hour into the proceedings. Not having expected him, we had no vibraphone around. Still, he offered to take part, playing drums on one number and his two-finger mallet-like piano on another. I asked whether there might not be a conflict, since he was under contract to Decca, but was assured that there was 'no problem, gates'.

Eric Bernay lost no time in taking advantage of the situation. Less than a month elapsed before labels were printed with the credit line 'Lionel Hampton Sextet with Dinah Washington'. In very little time, all hell – in the form of Joe Glaser, Decca Records and the Decca legal department – broke loose.

A story in *Billboard*, dated 29 January (exactly a month after the date), was headed 'L. Hampton Keynote Record Date Lands Right in the Middle of Decca Contract'. Was the Decca deal signed before or after Lionel recorded with Dinah? *Billboard* said it was not clear; however, Decca made threatening noises. Bernay, after offering to sell the masters to Decca for the money he had put into the date, changed his mind and reissued the two discs with the labels altered to read simply 'Sextet with Dinah Washington'.

By this time it really didn't matter. Keynote was off to a roaring start, not only with Dinah's immediate success but also with another session cut the same week, a Lester Young quartet date

that was the first of a splendid series produced for the company by
Harry Lim.

My own troubles were by no means over. Gladys Hampton,
Lionel's wife, was a formidably strong-willed woman who ruled her
husband's career, allegedly kept him on a token allowance and
exercised shrewd business judgement in controlling his every move.
(When she died, Lionel became a very wealthy widower.) Because
of Gladys, unbeknownst to me all four songs were placed in
Lionel's publishing company – with his name added as co-
composer.

Lionel was virtually an innocent bystander in all this, but he had
a canny lawyer and a determined wife. It became necessary to bring
both him and Gladys to arbitration court. After a series of long and
painful meetings over a period of a year or more, I retrieved the
songs, though how much had been lost in royalties I never
found out.

By the end of 1944 Dinah was famous, yet she remained with the
Hampton band, and incredibly Decca continued to ignore her,
recording Lionel only in instrumentals. Not until May 1945 was she
allowed to take part in a Hampton Decca session, singing 'Blowtop
Blues' with a small combo.

I had already recorded 'Blowtop', as well as cover versions of
'Evil Gal' and 'Salty Papa', for a new company, Black & White
Records, sung by an even younger discovery, the sixteen-year-old
Etta Jones, whom I had heard in a 52nd Street club. With her was a
seven-piece band led by Barney Bigard, one of my Ellington idols of
the 1930s.

This was one of three Bigard sessions, all during the same week.
On the first we made four twelve-inch instrumentals, cut the same
day as Etta's songs. A week later I put together a different group,
with an addition that amazed everyone. A few nights before the
date I ran into Art Tatum along 52nd Street, told him about the
session and, feeling there was nothing to be lost, asked him if he
would work it, for leader's scale, as a sideman.

'Sure, why not?' he said. As it turned out, the only two
instrumental sessions on which Tatum ever worked as a sideman
were my productions: the *Esquire* All Stars and the Bigard group,
which also included both Joe Thomases (the trumpeter and the
tenor saxophonist).

Stan Levey, the drummer, remembers the shock of walking into
the studio that day. 'I was nineteen years old, just an inexperienced

kid; except for your other Bigard date the week before, I had never made a record session, so when I looked around and saw Tatum there I was terrified! He was very kind, though; at the end of the session he put his arm around me and said, "Nice work, young fella." '

Because of the success with Dinah Washington, I was at a crucial point. With these blues hits to my credit, perhaps the moment had come to turn to writing and producing music on a full-time basis. Along with convictions, of course, courage is required. It took more courage than I could summon to give up my associations with *Esquire, Metronome, Look*, the *Melody Maker* and the rest. As a result, I found myself wearing half a dozen hats. It may have been all for the best, for by 1947 another recording ban loomed, and throughout all but the last two weeks of 1948 the studios were empty again, except for a cappella vocal groups.

Meanwhile, there was intense activity on the blues front. The genre of urban blues with which I was involved provided the basis for a long series of undertakings. Before the next ban overtook us I had recorded Cousin Joe, Doc Pomus, Wynonie Harris and Bob Merrell for Aladdin; Clyde Bernhardt for Musicraft; Laurel Watson for Apollo; Kirby Walker for De Luxe; Walter Brown for Signature; and even a two-piano date for Continental on which I teamed with Dan Burley of the *New York Amsterdam News*, who shared my enthusiasm for the blues.

Cousin Joe was a symbol of the rising urban blues phenomenon. Raised in New Orleans, he sang in a whisky-soaked, barrelhouse manner with strong overtones of humour and sophistication. At other times he was billed as Brother Joshua, Pleasant Joe and Smiling Joe; he was born Pleasant Joseph. Joe told me about his teen years, singing and playing piano for tips in gambling houses and on riverboats. He got as far as Havana with Joe Robichaux's band, made his way north, and was now a denizen of the same Swing Street clubs where much of the aspiring talent could be found: the Onyx, the Spotlight and others.

Aladdin Records, first known as Philo, was owned by two brothers in California named Ed and Leo Mesner. Like so many of the small operators, they were interested in jazz, preferably bordering on R & B. Cousin Joe was just their speed. He seemed almost as intimidated by the presence of the men I had assembled (among them Harry Carney, Al Sears and Dick Vance) as Stan Levey had been by the sight of Art Tatum. I wrote the charts for this full-bodied front line, played in the rhythm section and contributed two blues lyrics; the other two, by Joe, included the topical 'Postwar Future Blues' (this was October 1945). After this impressive debut, Smiling Cousin Joshua Joe Pleasant Joseph went on to other dates and other labels. When Bob Thiele, the young jazz fan whose Signature Records was building a fine jazz library, decided to record Joe, I helped out with the writing of lyrics and charts. Joe went home to New Orleans in 1948, but has never stopped travelling and recording; in early 1986 I received a new LP he had made in New Orleans just before his seventy-eighth birthday.

Clyde Bernhardt was no newcomer when we met. A professional trombonist and singer since 1926, he had worked with everyone from King Oliver and Edgar Hayes to Luis Russell and Jay McShann. Though he sang with the authority of Muddy Waters and the traditional spirit of a Joe Turner or Jimmy Rushing, he had never had a record date of his own. One night we met at the White Rose, at Sixth and 52nd, the gathering place for all jazzmen between sets.

'I'd like to hear you sing,' I said. 'Where can we go?'

Ben Webster, standing next to us at the bar, said, 'Bring him along to my joint – he can sit in.' We followed Ben to whichever club was then employing him. Clyde sang and played a whole set. The next morning I was on the phone to Albert Marx at Musicraft, and a date was set up. My 'Blue Six' included Joe Guy, Tab Smith, the greatly underrated guitarist Jimmy Shirley, Joe Brown on bass, Walter Johnson on drums and myself. A couple of months later Marx authorized a second date, this time with my perennially preferred alto blues artist Pete Brown.

Although Clyde Bernhardt went on to countless other sessions and jobs without my help, he wrote me a touching letter just a few years ago, saying, 'I will never forget you for giving me my start.' When I gave him his 'start' he had been an active professional musician for twenty years! Clyde's humility, coupled with his talents, kept him busy with few interruptions; he was over eighty and still working until shortly before his death in 1986.

Doc Pomus was a white singer, severely crippled by polio, whose work, I suppose, struck me as more than one expected from a young white artist in a predominantly black field. When I recorded him for Apollo with Tab Smith, Taft Jordan and a few others, we used two of his songs and two of mine. My confidence in Pomus was in one sense justified, in another misplaced, for he eventually gave up singing and became a well-established songwriter with a succession of R & B hits.

Of all the young singers whose paths crossed with mine, Laurel Watson remains in my memory as one of the most wrongly neglected. She had followed Louise McCarroll in Don Redman's band, recorded a few inferior songs with him, then gigged and recorded for a while with Roy Eldridge.

Laurel's big break should have arrived when she joined Count Basie, but her stay with the band was brief and she never recorded with him. When I brought her to Apollo, it was only half a session, split with another blues singer whose name escapes me. Laurel was closer to Billie Holiday in timbre and phrasing than most of the others who had been compared to Lady Day; she was also personable, strikingly attractive, and handled ballads as compellingly as she dealt with the blues.

Some artists, defeated by too many bad breaks, give up and are lost to music; others are willing to keep hanging in there for ever. Late in 1985 I read that Laurel Watson, presumably well into her seventies, was singing with the Harlem Blues and Jazz Band on a jazz festival cruise.

Though the blues, to the ears of some listeners, was a separate and distinct area, the borderline distinguishing it from jazz was extremely vague; this was exemplified in the case of Wynonie 'Mr Blues' Harris, one of the hottest attractions in black theatres. Wynonie toured with Hampton and several other jazz orchestras, but his records were all blues-inclined, with blues-orientated jazz accompaniment. On the Aladdin date I produced in late 1946, we had Joe Newman, Tab Smith, Allen Eager, Al McKibbon, Mary Osborne and others; I split the piano responsibilities with Bill Doggett. Just a year later, Harris began a mutually profitable association with King Records that lasted for ten years. Along the way 'Mr Blues' lost his image and his public; by the mid-1950s he was working at least partly outside music. Almost forgotten, he died in Los Angeles in 1959.

Too many of the great bluesmen and blueswomen dropped out of the picture early, victims of a lifestyle that seemed endemic to much of blues society. Another case was that of Walter Brown, whose vocals with the Jay McShann band delighted everyone who was exposed to his nasal sound and archly original lyrics. I was able to record him only once, for Signature, with a small group under Tiny

Grimes' name. Later he was reunited with McShann for a series of superb dates produced by Dave Dexter for Capitol. Walter Brown was only about thirty-nine when he died, possibly of a drug overdose, in 1957.

Although we never worked together in a recording studio, I felt a special closeness with Louis Jordan, whom I had met in the 1930s when he was a member of Chick Webb's saxophone section. Louis left the band to form his own combo, which for no apparent reason he called the Tympany Five. He became a master of showmanship without any loss of musical integrity; for every novelty hit such as 'Caldonia' or 'Five Guys Named Moe' there would be several other recorded works that showed him to advantage both as alto soloist and singer.

As early as 1941 Jordan recorded a blues I had written for him, 'Brotherly Love', aka 'Wrong Ideas'. Much later he gave my career a valuable boost with a version of 'How Blue Can You Get?' that was picked up by B. B. King; but this is another story that belongs in another chapter. A little later, when he was leading a big band, Jordan recorded 'You Didn't Want Me Baby' (aka 'You Could Have Had Me Baby'), also the precursor of other versions by Jordan admirers.

During the early 1950s there was a gradual translation of the blues into harder and more aggressive R & B terms. Ruth Brown, Big Joe Turner and several others benefited from the R & B vogue of the 1950s. Momentarily, I too was a beneficiary of the trend. Steve Sholes, the corpulent and genial RCA executive who had given me a free hand to produce a long series of dates in 1946–7, was still in touch with me long after the end of the second record ban, even though he was now involved in other, more profitable ventures.

One day he called to say: 'I think I have something interesting for you. We have this new kid, who does a sort of R & B blues. A couple of the things you sent me would be just right for him. He's only fifteen and this is his first record date, but I feel something may happen; so watch out.'

The session took place in a radio station, WGST in Atlanta, 16 October 1951. My songs were 'Get Rich Quick' and 'Taxi Blues', sung with the support of a boisterous small band by the unknown teenager Richard Penniman, who had adopted the professional name of Little Richard.

The records enjoyed generous airplay and were reissued many

years later in retrospective LPs. I never met Little Richard, never saw him in person, and am sure he has never heard of me and is unaware of who wrote his first recorded songs. It was not until after he had moved to another label and recorded a long string of hits such as 'Tutti Frutti' and 'Good Golly Miss Molly' that Richard became a nationally known name.

It took Joe Williams, recording with the Basie band in 1955, to remind the American public that there was still a substantial audience for the blues in a more traditional jazz-related vein that went back to the 1920s and 1930s, to Jimmy Rushing and T-Bone Walker and Muddy Waters. Williams and Basie offered proof that despite any claims to the contrary, the blues and jazz have remained inseparable as a part of the fibre of twentieth-century music.

Happily Dinah Washington didn't forget. Despite all her successes with 'This Bitter Earth', 'What a Difference a Day Made' and the rest, she never broke her ties with the blues. The last time I saw her she was at a Los Angeles club, Basin Street West. By chance, as Jane and I walked into the crowded room she was singing the opening line of 'Blowtop Blues'. Dinah saw us and waved; then, during the brief pause between lines, she tossed in a spoken aside. 'Would you believe,' she said, 'that a white man wrote this song?'

Two weeks later the Queen, as she delighted in calling herself, was dead of an accidental overdose of liquor and pills. Like Billie Holiday, she could never be replaced; voices like hers are heard once in a lifetime, and I was grateful that her brief time coincided with part of my own.

GEORGE

The end of the 1940s produced irreversible changes in the course of jazz and, consequently, in the pattern of my activities.

The blues as I had known the idiom in the early to middle 1940s had begun to fade. Dinah Washington and many others were phasing out most of their blues repertoire and moving into pop songs or R & B.

Big bands also were beginning to pass their peak; by the end of the decade several of the most valuable ensembles would disband, some temporarily like Basie's, others for ever.

Overshadowing both these trends was the second Musicians Union recording ban. After experiencing, during 1946 and 1947, my most active and enjoyable years in the studios, I found it a serious blow to be shut out during all but the last two weeks of 1948.

The year was far from a total loss. I had a new radio series on WHN in addition to working, during the summer, on Duke's programmes. I presented two concerts with Dizzy Gillespie (the first including Charlie Parker) at Carnegie Hall. Bird, Joe Newman, J. J. Johnson, John Lewis, Tommy Potter, Jimmy Jones and Max Roach all played in the first of a series of jam sessions I produced on Tuesday nights at the Three Deuces.

Best of all the events that year was my final citizenship hearing: I became an American at 9.15 a.m. 26 April 1948 after duly recalling the correct answers to a number of questions about the country's history, most of which might stump me if I were asked them again today.

Unhappily, I was involved for some time in a rather disagreeable job. Late in 1947 I had been hired as a programming consultant for a daily record show hosted by Tommy Dorsey. It was one of the very few times in my life when I had to report for work at a certain hour and stay all day. This would not have mattered if I had had even a token measure of artistic freedom, but on the occasions (fortunately few) when I had to deal directly with Dorsey, he would quench whatever enthusiasm I might have mustered with some remark such as: 'Take out that Dizzy Gillespie record. You know I don't want any of that bebop shit on my show.' Musical opinions aside, Dorsey was one of the least pleasant people I ever worked for.

Consequently, it came as a source of relief when, later in the year, I stopped working for Dorsey and was hired to write for a similar show with Duke Ellington as the host. There were no problems with Duke except for the minor one that because he was too vain to wear glasses and had trouble reading the scripts, they had to be transferred to a machine with extra-large type. Duke's show did not enjoy as much commercial success as Dorsey's, but he and I enjoyed the process of putting it together.

Undoubtedly the most auspicious event during those last two years of the decade, in terms of the gratification it gave me rather than the financial reward, was the slow but inexorable rise to prominence of George Shearing.

George and I had first met late in 1938, when I was conducting a meeting of the No.1 Rhythm Club in London. After some of my recently imported American records had been played, the time arrived for a session of live music, and someone brought in the nineteen-year-old alumnus of Claude Bampton's band, all of whose members were blind except the leader.

In a country where live jazz from America was almost non-existent and even records were in relatively short supply, one did not look to domestic talent for creativity or originality; but when this blind teenager began to offer his impression of how jazz should sound – clearly inspired by the records of Meade Lux Lewis, Earl Hines, Art Tatum, Joe Sullivan, Teddy Wilson and whoever else he had heard on imported records – there was a minor commotion in the room. Here was a young man clearly wise beyond his years. I also found out a little later that he was an accomplished jazz accordionist. Since I had been recently engaged in a running battle with the magazine *Accordion Times*, claiming that 'jazz accordion' was a contradiction in terms, I felt obliged to write a follow-up confessing that George Shearing had proved me wrong.

It might have been better if I had left it at that; instead, when I was able to set up a Decca recording session for George a few weeks later, one of the tunes was an ad lib accordion solo, 'Squeezin' the Blues', for which I provided the very inept piano accompaniment.*

George soon established himself solidly in England, playing on his own radio series, working often with Vic Lewis and Stéphane Grappelli, and appearing as a guest with the popular Ambrose orchestra. By the time he had won the *Melody Maker* poll for several years, it began to become clear to him that there was no place to go above the top, except by moving to the US.

We had kept in touch, and by 1946 George's wife, Trixie, wrote to tell us that they and their daughter, Wendy, would come to New York, strictly for a visit, later in the year.

The Shearings' first visit was purely exploratory. George's records had not been released here, which meant that he was totally unknown in this country. Much of the time during this three-month visit was taken up inspecting the New York jazz scene, particularly along 52nd Street. One night we ran into Teddy Reig, of Savoy Records, who arranged to produce a date in February 1947, with Gene Ramey on bass and Cozy Cole on drums.

Having tested the water, the Shearings returned home. He worked a variety of jobs (in London that summer, to my surprise, I found him playing accordion in a band led by Frank Weir), but before the year was out he came back to New York, this time for good, and Teddy Reig gave him another date, using Curly Russell and Denzil Best.

Once again, though, George found that the assurance he had been given in London that the American public would greet him with open ears was wildly exaggerated. At least one club owner whom I approached told me that a blind artist would be too depressing a sight (this despite the huge success of another British artist, also blind and now living in the States, Alec Templeton). George played a Monday off-night at the Hickory House, then settled in for a long run at the Three Deuces, where the scale was $66 a week.

At the club George slowly built a local following, working at first solo, then with Oscar Pettiford or John Levy on bass, J. C. Heard on drums and, for a while, Eddie Shu on alto sax and trumpet. By

*I was not the first record to George. Vic Lewis, an old friend with whom I co-produced a session in 1937, had him at the piano on several small-group dates in 1938–9, released on Lincoln Rhythm Style and Days Rhythm Style 78s.

late 1948 he was hired for the Clique Club, on the site of what later became Birdland. With him were John Levy, Denzil Best and the imcomparable clarinettist Buddy De Franco.

The recording ban, which had begun 1 January, ended 15 December, and I at last succeeded in landing a date for George with his own group, for Discovery Records, run by Albert Marx, whose Musicraft company had brought so much durable jazz to the studios.

We planned to use the Clique Club personnel, but a hitch developed: De Franco was under contract to Capitol.

Some years earlier I had experimented with a quintet sound, using piano, vibes and guitar, first at a Slam Stewart session using Johnny Guarnieri, Red Norvo and Chuck Wayne, then in 1946 on the all-woman Mary Lou Williams date with Margie Hyams on vibes. 'Why not,' I suggested to George, 'get Chuck and Margie, and try out a group along the same lines?'

George liked the idea. We set a studio for 31 January 1949; but meanwhile, MGM Records had expressed interest in signing George to an exclusive contract. Preferring to save his own music for this major record label, George had me write most of the originals for the Discovery date.

That maiden voyage came off remarkably well. George displayed his locked-hands technique in my 'Life with Feather' and 'Midnight in the Air', played accordion on 'Cherokee' and a blues, and distinguished himself throughout this auspicious day.

By the time we were due to make the first MGM recordings on 17 February, George had developed a new and unprecedented blend for this instrumentation. He would play four-note chords in the right hand, with the left hand doubling the right hand's top-note melody line, the guitar doubling the melody, and the vibes playing it in the upper register. This was the basis for 'September in the Rain', the big hit of the first session, as well as for 'I'll Remember April', 'Ghost of a Chance' and most of the other ballads.

For the jazz instrumentals the formula would usually consist of a unison theme statement, followed by guitar and vibes solos and a two-stage statement by George, beginning with rapid single-note lines and evolving into sumptuous, brilliantly executed 'locked-hands' or block-chord improvisation.

Though this sound remained essentially unchanged through the years, the personnel underwent many changes. In 1953 George began adding Latin percussion. But the 'Shearing Sound' by now was so well established that the group became one of the most popular in jazz, with a reputation that was soon worldwide.

With Harry Meyerson of MGM, I produced all the sessions for the first two years of the five-year Shearing contract. The pattern for the group had been so firmly set, and in such continuous demand, that George was reluctant to make any changes. Not long after I had moved to Los Angeles, the Shearings also decided to make their home on the West Coast, where we lived only five minutes apart.

At one point I tried to interest George in a new concept, using two horns and accordion; we even made some trial tapes, but nothing came of it. The quintet went on its way, occasionally with such illustrious sidemen as Joe Pass, who toured with George from 1965–7. On the twentieth anniversary of the quintet's formation, George was working at the Hong Kong Bar in Century City, which gave me an opportunity to spring a surprise on him. I called several former members of the group to drop in at the room. During one number Colin Bailey quietly eased on to the bandstand and took over from Stix Hooper; Al McKibbon replaced Andy Simpkins on bass; Dave Koonse turned over his guitar to Joe Pass, and Charlie Shoemake handed his mallets to Emil Richards.

'I knew something strange was going on,' George said later, 'and when I heard the vibes played in octaves, which was Emil's style, I had a pretty good idea of what had been happening. That was one of the nicest surprises of my life.'

Another nine years elapsed before George finally decided that enough was enough. He began phasing out the quintet in 1978; the time had come to work within a more intimate framework, a duo that would leave room for more freedom of expression. 'I said when I gave up the quintet,' he told me recently, 'that I'd never do it again except for Frank Sinatra or Standard Oil. Well, Standard Oil never came through, but Sinatra wanted a quintet for two weeks at Carnegie Hall in 1981, and I did it. That was all.'

During the early years of the quintet George was often treated with disdain, or at best faint praise, by many of the critical establishment. Ironically, today he is enjoying more acclaim than ever; in his mid-sixties, he seems to have reached a new level of creativity. It's an encouraging thought that this is the same artist whose very appearance was once considered 'too depressing' even for a one-night stand on 52nd Street.

A few years ago George moved back to New York, where he lives on the upper East Side with his second wife, Ellie, a group singer. He records for Concord Jazz, and was teamed with Mel Torme, his frequent concert partner, for a Grammy award-winning album. Almost forty-eight years after he sat in at that Rhythm Club session in London, our friendship survives.

Not long ago I was a guest on his WNEW radio programme; we played four hands for a couple of minutes, and George said 'Let's play "Mighty Like the Blues".' That was the theme song on his British radio series. Who said nostalgia isn't what it used to be?

MGM AND EOJ

At the time I resumed my association with Duke, in 1950, jazz was at a watershed stage in terms of the acceptance it had been seeking on intellectual, social and political levels. The 1940s had ended with the permanent break-up of Dizzy Gillespie's orchestra and the temporary dissolution of Basie's, but there were many compensatory factors. Norman Granz and his Jazz at the Philharmonic tours were growing in importance; jazz in the concert hall was no longer taboo. Ellington was beginning to think about his 'Harlem' suite, which he would introduce at the Metropolitan Opera House early in 1951.

The print media started to show signs of awareness that jazz deserved specialized attention. By 1952 John S. Wilson had begun writing for the *New York Times* and Whitney Balliett for the *Saturday Review*. Leaving *Metronome*, I took over from Wilson at *Down Beat* and brought the 'Blindfold Test' into its pages.

More significantly, a branch of the US government was becoming interested in a source of international goodwill it had never before noticed. Not long after I had gone to work for Duke, a call from Washington invited me to meet Harold Boxer of the State Department's 'Voice of America'. I was invited to assemble a series of programmes which I called 'Jazz Club USA', to be beamed around the world.

A strictly enforced rule was that my talk was not to involve any hint of propaganda; I was simply to discuss the music at hand. This consisted not only of recordings, but of various airchecks and tapes of whatever events seemed to be worth beaming overseas.

To my surprise, one tape I received was listed as 'Wilkes Barre, Pennsylvania, Jazz Festival'. I had known about jazz festivals in Nice and Paris in 1948–9, but there had been no event so characterized in the United States. Evidently the budget in Wilkes Barre was small, since the groups were all unknown except for one led by Sonny Greer, who had just quit Johnny Hodges' small band.

Since this was in the autumn of 1951, almost three years before the first Newport Jazz Festival, it is an interesting footnote to history that the honour of bringing America its first jazz festival belongs in fact to a small Pennsylvania city.

'Jazz Club USA' was well received, particularly in the Soviet Union. In his book *Red and Hot* on the history of jazz in the USSR, S. Frederick Starr pointed out that 'American diplomats in Moscow . . . had noted that Leonard Feather's "Jazz Club USA" was attracting many listeners to the Voice of America, and sensed that a jazz programme designed specifically for Soviet youth would have a large audience.' In 1955 a popular Washington disc jockey, Willis Conover, began his landmark 'Music USA' series, which was still in full force in 1986.

Even though my own series had ended some nine years earlier, I found on visiting Moscow and Leningrad in 1962 that my name evoked the response: 'Ah, yes! Jazz Club USA!' It turned out that there had been a lively exchange of bootlegged copies of my shows, and since then Willis Conover had become a lifeline to the United States for countless jazz fans all over Eastern Europe.

The 'Voice of America' experience was one of several that helped to launch the 1950s on an auspicious note. Early in the decade, too, we decided that the time had arrived for a move; we had outgrown our small Sheridan Square penthouse, much as we enjoyed the location and the proximity of Cafe Society. The reason for the outgrowth was that there were now three of us.

When we first discovered that Jane was pregnant and I told Billie Holiday the news, she said: 'Wonderful! Hey, I want to be the godmother.' Her wish was granted, and Billie became our daughter's first name. But my sentimental attachment to Nat Cole's record of 'Sweet Lorraine' had decided me on that name for her; in addition, it seemed appropriate to name her after her mother and after Peggy Lee, who had brought us together. As a result, her full name was Billie Jane Lee Lorraine Feather. She was an adorable child who, without any coaching from either parent, became a talented singer and an award-winning songwriter.

Our new home was a six-room apartment with a view of the Hudson, at the corner of Riverside Drive and 106th Street.

Coincidentally, Duke Ellington owned some property on Riverside in the next block, and Ruth Ellington lived there with her two sons, one of whom, Stevie, was about Lorraine's age. (Later, the block of 106th Street that we looked out on was renamed Duke Ellington Boulevard. It was hard to believe that this was all a matter of chance.)

Our new uptown neighbourhood was within a reasonable distance of both the midtown music scene and the uptown action. We could catch Miles Davis or Dave Brubeck at Birdland, perhaps Marian McPartland or Joe Bushkin at the Embers, Earl Hines at Snooky's, and occasional attractions still at the Savoy, the Apollo, Smalls, Cafe Society and several other shorter-lived jazz rooms.

A new development was the emergence of Sweden as a major jazz force. It was there that Dizzy Gillespie had taken his band on its first overseas venture, and by 1951, aware that Stockholm was a hive of activity for the newer jazz forms, I took off for Copenhagen and a weekend with my old friend Svend Asmussen, followed by a series of record dates in Stockholm. They were the first to be made specially for American consumption, on a Prestige LP.

Of my 'Swingin' Swedes', the trumpeter Rolf Ericson became best known, working with Ellington, Herman and dozens of other US and European bands. The sound of Lars Gullin was so distinctive that in 1954 he became the first non-American ever to win a *Downbeat* Critics' Poll (as New Star on baritone sax). Gullin, the splendid trombonist Ake Persson (who later worked with Gillespie and Quincy Jones) and the bassist Simon Brehm all died young. Two non-Swedes sat in on one date: the Belgian harmonica virtuoso Toots Thielemans and Svend Asmussen.

Although there were frequent side ventures with other companies, the 1950s kept me occupied principally with MGM Records, where the success of George Shearing had left me free to suggest, with rare chances of rejection, a series of album ideas, and subsequently to launch a subsidiary label, MetroJazz.

Several of these projects were based on a premise that some critics found questionable. Titles such as *Hot Vs. Cool* and *Dixieland Vs. Birdland* suggested a competitive spirit that was in fact neither intended nor carried out. The first title was a misnomer, since Dizzy Gillespie's group had none of the characteristics associated with cool jazz. What this album seemed to prove, during a well-received live taping at Birdland, was that such tunes as 'Muskrat Ramble', 'Indiana' and 'How High the Moon' were just as easily negotiable by Gillespie's group as by the Jimmy McPartland combo (with Vic Dickenson, Edmond Hall, Dick Carey on piano, Jack Lesberg and George Wettling). For a 'Battle of the Blues' finale two members of the other camp, McPartland and Dick Cary (on trumpet), joined forces with Dizzy, Ray Abrams, the British pianist Ronnie Ball, Don Elliott, Al McKibbon and Max Roach.

For the follow-up album, *Dixieland Vs. Birdland*, we had two trombonist-led groups: Bobby Byrne's NBC Dixieland band, with Yank Lawson, Bobby Rosengarden and others, pitted against Kai Winding's Septet with Howard McGhee, Eddie Shu, John Lewis, Percy Heath and Kenny Clarke. Again the album consisted of alternating tracks in which either band offered its version of the same theme: 'Get Happy', 'Perdido' and even 'That's a Plenty' offered no hazards, and again members of both bands joined forces for a blues finale.

The most important message of these albums was that the internecine hostility of the 1940s had all but vanished, and that musicians representing wrongly contrasted values could negotiate the same material and could even join forces amicably. By now Ertegun, Avakian and most of the others who had been the fiercest champions of reaction, arguing that swing and bop were not jazz, had made a convenient switch to the more profitable belief that modern jazz was not only valid, but was worth recording. Avakian busied himself at Columbia with sessions by Brubeck and others; Ertegun, who became a producer at Atlantic, had everyone from Gillespie to Coltrane in his catalogue.

After these two albums and *Cats Vs. Chicks*, which became the best remembered of the three, I felt the moment had arrived for something with a less contentious premise. MGM had approved the concept of a Christmas jazz album; with this in mind, I wrote a suite of eight short original pieces, named after the traditional reindeer, each designed as a mini-concerto for a different soloist. Ralph Burns, whom I knew well from the Woody Herman days, wrote the arrangements, for which I furnished sketches.

The result, which we called 'Winter Sequence' (with Ralph's 'Summer Sequence' for Herman in mind), provided frameworks for Herbie Mann on flute (then a rarely heard jazz solo vehicle), Oscar Pettiford on cello in the 'Comet' movement (fittingly, I based the melody on a descending cycle of fifths) and, best of all, a vastly underrated trumpeter named Joe Wilder, who played the title role in the concluding 'Blitzen'.

All these recordings were made during the era of the ten-inch LP. The transition to twelve-inch albums was almost total by 1955, but before then I had completed a series of undertakings for the shorter discs, many of them for Period, another independent company that glowed brightly for a few short years. On Period I recorded Ralph Burns in two piano albums; several sessions with the ageless Maxine Sullivan (one composed entirely of songs with lyrics by Andy Razaf, to whom an album had never been devoted), and others led by Osie Johnson with some Basie sidemen, as well as three Jack Teagarden sessions and some Thad Jones dates, for one of which Quincy Jones played flugelhorn as a union-scale sideman.

It was around this time, in 1954, that I persuaded the Gabler family, who still owned the long dormant Commodore label, to let me produce some sessions. Two ten-inch LPs were made, led by Frank Wess and featuring Joe Wilder and Henry Coker. They turned out to be Commodore's swan song.

Probably the most important date that year had nothing to do with recording. On 26 February, John and Esme Hammond came over for dinner, after which we planned to catch a set by the Basie band at the Rockland Palace in Harlem.

During a talk over dinner the subject came up of a glaring lack in the jazz world: we had no reference book to turn to. As usual, America lagged behind Europe: in 1953 a biographical dictionary of jazz musicians had been published in Copenhagen. Why couldn't something comparable be put together in the States?

As always seemed to be the case when a need arose, John knew the right person in the right place. 'I'll talk to Ben Raeburn at Horizon Press. He's just the man for this.'

Three days later John and I met at the office of Ben Raeburn, a soft-spoken, distinguished-looking man best known as the publisher of Frank Lloyd Wright's books. As we batted the prospects for a jazz *Who's Who* back and forth, Ben made one classic comment, of which he has often reminded me:

'I suppose the reason there hasn't been a book of this kind is that there's no demand for it.'

Of course, another half-hour of the Hammond enthusiasm, backed by my own, was all it took to change his mind. Within a month I was drawing up plans and designs for the book's format. Soon I had a contract, and the need arose for secretarial and editorial assistance.

Jan Rugolo, Pete's ex-wife, and Jane Feather became my secretarial *aides-de-camp*. As my editorial assistant I hired a young man named Ira Gitler, then twenty-five, whom I knew through his work for Prestige Records. This was the beginning of a business and personal relationship that has lasted successfully through the decades. For the *Encyclopedia of Jazz in the Seventies* Ira became a full partner with co-author credit.

The decision to call the first book *The Encyclopedia of Jazz* – a somewhat pretentious name, it seemed to me – was arrived at partly because the more logical title, *Who's Who in Jazz*, was unavailable for legal reasons – or so I was told, although many years later a jazz book using the term *Who's Who* did appear with impunity. In any event, what mattered would be the contents, and with that in mind we went about the laborious task of sending out questionnaires to musicians around the world, compiling a chronology, lists of musicians under places of origin and under birth dates, a historical survey and various other features.

While all this was going on I conducted my normal activities, writing for *Down Beat* and other magazines, running 'Platterbrains' every week, visiting Minneapolis to see Jane's family, and Los Angeles, where the Benny Carters hosted a party for us and where I recorded some less than triumphant 'Best from the West' albums for Blue Note.

Early in 1955, along with frantic work on the book, there was the pleasure of having Gerry Mulligan every week for three months as a 'Platterbrains' panelist, and the pain of hearing about Charlie Parker's death. Confusion surrounded the funeral, at which Charlie's wife and common-law wife vied for priority, and for which I served as a pallbearer. That was, in every sense, a heavy load to carry.

On 14 October we received the first copies of the book. Soon after, on a Friday evening, a Rev Kershaw was appearing as a jazz expert on a national TV show called 'The $64,000 Question'. One of his prizes, it was announced, would be a copy of *The Encyclopedia of Jazz*. That one momentary plug was magical; between the show and the following Monday morning, Horizon's office was flooded with mail requests and phone calls. As Ben Raeburn soon granted, 'I guess there was a need for it after all.'

Raeburn kept the momentum going by publishing several more books aimed at the same market. In *The Book of Jazz* I wrote an 'Anatomy of Improvisation' in which solos by everyone from

Armstrong and Tatum to Goodman, Christian, Gillespie and
Parker were transcribed and analysed. Though I felt that because it
necessitated the ability to read music this might prove too technical
for the average reader, it was the best received chapter in the book.
(In fact, for some who objected to my adducing evidence that jazz
was not born simply in New Orleans, it was the *only* well received
chapter.) After two *Encyclopedia Yearbooks* that fell below our sales
expectations, we went to work on a completely updated version of
the original volume. Published in 1960, it has remained on the
market ever since, along with later books devoted to the 1960s and
1970s.

During those years my recording plans continued; in several
instances they were brightened by the presence of an amazing
young man named Dick Hyman.

I first met Dick when, at twenty-one, he was working in tandem
with an organist at Wells' in Harlem. During the next few years I
heard him in every conceivable setting: playing staff jobs, joining a
series of jazz groups including Norvo and Goodman, making a
series of pop singles for MGM, one of which, 'Moritat' ('Mack the
Knife') became a No.1 best-seller. Our collaborations began in
1955, when he played on some of my Maxine Sullivan sessions for
Period, but they got under way on a more ambitious level when, at
MGM, he took part in various capacities – co-leader, co-composer,
arranger, pianist, organist – on several of my albums and live
concerts.

Dick Hyman is a phenomenon. His placid, seemingly emotion-
less demeanour is at odds with the spirit and authenticity he brings
to the interpretation of every keyboard style from Scott Joplin to
Cecil Taylor. As an arranger he has transcribed and enlarged many
classic recordings by Armstrong and others. As a collaborator on
our numerous ventures over the years I have found him invaluable.

West Coast Vs. East Coast was the last in my series of synthetic
battles. Dick led the New York group, with Thad Jones, Benny
Powell, Frank Wess, Oscar Pettiford and Osie Johnson. Pete
Rugolo wrote some charts for the Los Angeles combo, notable
mainly for the presence of André Previn, whose ability as a
swinging pianist I continued to admire even after he himself had
phased out his activities in jazz.

High-fidelity sound reproduction had now become the in thing
and we were on the verge of the stereophonic age. Bearing this in
mind I wrote a 'Hi Fi Suite', with Dick leading two strong groups.

The album set two precedents. One was a mini-concerto for jazz piccolo, played by Jerome Richardson and titled 'Tweeter'. Better remembered is 'Bass Reflex', my first attempt to write in 5/4. (More about this later in the 'Music' chapter.)

Dick and I produced an LP based on the score of a Broadway musical, *Oh Captain!* Despite Coleman Hawkins and Sweets Edison on one date, Art Farmer on the other, and two excellent singers, Jackie Paris and Marilyn Moore, the album, like the show itself, was a resounding flop. More to the point was a show we put together, 'The Seven Ages of Jazz', which we presented at several concerts. One of them, with a cast that included Billie Holiday, Buck Clayton, Hawkins, Willie the Lion Smith, Georgie Auld and Brownie McGhee, was taped for a live two-LP set on MetroJazz. Lonely and depressed, Billie still gave us her incomparable 'Lover Man' in what turned out to be her last recorded version.

One curiosity in that show was the Dixieland sequence in which, while The Lion took over at the piano, Dick Hyman played very competent traditionalist clarinet, an instrument he had not touched in years.

Anxious to establish the MetroJazz label with a powerful new name, MGM signed Sonny Rollins to a year's contract. For his first date it was agreed that he should be provided with a big band, with eight brass and Sonny as the only reed player. A trio session was taped to complete the album, which sold moderately.

MGM wanted to put out another album soon afterwards. Following several delays Rollins called me from Los Angeles: 'Come on out – it's nice and sunny here, and I'm ready.'

I flew to the coast, checked in at my hotel, and that evening, with Jesse Kaye of MGM, dropped by to see Sonny at the club where his trio was working. 'Everything's fine, Leonard,' he said. 'See you in the morning.'

The morning arrived; the bass player and drummer arrived, but no Rollins. We waited a half-hour, an hour; his phone did not answer. Desperate, I took a long cab ride to South Central Los Angeles and was greeted at his front door by Dawn, Sonny's wife at the time.

'I'm sorry,' she said, 'Sonny just doesn't feel like recording.'

I could not even get inside the door to talk to him. Back at the studio, I told the men; we packed up and left, and the next day I flew back to New York. To this day I have no idea why this happened.

No such problems hampered my encounter with Langston Hughes, one of my happiest MGM assignments. I had known about Langston since an evening at Red Norvo's home in 1935 when I noticed a book lying on the coffee table. It was Langston's *The Ways of White Folks*. Intrigued by the title, I picked it up. 'That'll tell you some things you'll need to know about America,' said Mildred Bailey. 'Take it along.'

The book consisted of sardonic vignettes about black and white lifestyles and attitudes. I took it back to London and was delighted when, a couple of years later at an after-hours club in Soho, someone introduced me to Langston Hughes.

Langston, I found, loved jazz and seemed to have a deep feeling for the blues. Much later he wrote a short book for children called *The First Book of Jazz*.

When the fad for poetry readings with a jazz background took hold briefly around 1958, it struck me that the poets had all been white and their work bore no relationship to jazz. Langston had written poems about the black experience; why not an album of his work?

'I'd love to try it,' he said, 'but who's going to do the music?'

Because he leaned towards an earlier style, I arranged a compromise: for one side I hired Charles Mingus to write the music, with his quintet (nominally led by Horace Parlan); for the other, on which we used the more blues-orientated poems, I wrote several blues and quasi-gospel charts and assembled a small swinging group to play them: Red Allen, Vic Dickenson, Sam the Man Taylor, and a rhythm section to match.

At first things went smoothly; then we came to a poem that was based on the orthodox A-A-B blues lyric pattern, with corresponding music.

Langston couldn't feel where 'one' was! Time after time he came in early or late. I realized that his love of the idiom did not extend to a deep sense of its structure. For the next take I stood behind him, tapping him on the shoulder when it was time for the next line. *The Weary Blues*, as we called the album (after his book) was issued on MGM and reissued a few years before his death.

His recording was most memorable for the 'Dream Montage' sequence, in which he spoke the lines that would provide the title for a celebrated play and movie: 'What happens to a dream deferred? Does it dry up, like a raisin in the sun? . . . or does it explode?'

My last recollection of Langston goes back to February 1967. He was in Los Angeles for a tour of bookshops organized by his publisher. Jane and I invited several friends of his and of ours to a party in his honour.

I had amassed a collection of his books and asked him to sign one. Instead, he sat down and inscribed a different message in each book; it took him close to a half-hour.

Six weeks later I heard on the radio that the man whose book had fascinated me more than thirty years earlier, that night at the Norvos', had died in a New York hospital.

A brilliant and perceptive writer, Langston was also an essentially gentle man, capable of turning a potentially bitter diatribe against racism into a masterpiece of sly, subtle humour. Langston was a militant in the most oblique sense, a fighter who remained ahead of his time and far beyond his contemporaries in understanding the ways of white folks.

PART FIVE

Travels

WESTWARD

Of all my experiences as a producer, none was more traumatic than the attempt, in 1960, to record an album for Mercury Records with Charles Mingus.

We had worked together without difficulty on the Langston Hughes album; I saw no reason for not making an LP by the quintet on its own. Mercury agreed. Mingus later asked whether he could add a couple of horns. This also was agreed to.

One afternoon I walked into a rehearsal to find that not two, but four men had been added. Mingus also mentioned some old arrangements he wanted to try out – material that dated back to his days in the Lionel Hampton Orchestra of the 1940s. 'The music is available and paid for,' he said, 'so it would be a shame not to use it. Let's add a few men for some of the tracks.'

Before I knew it, the band had expanded to fourteen pieces. Mercury balked. Mingus screamed. He sent long, threatening telegrams to the Musicians Union and to me, insisting on the larger band. Figuring that the end justified any means, he called my home and, since I was out, told Jane that he was dying of cancer and, because he had only months to live, the record would be historically valuable.

After two days of crisis during which it seemed the album might never be made, I walked into the studio on the date of the session and could hardly believe my eyes. We had a twenty-two-piece orchestra, with Gunther Schuller conducting! Eric Dolphy, Clark Terry, Slide Hampton, Jimmy Knepper, Joe Farrell, Booker Ervin, Yusef Lateef and Paul Bley were among the participants.

The album was entitled *Pre-Bird*. In a predictable postscript, Mingus later sent a bill to Mercury for several thousand dollars in charges for the charts he had said were 'available and paid for'. He was duly paid, and in retrospect I understood how right he had been in desperately wanting to put this music on record.

'Mingus's intensity killed him,' Red Callender said on learning of the bassist's death almost twenty years later (not from cancer but from amyotrophic lateral sclerosis). Mingus's intensity also did nothing to lengthen my life; after this experience Jane extracted a promise from me that I would never again work with him. She didn't need to ask.

This experience and other manifestations of the tension inevitably brought about by life in New York played a part in a decision that had long been in the back of my mind and Jane's. We needed a better place to send our daughter to school; we wanted a home of our own instead of the apartment life. It was decided that we would rent a house for two months from a friend in West Los Angeles, stay there with my mother-in-law and, if we all agreed that this was as pleasant a place to live as our previous visits had indicated it might be, Jane and her mother would go house-hunting.

It took only a couple of weeks to convince us. Jane and Tody found a fine, spacious house up in the hills overlooking the San Fernando Valley. Our trial visit ended on 15 August. On 28 October, Jane and I took off in our car with Lorraine, accompanied by a small Pekingese named Scampi. Seven days later, after an easy-going cross-country trip, we arrived in North Hollywood on a Friday – the Friday before John F. Kennedy was elected president. It seemed like a good time for both changes.

California was everything we had expected. The sunshine, yes, but the smog too; we missed our New York friends, but most of our new circle consisted of transplanted New Yorkers: Shelly Manne, whose Manne Hole opened on the same night we arrived in town; Irving Townsend of Columbia Records, who had been a neighbour of ours during several summers in Westport, Connecticut; the Shearings, who moved out not long after we had, to a house only minutes away; the Carters, of course, with whom we had never lost touch; and a few Hollywood/Las Vegas acquaintances such as Tony Bennett, as well as such long-established friends as the Dick Hazards, the Harold Joviens, the Nat Coles and Virginia Wicks, who had been a panelist on 'Platterbrains'.

Some of my New York work could be continued: features for *Down Beat* and for *Playboy* (I had been their nominal jazz consultant since 1957, when Hugh Hefner lured me to the ranks mainly, it seemed to me, because he was glad to hire anyone who, like him, had worked for *Esquire*). But new sources of income were needed, and the man who came to my rescue was Les Koenig, one of the greatest and most respected men in the business end of music.

Though he never talked about it, Les had been blacklisted out of his previous career as a movie producer. For several years he had been building Contemporary Records into its present stature as one of the best modern-jazz catalogues in the world. Les hired me to come to his office every morning, write and edit the house magazine he was then putting out, and make myself generally useful. He was a strict taskmaster only in that he insisted on perfection, on correct spelling and grammar and punctuation and proofreading. This made him a unique figure in his field; it also made me very content, and the few months I spent working with him established a close friendship that lasted until his sudden death in 1977.

It had been my aim to use California as a stepping stone into greater music-writing activity, and for a moment it seemed that I had started on the right foot. Only weeks after my arrival, when the Ellington band came to town, I suggested to Johnny Hodges an idea that seemed perfect for his romantic alto: why not a suite of original works named for the great lovers of history? Don Juan, Lothario, Casanova, Romeo, John Smith and others could each constitute an individual movement.

'It sounds fine,' said Johnny. 'Let's go ahead and book a studio.'

Mercer Ellington became a partner in the concept: I wrote several melodies and left it to him to score them for four Ellington horns (the others were Nance, Lawrence Brown and Ben Webster, who to my mind was still one of the family).

We began recording on 21 February 1961. Despite delays due to copying errors, two ballads come out flawlessly, and a third tune, though very short and of far less melodic interest, was completed. Then came more and more delays as more and more copying goofs were found; finally a restless voice in the control booth said, 'Let's get on with it!' whereupon Hodges & Co began taping ad lib variations on the blues and 'I Got Rhythm' until we reached our time limit.

Before another session could be scheduled, there was a changing of the guard at Verve Records, the products of our date went on the shelf, and the 'Great Lovers Suite' was never completed. All I have to show for it can be heard in tapes of the tunes we did complete that day. One of them appealed to André Previn, who recorded it a few months later in a luscious string arrangement. His wife Dory wrote lyrics to it under a new title, 'Meet Me Halfway'. Though her lyric was never used, the Previn record was issued under that name.

The other slow ballad, 'Romeo', was included in an album I made with Roy Ayers, back in his jazz days, and later was recorded by the Louie Bellson orchestra, retitled 'I Remember Duke'. Although the Hodges venture can never be completed, I live in hope that eventually Verve, or whoever now controls that conglomerate, will dust off those three tunes and bring them to the public.

There were a few other encouraging signs during that first California year. Ella Fitzgerald made an exquisite version of 'Signing Off'. I produced an Atlantic session with Ann Richards, notable mainly for its inclusion of the only vocal version of my 5/4 piece 'Bass Reflex', with ingenious lyrics by Milton Raskin under the title 'Love is a Word for the Blues'.

To keep my typewriter from rusting over I took on a weekly column for a local paper, the *Valley News*, at $10 a shot; this enabled me to report on such occurrences as the Monterey Jazz Festival, to which I paid my first visit that September. In those days it was an exciting, innovative affair, with all sorts of splendid initiatives: all-star bands of great musicians were brought up from Los Angeles to introduce new major works such as Lalo Schifrin's 'Gillespiana'. But success, and false economy, eventually ruined Monterey; the crowds became louder and less discriminating, the new works were played not by pros but by high-school bands, and hardening of the creative arteries set in.

Locally, there was no shortage of live action. We had the Parisian Room, the It Club, the Renaissance, Shelly's Manne Hole, the Black Orchid, the Cocoanut Grove, the Ash Grove and others, all now long gone. For two or three years a bunch of us formed an unofficial record listening club, visiting one another's homes about once a week to examine and argue about the latest releases. This pleasant social group included John Tynan, then the West Coast editor of *Down Beat*; Lester Koenig and his wife Joy; Charles Weisenberg, who like me had a programme on KNOB, then a major jazz station; George Shearing (during a period when he took a year off to study classical piano); Howard Lucraft, the British-born composer and critic; and a new friend who would become central to my California life, Jimmy Tolbert.

Jimmy and I met through our mutual friend Patricia Willard, a bright young writer and Ellington camp follower. We also had a common interest in the local NAACP, which I had joined in the naive belief that this was the organization through which local segregation could effectively be broken down.

Somewhere along the way Jimmy and I became disillusioned with the petty bickering at the assocation's meetings; there was a political upheaval and in 1963 Jimmy became president, and I was appointed vice president, of the Hollywood-Beverly Hills NAACP.

That aspect of our collaboration did not last very long; however, over the years Jimmy and I remained close. He was a loyal friend and, when it was required, my lawyer and my business manager. I could hardly have imagined a more appropriate association, since aside from his enthusiasm for jazz and his background as an amateur trumpeter, James L. Tolbert Esq also happened to be the nephew of Lee and Lester Young.

Overall, my West Coast years, though I could never have foreseen it, have been less memorable for local musical events than for the extent to which I have become a global traveller. From festival to festival, country to country and, a little later, from jazz cruise to jazz cruise, the world became my stage.

USSR

The news that Benny Goodman was due to make a tour of the Soviet Union, under the auspices of the State Department, reached me in April 1962. Since no real jazz orchestra from the United States had undertaken such a venture (despite the visits of Sidney Bechet and a few others in the 1920s), this promised to be an event that would make history.

I had almost no contact with Benny Goodman prior to the trip, and none with any government body, yet my reaction was immediate: 'I want to be there when the band starts playing.' It was not difficult to line up a few magazine assignments, just enough to cover my plane fare; nor was there any problem in transportation.

One little snag arose: until arrival at Moscow Airport, nobody knew to what hotel he had been assigned. Nor did I know where the Goodman orchestra would be staying. Somehow, after checking in at the Hotel Ukraina, I managed to find out that the musicians were only a few blocks away.

I ran into Benny and some of the sidemen, but learned that no rehearsal was planned. The orchestra, specially organized for this tour, had played a break-in week at the World's Fair in Seattle.

'I just hope we get to do some of the new things,' Zoot Sims said. Benny had commissioned Tommy Newsom, the band's other tenor player, as well as his pianist, John Bunch, and Tadd Dameron, to write charts in contrast to the traditional Fletcher Henderson material.

Word of the band's presence had circulated fast; before the first concert at the Central Army Sports Arena on 30 May (Goodman's fifty-third birthday) I had met enough Soviet fans and musicians to discover that they were at least as excited by the presence of Joe Newman, Joe Wilder, Teddy Wilson (pianist in the small group),

Phil Woods, Victor Feldman (on vibes) and Mel Lewis as they were about Goodman himself.

The big question buzzing around was: will Nikita Khrushchev really be there? Arriving early, I saw the Premier and his wife file in shortly before curtain time.

The concert was received with prolonged applause, but there was none of the hysteria that Soviet officials had feared might arrive if, say, a Louis Armstrong had been invited. (That, supposedly, was a principal reason Armstrong never did play in the Soviet Union. He was too popular.)

Goodman played superbly; Wilder's solo feature, 'I've Got It Bad', was a model of pristine beauty. Joya Sherrill was particularly well received, but told me later, 'I was very disappointed I didn't get to sing my number in Russian.'

She performed the song ('Katusha') on the second night, but Khrushchev was absent, thus denying himself the pleasure of hearing what might well have been, for him, the only comprehensible moment of the evening; he was later quoted to the effect that he just didn't understand this stuff.

After the concert we repaired to the American Embassy, where a birthday party was staged for Goodman. I asked Ambassador Llewellyn Thompson, 'Do you think this exchange will accomplish something worthwhile?' 'It already has,' he said. 'Premier Khrushchev's presence at the concert was very significant in itself.'

(As it turned out, Goodman's visit paved the way for successful tours by Earl Hines in 1966, Duke Ellington in 1971, Thad Jones/Mel Lewis in 1972 and a few others, though by the late 1970s the thaw in the cold war was almost at an end, and cultural exchanges dried up.)

Most surprising to me was the reaction of some of the Soviet listeners to a so-called 'Anthology of Jazz' presented by Goodman. Through his omission of Gillespie, Miles Davis, the Modern Jazz Quartet, even Fletcher Henderson, and the inclusion of George Gershwin, Glenn Miller and Paul Whiteman, the suggestion that the latter were major jazz figures was fostered rather than dispelled. Yet the new wave of musicians and aficionados seemed too alert to be confused by this odd pastiche. The situation was explained to me by Alexei Batashev, a twenty-seven-year-old physicist who served as president of the Kirov Musical Youth Club's jazz department.

'The first music that came to this country labelled as jazz,' Batashev said, 'was played by pseudo-jazz bands of the worst kind that flourished in the 1920s and 1930s. Entertainment and variety music were confused with jazz until the early 1950s, when the real jazz finally began to reach our ears.

'By 1960 a good number of musicians had reached a professional level as jazzmen, and some local historians founded the Moscow Jazz Club. We now have similar clubs in Kiev and Leningrad.'

A new movement at the time of my visit was the emergence of the 'youth cafes', of which there were two in Moscow. Writing about the Club Aelita, I observed: 'It is the closest Moscow comes to a nightclub . . . serves only wine, closes at 11 p.m., and is decorated in a style that might be called Shoddy Modern, though radical by Moscow standards . . . the shocker was the trumpeter, Andre Towmosian, who is nineteen but looks fourteen and plays with the maturity of a long-schooled musician, though in jazz he is self-taught . . .'

I learned that Towmosian was acclaimed at the fourth annual jazz festival in Tartu, Estonia. He had been featured with his own quartet at the Leningrad University Jazz Festival. I found his work quite adventurous, and at times, original, as he played his own compositions and others by Miles Davis and Monk.

The next night, at the Cafe Molodozhnoe, I heard the guitarist Nikolai Gromin, who swung so hard that it was difficult to accept how limited his exposure had been: mainly a few records (including Django Reinhardt's) and, of course, Willis Conover's 'Voice of America' programme.

Attempts to incorporate their own ethnic elements were already under way: Gromin had experimented with the balalaika, Towmosian used Russian folk melodies, as did the composer and tenor saxophonist Alexei Zubov, who in recent years has been living in Los Angeles.

The young, adventurous, new-wave jazzmen were and still are better versed in the realities of the music than, for instance, Leonid Utyosov, the veteran dance-band leader from Odessa, whose claims to have fought for jazz since the 1920s were negated by his citing of Paul Whiteman and Ted Lewis as his main influences.

Goodman's statements at a meeting of the Union of Soviet Composers hardly cleared up anything. 'I've always felt,' he said, 'that jazz has something to do with dancing. The concert hall is not the real place for this kind of music.' This from an artist who had flown 8,000 miles to undertake a tour composed entirely of concerts.

While Goodman went on his way to Sochi, Tiflis and Tashkent, I flew directly to Leningrad, where the band was due later to wind up its tour. Alexei Batashev had put me in touch with Valeri Mysovsky, a drummer and jazz student who had written what was then the only Soviet book on jazz. Through the efforts of men like Mysovsky, modern jazz had established a firm foothold and was played at Soviet festivals. Today, as S. Frederick Starr makes clear in his well documented book *Red and Hot: the Fate of Jazz in the Soviet Union*, considerable headway has been made; the Soviets have embraced both fusion and the avant garde and have been turning out some records of remarkable originality.

One evening Mysovsky took me to visit the apartment of an alto saxophonist named Gennadi (Charlie) Golstain, nicknamed after Charlie Parker. As I walked in the living-room, I saw photographs, side by side, prominently displayed on a wall, of his two idols: Vladimir Ilich Lenin and Julian Cannonball Adderley.

Golstain, like all the young musicians I met in Leningrad, was right on top of the latest developments. Why had we sent Goodman rather than John Coltrane or Art Blakey? What was Charles Mingus up to these days?

Though he was not working at the time, Golstain played me some tapes that revealed him as a soloist of considerable passion, undisciplined and subject to diverse influences, but clearly dedicated and intelligent both in his writing and playing. He was then working regularly with a big band led by Yusef Weinstain and writing most of its book.

The most durable recollection of my Soviet journey is of the pride of the musicians in their accomplishments, their seeming indifference to social and material obstacles, and their sensitivity to criticism.

Though jazz reflects an aspect of our culture that they admire, while acknowledging the source, they were concerned with the idea of fashioning, out of this music, something they could honestly call their own. This was due in part to the problems they faced in presenting anything that was redolent of pseudo-Americanism.

This was also true of any imitation of US social patterns. One night Mysovsky took me to a small town twenty kilometres out of Leningrad, to see a typical young group, mostly teenagers, in an open-air 'dance hall' – actually a walled quadrangle with plain green paint.

No food or drinks were available. The admission price was forty kopeks (forty-five cents). The music was played by a group of eight young semi-professionals. When the manager announced a 'change partners' dance, the band played Bobby Timmons' blues hit 'Moanin'' followed by Benny Golson's 'Whisper Not'. Next came one of the Soviet fans' traditional favourites, 'Some of these Days', played in Dixieland style with the tailgate trombone, after which the audience lined up in formation for a Polish folk dance. Mysovsky remarked to me: 'The people like this dance, but the musicians don't dig playing it.'

The men were working hard for the six roubles ($6.60) this gig paid. The audience seemed to be working almost as vigorously. At one point the jitterbugging became so wild that the manager stepped up on the bandstand to deliver what sounded to me like a tongue-in-cheek tirade, though he played it straight-faced: 'This wild dancing must stop! This is not in keeping with our standard of Soviet morale! If there is any more of this behaviour, the band will stop playing!'

To cool things off, a Soviet dance was played, then a tango. But before long the band edged its way back to the preferred groove, first with a Dixieland 'St Louis Blues' and then more boldly with Horace Silver's 'The Preacher'. By that time the jitterbugging had recommenced, and a new warning was issued, over the PA system. A silent, grim-faced militiaman led one recalcitrant couple out of the hall.

The evening ended a little before 11 p.m. (in the Soviet Union, I had begun to realize, everything public ends by 11 p.m.), with a fast waltz, 'Lover'. The mild night by now had turned bitterly cold, yet not many of the younger dancers wore top coats and none seemed disturbed by the chill as we crossed the street to board the last train back to Leningrad.

What happened in the dance hall pointed up to me the paradox that still faces many Soviet citizens: how to reject what they basically admire, and how to convince their elders that cultural manifestations, whether they be a jitterbug dance, a Basie-style arrangement or a Frank Lloyd Wright-style art gallery, are supranational.

By 1962 the citizens of the USSR were getting to see and hear much more of our life and folkways than they could in the Stalin era. Some had access to a magazine called *Amerika*, which appears there in exchange for the distribution in the US of *USSR*.

Most of the people I met, though they couldn't send a kopek out of the country, knew there was always the chance of meeting some American who had a few spare copies of *Down Beat* or who would send them the latest Miles Davis LP. (One fan told me that a friend of his had laboriously transferred a borrowed copy of my *Encyclopedia of Jazz* one page at a time on to microfilm, so hard was it to find.)

The friends I made in Moscow and Leningrad were hospitable, amiable, desperately anxious to learn and understand. Contrasts in our attitudes, or in those of our leaders, never seemed to come up; most of the musicians seemed apolitical and more eager to talk about shared interests.

Though the Goodman band arrived in Leningrad after I had left, I later heard about its visit from Victor Feldman and Mel Lewis. 'Leningrad was the most fantastic of all,' Lewis said. 'Even after I'd taken my drums apart, they yelled for more. Benny had to play a solo all by himself, finally they turned the lights off. The people just stood there, shouting "Friendship! Friendship!" It was beautiful.'

'How about the friendship within the band?' I asked.

'There was no discord among the men – only between us and Benny. What you saw in Moscow was nothing – as soon as we started travelling, the trouble began.'

Feldman said: 'Between all the tension and the bad food and catching a cold, I wound up in a hospital in Kiev. I was literally sick and tired of the whole thing.'

'Did he ever get around to playing the modern arrangements?'

'Not until the last three nights, and then he just did a few in order to get them on the live album, because all these old tunes we'd been doing had been recorded so many times before.'

'How about that idea he discussed in Moscow of helping some of the young Soviet jazzmen, by letting them sit in with the band?'

Lewis said, 'He never even went to hear them.'

'Didn't anyone try to get through to Benny, to tell him about the discontent in the band?'

'I tried once,' said Feldman, 'but it was futile. He doesn't care how the men feel about him. We did talk about other big bands, and he seemed to have negative thoughts about all of them; he even put down Duke Ellington's as too much of a bunch of stars.'

'That's because he doesn't like sidemen to shine too much,' said Lewis. 'After I broke it up with my solo on "Sing, Sing, Sing", he took the solo away from me. Same thing happened to Phil Woods when he got a great hand on "Greetings to Moscow".'

'Well,' I said, 'I'm sure Benny appreciated how good you made the band sound. Even though most of you quit him at the end of the tour, he must have expressed his gratitude. What did he say when you said goodbye?'

'What goodbye?' said Lewis. 'On the plane home he was up front in the first-class section. Never came back to see us, never said a word to us. Benny cares about one person.'

'Tell me,' I said, 'if you had it to do all over again, would you go?'

'Sure,' said Mel. 'But next time I'd take Dizzy Gillespie along as leader.'

A couple of months after this conversation, Victor and I got together and recorded what we called *The World's First Album of Soviet Jazz Themes*, using material from tapes of manuscripts given us by Golstain and Towmosian. Joe Zawinul, Nat Adderley and Harold Land were on one date; Carmell Jones, Herb Ellis and Land on the other. Ironically, the composers had never had a chance to record these tunes on home ground. (Regrettably, too, the LP was for Ava, a company that promptly went out of business.)

Since those days, jazz has been established beyond a doubt as the musical *lingua franca*. Only two months after leaving Moscow in 1977, the trumpeter Valeri Ponomarev secured a job with Art Blakey, which he held with distinction for five years. The walls are crumbling; only the politicians are keeping us apart.

EAST

From my perhaps limited observation post during the 1930s, it appeared that the first countries to challenge the United States in terms of public appreciation of jazz, and in developing a few genuinely original creative performers, were France and England. The accomplishments of the Hot Club of France and of the British Rhythm Clubs were well known, as were the performances of Django Reinhardt, Stéphane Grappelli and, a little later, George Shearing.

Somehow it escaped the attention of many of us that in other parts of the world a keen sense of the significance of jazz was evolving, and with it a level of media coverage of which we knew far too little. Through working for *Orkester Journalen* and *Estrad* I had become aware of the existence of some promising Swedish talent, and the Danish jazz community already had reason to be proud of Svend Asmussen in the late thirties.

In 1947 the arrival in New York of Ake (Stan) Hasselgard, who became the first and only clarinettist ever to be featured officially alongside Benny Goodman, came as a shock to American audiences. His death the following year in a car accident robbed us of a potentially phenomenal artist. But by 1948 the Chubby Jackson combo and the Dizzy Gillespie band had learned at first hand about the enthusiasm of Swedish audiences and the growing cadre of brilliant young jazz musicians in and around Stockholm.

What too few of us realized was that almost simultaneously, Japan had begun to develop as a vital centre for the appreciation and performance of jazz. My 1960 edition of *The Encyclopedia of Jazz* listed only six Japanese musicians, along with two who had moved there from Manchuria. One of the latter was Toshiko Akiyoshi, who was unknown in the States until she arrived, in 1956, in Boston to study at the Berklee School of Music.

By that time it had become clear that the long burning fuse of jazz interest in Japan had ignited a great explosion. Members of the UN forces stationed in Japan after World War II had given Hidehiko Matsumoto his nickname, 'Sleepy'. A gifted tenor saxophonist, he admired Gene Ammons, Sonny Rollins and Sonny Stitt. Sadao Watanabe, born in 1933, had played in Akiyoshi's quartet for three years before she left for the US, then took over leadership of the group. Long before any of them there had been such pioneers as the late Fumio Nanri, whom Louis Armstrong had called 'the Satchmo of Japan', and who had spent six months in this country in 1932.

By the early 1960s the Westernization of Japanese culture had reached an advanced stage. Tokyo promoters had been engaged in a highly competitive struggle, outbidding one another for the services of Ellington, Basie, Oscar Peterson, Brubeck, Mulligan and dozens more. This intense concern reached a peak during the summer of 1964 when Tokutara Honda, a young impresario and head of the Japan Booking Corporation, decided to outdistance his rivals by staging what he planned to bill as a World Jazz Festival. To assemble talent for this precedent-setting event he called on George Wein, who since his first Newport presentation in 1954 had been known around the world as the pre-eminent jazz-concert impresario.

A plan evolved of bringing over three different packages, each appealing to a different element of popular taste. Japanese musicians were added to each unit, but the chief attractions were all US artists. Invited by George Wein to travel with this group, I arrived in Tokyo with the entire company on the muggy evening of 9 July 1964.

One of the three units was the 'modern' group. Except for Sleepy Matsumoto's quartet and Akiyoshi, who was a member of J.J. Johnson's group, this show was composed entirely of black Americans. Miles Davis was the main attraction, bringing with him Sam Rivers on tenor, Herbie Hancock, the eighteen-year-old Tony Williams and Ron Carter. The programme also included Carmen McRae and her trio headed by the pianist Norman Simmons; the pianist Wynton Kelly's trio, with Paul Chambers and Jimmy Cobb; and the J.J. Johnson All Stars, featuring Clark Terry and Sonny Stitt.

A second show, billed as 'Dixieland-Swing', comprised the Dukes of Dixieland (with Edmond Hall as guest soloist), the singer

Dakota Staton backed by a Japanese trio, the Red Nichols combo and Gene Krupa.

The third show was pop-orientated, with the Tommy Dorsey ghost band (led inexplicably by a saxophonist, Sam Donahue), Frank Sinatra Jr, the trumpeter and singer Charlie Shavers, who was featured with the Dorsey band, and a popular Japanese big band, the Sharps and Flats. In addition there were the Pied Pipers, and Louie Bellson, who was a guest drummer with both bands.

On arrival in Tokyo we were met by a line of attractive girls who handed bouquets to everyone. Before leaving for the Okura Hotel the musicians were introduced to reporters in the airport's VIP room.

Our hotel was luxurious and spacious; we were assured that Ellington and most of the visiting heroes had stayed here. (Out-of-town accommodations were less agreeable; as Wynton Kelly put it, 'In my hotel bedroom in Osaka, you had to go out to the hallway to turn over.')

Each of the three units played in a different city every night, shuttling by train between Tokyo, Kyoto, Osaka and Nagoya. By the end of the week it was very clear that the modern show was by far the strongest, musically and commercially, and that Miles Davis was the most powerful box-office attraction in our midst.

The mystique surrounding Miles, even back in 1964, was already as potent a factor in Tokyo and Osaka as in Texas or Ohio. For weeks before the festival, rumours had spread in Japanese circles that he would not appear. There was some foundation for these reports, since Miles, suffering for months from a condition in his hip caused by calcium deposits, had been in considerable pain. This, coupled with his professed diffidence about festivals in general, prompted him to tell friends that he positively was not going.

The uncertainty served to strengthen the Miles Davis legend. When he finally agreed to make the tour, he travelled like royalty. No other performer went first-class, had an air-conditioned limousine to take him from hotels to concert halls, or insisted that no photos be taken while he played. His fee for six concerts in four cities was over $15,000 plus round-trip fares for himself, his sidemen, his wife Frances and his booking agent Ben Shapiro. Though this seemed unthinkably high at the time, it was considerably less than he would charge today for a single performance.

Expensive though his services were, Miles proved his worth every night. No other moment during the entire week could compare for excitement with the first appearance, to thunderous applause, of the small, trim American in the Italian suit, walking across the vast Japanese stage and plunging into the sombre first chorus of a French song ('Autumn Leaves').

Davis elicited from the crowds a degree of sensitive attention that surpassed anything I had seen in America. So deep was the fans' involvement that some expressed surprise at a change of personnel: they had expected George Coleman on tenor rather than Sam Rivers.

The modern show made two Tokyo appearances. My small contribution was an opening speech in Japanese, which I had learned by sitting next to Toshiko on the plane from Los Angeles. At the first show, held in a 5,000-seat outdoor amphitheatre in Hibiya Park, despite seat prices that seemed unusually high ($2 to $9.50) the house was almost sold out. At the second show, held indoors at the 2,400-seat Kosei Nenkin Hall, the house was packed and hundreds of disappointed fans were turned away.

The audiences were younger than most of us had expected. As Carmen McRae remarked, 'Kids this age in America would all be rock 'n' roll fans.' They were not only young but tenacious, as we observed in Kyoto during the most memorable evening of the tour. This 1,200-year-old city, for more than a thousand years the capital of the empire, turned out to be as up-to-date as the latest space missile.

During Miles Davis's set a light rain began to fall. A few spectators ran for cover. The rain became heavier. Hundreds of umbrellas were raised; at least thirty youngsters jumped up on to the partially covered stage. But thousands sat patient and unprotected. A photograph I took that night at the Mariyama Music Hall looked like a sea of umbrellas. After the customary presentation of a bouquet to Davis at the end of the set (each artist received flowers every night), Carmen McRae took to the stage and sang 'Here's that Rainy Day'. Immediately, the rain stopped.

During a week spent in perpetual motion, measures were taken to make us feel very much at home. One morning George Wein called to tell us that we were invited to the American Embassy to meet Ambassador and Mrs Edwin Reischauer. The Ambassador, recovering from a wound inflicted in an assassination attempt, got up from his sick bed to meet the few of us who were able to attend on short notice: Wein, the promoter Honda, Carmen, Louie Bellson and me.

Some of the musicians were invited to a musical instrument shop in Kyoto to hear a demonstration of the koto. J. J. Johnson was escorted by Reiko Hoshino, the gracious owner of a Kyoto coffee shop, to relax in the quiet serenity of a Japanese garden and lake area. A group of schoolchildren was brought to meet Clark Terry.

We soon learned that the young Japanese was interested mainly in the latest jazz developments. The Dixieland show did not enjoy the same good fortune as the modern unit; though the artists were well received – especially Edmond Hall, whose unaccompanied solo of 'Dawn on the Desert' was a highlight – attendance figures were erratic. The Dorsey show did even less well, but Louie Bellson and Charlie Shavers were big favourites.

The adoption of jazz was part of an overall Westernization that resulted in the gradual displacement of kimonos by copies of Dior or Cardin. Even the ancient Kabuki theatre and modern Japanese films were being bypassed to some extent in favour of American westerns. Coffee mills, jazz bars and soda fountains were becoming the rendezvous of the young, while the green tea and Japanese sweets of the older generation lay deserted in some of the old-style tea houses.

The rain, heat and intense humidity would normally have bothered us more than they did, but the charm and hospitality of our hosts were compensation enough. 'It took me sixty-three years to get here,' said Edmond Hall, 'and I'm just sorry I had to wait so long.' Hall died three years later; Red Nichols, already an all but forgotten figure of the 1920s and 1930s, died less than a year after the visit.

Even the supposedly taciturn Miles Davis enjoyed the experience, chatting amiably with new friends about karate, boxing and his expertise in the art of Oriental cooking. Still, the climate proved hard on him. As the week drew to a close, he told me, 'I've lost twelve pounds in six days. I've got to go to Mexico for a rest.'

Early in the week two panel discussions were held at which twenty-six reporters heard a battery of Japanese jazz critics ask questions of George Wein, Jimmy Lyons, Mel Isenberger (producer and president of the Monterey Jazz Festival) and me. A typical question, asked by a writer from *Swing Journal*, was, 'Why were no avant-garde musicians included in this festival?'

On the topic 'Jazz and Race' the critics showed a fairly perceptive insight, based partly on their study of the writing of James Baldwin and Leroi Jones (Amiri Baraka). One critic was rebuked for putting the issue on the basis of a racial contest; the US panelists reminded him that integration is more common in jazz than on other levels of US society. Bogged down by the long waits while interpreters translated, the discussion was further hampered by the fact that most of the musicians were en route between cities and consequently we could not include a black panelist.

Though they equated authenticity with the black experience, the Japanese had already welcomed many white or interracial groups. Shelly Manne, who had toured Japan a few months earlier in a percussion ensemble with Max Roach, Philly Joe Jones and Roy Haynes, had told me, 'We all got along beautifully, with each other and with the public.'

The week ended on an international note as Toshiko took Paul Chambers, Jimmy Cobb and Sleepy Matsumoto along with her to record an all-night session for Nippon Columbia, with a big band on some tracks. Chambers and Cobb each received a Nikon F camera, worth $450, for playing the date.

What our three-rhythm circus showed us was that a social revolution was well under way. The Occidental clothes, the chewing gum and Yankee soft drinks, the English lettering in the signs, the entire ambience were parts of a picture that spelled Americanization in the arts, attitudes and mentality of a substantial segment of the younger Asian generation.

'Jazz,' the critic Jiro Kubota told me, 'is today a form of intellectual snobbery as well as entertainment for our young audiences. Our old pentatonic scale actually sounds less natural to these kids than the European diatonic scale.'

During the decade following the festival, Japan experienced an avalanche of jazz action, both domestic and imported. When I returned to Tokyo in 1977, the main reason for my visit was the tenth annual *Swing Journal* poll awards presentation. Held in a hotel banquet room, attended by some 300 record company, TV, radio and press representatives, this was the most pomp-and-circumstantial occasion since the golden days of the 'Esky' awards. *Swing Journal*, in the *Esquire* tradition, presented statuettes to winners chosen by a board of twenty-two Japanese experts.

This year the Gold Award went to *Insights*, an LP by the Hollywood-based Toshiko Akiyoshi/Lew Tabackin Orchestra. The Tabackins and I had flown over together to attend the ceremony. 'I am deeply honoured,' said Akiyoshi, adding less formally, 'Wow! Just think, they chose ours out of 1,300 jazz albums released in Japan last year!' She might have added that this was more than twice the US figure, and included albums made in the US or Japan by American musicians but never released in the States, as well as countless reissues, and some 170 albums by Japanese artists.

The Silver Award went to Charlie Haden, a prophet more honoured in Japan and Europe than at home, for an album of duet performances with Ornette Coleman, Alice Coltrane and others. Reissue awards went to a 1930s Dorsey Brothers set and to Lennie Tristano's *Descent into the Maelstrom*, a set of private tapings that had not been released in the US.

No doubt *Swing Journal* was part cause and part effect of the astonishing Japanese jazz boom. Founded in 1947, it was already by far the world's fattest jazz magazine, close to an inch thick with its 300 to 500 pages monthly and a circulation close to 200,000 (more than double that of *Down Beat*). It included hundreds of photographs, many of them glossy full-page colour reproductions, an enormous audiophile section, and scores of record reviews and features catering to every conceivable taste.

Kiyoshi Koyama, the editor at that time, told me, 'Our average reader is between eighteen and twenty-six; most are university students or graduates. We also have a big following among record buyers in their thirties who love all kinds of jazz, bebop to contemporary.'

Returning to Tokyo and Kyoto, I had a chance to divide a week between visits to shrines and temples, coffee houses named Dig and Dug and Lady Day and Basie, to observe statues of Buddha and listen to disciples of Coltrane; to hear the twenty-three-year-old guitarist Kazumi Watanabe string out a dozen choruses of Sonny Rollins' 'Oleo', to listen to new releases on Japanese labels called East Wind, Three Blind Mice and Why Not Records, played for me at the Django coffee shop, and to catch Teruhisa Togo singing 'Alright, Okay, You Win' at the Club Misty.

In Kyoto Lew Tabackin and I dropped in at the Big Boy, where Miles Davis's 'Nardis' was piping through a pair of elaborate speakers. The small room was packed with young fans, many in jeans, drably dressed. Introduced to Lew and me, the owner promptly turned to his collection of 3,000 records that lined the walls and whipped out two Tabackin albums, as well as a Leonard Feather bebop LP I had produced twenty years earlier.

Record sales are stimulated by Japan's 400 coffee shops. Jazz in general is helped by the existence of live music on radio, by now all but obsolete in the US. Sadao Watanabe told me, 'My quartet has a regular radio programme every Saturday night. The jazz life is good for me; I can do what I like, when and where I choose. For a long time it was hard to find a Japanese rhythm section that swung. Today I have no such problem.'

The difficulties confronting big bands in America have no counterpart in Japan. Toshiyuki Miyama, then fifty-five and leader of the long-established New Herd, said, 'Half of our activity in any given year involves TV. The rest of the time we play two or three months of concerts, other concerts backing up singers or visiting stars from the US. Our band records five or six albums a year.' (I told him that most of America's big jazz orchestras were lucky to make two or three albums a year; some had no recording contracts at all.)

By learning from visiting Americans, or in many instances by studying at Berklee, Japanese musicians had grown beyond the imitative stage. Originality was now feasible not only through living the American experience, but also on home grounds. Not for nothing had Toshiko, taking her cue from 'black is beautiful', composed a number entitled 'Yellow is Mellow'.

It is still not easy to arrive at a full explanation of the cultural crosswinds that established Japan as the world's second most active jazz centre. There are times when, observing how many fine musicians in Los Angeles are scuffling for scale jobs, I wonder whether it might not be advisable to omit 'second' from that last sentence.

TIMES

The timing of my first visit to Japan in mid-1964 could hardly have been more convenient. The first few years in Los Angeles, despite plentiful opportunities for good listening experiences among good friends, had not provided a firm path along the lines I had hoped for. There had been the occasional recording session, and once in a while some encouraging incident: a lecture scheduled here, a song recorded there, and a slight expansion of my weekly column, achieved through personal syndication: for a while it ran in the *New York Post*, a few other out-of-town papers, and in the *California Eagle*, a black-orientated weekly then owned by Jimmy Tolbert.

I had co-written *Laughter from the Hip*, with Jack Tracy, the former editor of *Down Beat*, and was working on a revision of *The Book of Jazz*. I had also completed, for Irving Mills, an elaborate history of jazz styles, with a record session specially designed to correspond with each chapter of the book.

To my dismay, just after this ambitious venture was completed (with sessions by Wally Rose, Johnny St Cyr, Wild Bill Davison, Olive Brown, Dick Hyman, Paul Horn, Shorty Rogers, Benny Carter, Curtis Amy, Johnny Hodges and Lalo Schifrin), Mills sold his company. The new owners were aware of the material but did nothing to make it available. Many years later some of the recordings were released piecemeal, but what could have been a unique and valuable book-and-record package never saw the light of day.

By 1965, despite a variety of work opportunities in radio, recording, television and lectures, along with magazine pieces for *Down Beat, Melody Maker* and various others, there seemed to be no definite direction to my California career. A bright ray of light entered the picture with the arrival in Los Angeles of Charles

Champlin, who took up the post of arts editor for the *Los Angeles Times*.

I wrote to Champlin, suggesting that there seemed to be considerable room for expansion of the newspaper's jazz coverage. The reply, and our lunch meeting soon after, could not have been more encouraging. It turned out that Champlin had played cornet as a young man, idolized Louis and Bix and Wild Bill, and one of his most cherished memories was a meeting with Duke Ellington during his college days. In other words, he did not have to be persuaded. He knew me well enough by reputation to offer me an occasional freelance reviewing assignment, starting immediately.

Some time in the early autumn of 1965 my first byline appeared in the paper. In January 1966 a regular arrangement was agreed on: I would write a feature to appear every Sunday in the 'Calendar' entertainment section, and an average of two nightclub or concert reviews a week. In addition, there were occasional special assignments such as book reviews, not only on jazz but on other subjects that interested me (principally civil rights and the uses and abuses of the English language).

That has been my principal occupation ever since. Once my name began appearing regularly with the words '*Times* Staff Writer' under my byline, I began to feel not only a security unknown since my arrival on the coast, but also a sense that I was a useful member of the jazz community. To sweeten the job, Champlin arranged for my Sunday pieces to be syndicated worldwide through the *LA Times–Washington Post News Service*, which then numbered some 200 papers but has now expanded to more than 500.

Along with the advantages of these valuable outlets came almost unlimited freedom: during the next twenty years I would file stories for the *Times* from dozens of cities around the world, from festivals and cruises and White House receptions. Until I took a leave of absence to work on this book, my features appeared fifty-two Sundays a year almost without exception, since I would backlog stories whenever I planned to go to some distant point.

Many of these articles were incorporated into two of my books, *The Pleasures of Jazz* and *The Passion for Jazz*. Some of the journeys I took with the newspaper primarily in mind have provided the foundation for much of the latter portion of the present book. Aside from the *Esquire* affiliation my *Times* job turned out to be the happiest, most productive and proudest association of all my years in jazz.

Fortunately several other developments, some shortly before and others after the start of my _Times_ association, kept me active in areas that I found challenging and creative.

Early in 1965 I was approached by executives at MCA. They had been receiving requests from a German television station to supply them with a series of short jazz films for use on TV. Since MCA was affiliated with Universal Pictures there was a wealth of material available, much of it hidden in the vaults.

I was hired to assemble thirteen films, none more than ten minutes long, each dedicated to a specific subject. Because I could still speak German (with the help of scripts on which I worked long and hard) it was also decided to include some voice-over narration, and to record special theme and background music, for which Benny Carter assembled an all-star unit.

Since it would involve only a little extra time, I also recorded the narration in English. It was a typical irony that although the series was well received in Cologne and I was commissioned to assemble thirteen more shows, the English versions were never sold.

Digging out footage for these shows had all the characteristics of a treasure hunt. I had three main sources on which to draw: 'band shorts' that had been filmed between about 1940 and 1955; certain Universal feature films that happened to include segments by jazz groups or singers; and some Paramount features containing similarly excerptable sequences.

During the two or three months of research I was shocked to find how carelessly these works had been treated. In some instances they were supposedly lost, though eventually most of them turned up. Others, such as a 1937 short by the revived Original Dixieland Jazz Band, had been filmed on nitrate stock that had disintegrated. On the other hand, a short entitled _Sugar Chile Robinson_ (named after a small and not very talented youngster playing boogie-woogie piano) turned out to include two wonderful songs by Billie Holiday, 'God Bless the Child' and 'Now Baby or Never', and a 'One o'Clock Jump' by the 1950 Count Basie septet.

The series, for which the English title was _Feather on Jazz_, brought to life a goldmine of early works, all in black and white, all lying unused until then, by Ellington, Goodman, Nat Cole, Hampton, Norvo, Sarah Vaughan, Kenton, Louis Jordan, Krupa, Herman and Barnet. A complete set of the twenty-six shows, with English narration, was presented to me, but they have still not been seen in the US except when I occasionally use a few of them in the course of lectures in colleges or on cruises.

Colleges, as it turned out, began to take on an unprecedented importance for me during the 1960s and 1970s. After the ground-breaking series with Goffin in 1942 I had given occasional lectures, but the growth of the jazz-education field enabled me to incorporate into my schedule visits to North Texas State University, Berklee College in Boston and other campuses that had pioneered in the teaching of jazz styles, history and techniques.

At one time or another I lectured at all the eight University of California campuses. One particularly rewarding venture was a short tour organized by the University of California Extension, entitled 'American Art and Culture: the Negro's Contribution'. The first part of each programme was a symposium in which Duke Ellington, Quincy Jones and I discussed the Afro-American musical tradition; after an intermission, the Ellington orchestra was presented in concert. Travelling from San Diego to San Bernardino to Irvine and Los Angeles, with a delightful, jazz-sensitive woman named Mary Jane Hewitt as our programme co-ordinator, we all found the experience stimulating and as educational to us as it was to the students. In a sense that tour, in 1966, was a prologue to a more comprehensive adventure that brought me into academia on a regular basis. In the spring of 1973 I was invited, under a Regents' Lectureship, to give a full series of classes on jazz history on the University of California campus at Riverside.

Riverside being about eighty minutes' drive from my home, I set out early every Tuesday and Thursday morning, from early April through to June 1973; my classes lasted from 11 a.m. to 12.30 p.m. and I would often stay behind to chat with the students. I used my film collection, which by now was quite substantial, to illustrate various aspects. Though there was a minimal budget for guests, a few enthusiastic musicians, glad to find jazz dealt with so extensively, volunteered their services. To celebrate Duke Ellington's birthday I invited Barney Bigard, Cat Anderson and Louie Bellson to speak, and to join with a student group for a jam session.

The Riverside experience was a revelation. Sometimes one tends to assume too much knowledge on the part of a young audience, taking for granted that anyone who has bothered to enrol for a jazz class must know the basics. As I soon learned, I was dealing with some students who were novices. In a written test, one of them listed Miles Davis as one of his favourite saxophonists. I was asked whether Benny Goodman was dead.

It soon became clear that these students (the class numbered over 200) could be drawn into the subject more readily if they dealt not with abstracts in dry, documented dissertations, but rather with men and women whose acquaintance they could make through films, or even more valuably through personal visits. One morning, after I had shown a film about the international influence of jazz, with a 1958 clip of Toshiko Akiyoshi, I presented Toshiko and Lew Tabackin as guest speakers. Such events proved stimulating and were certainly the best way to keep the class involved.

I was invited back to Riverside for the spring season the following year. Eubie Blake, ninety years old but eager to help and refusing all offers of payment, came out with me one morning and kept the class totally fascinated as he reminisced about his parents, who were slaves, and about his teenage years playing piano in a 'house of ill repute', as he called it, then performed several numbers with a long-time associate, the eighty-one-year-old singer Ivan Harold Browning.

Not long after my second season at Riverside, a campus much closer to home, Loyola-Marymount University in Los Angeles, extended an invitation to offer a similar course there. Once again the experience was gratifying, and again the best remembered class was one attended by a guest speaker and performer, this time B. B. King, whose amiable personality established an immediate rapport.

After three seasons at Loyola-Marymount I gave one series of classes at California State University at Northridge, where Gerald Wilson has been offering jazz history classes for almost twenty years. This too was enriching, reminding me again that there is a good reason why teachers in general are willing to work in the United States for such abysmally low salaries: it may do little for the bank balance but it is balm for the soul.

The President and Mrs. Carter
request the pleasure of your company
at a concert to be held at

The White House

on Sunday, June 18, 1978
at five o'clock

South Lawn   *Buffet*

On 18 June 1978, President Jimmy Carter celebrated the twenty-fifth anniversary of the Newport Jazz Festival by holding a jazz concert utilizing thirty musicians, on the South Lawn at the White House. I was among the guests.

Beginning with a buffet, with music by the Young Tuxedo Brass Band from New Orleans, the concert got under way with a moving speech by the President. Using no notes, and speaking with evident knowledge and enthusiasm, he dealt with every relevant point, from the unique value of jazz as an art form to the racism that had held it back for so long.

Eubie Blake, ninety-five, played 'Memories of You', and W.C. Handy's seventy-six-year-old daughter, Katharine Handy Lewis, sang 'St Louis Blues' backed by Dick Hyman, Doc Cheatham and Milt Hinton. The programme continued with a capsule history of jazz piano by Mary Lou Williams. A swing-style session with Roy Eldridge, Clark Terry, Illinois Jacquet and Benny Carter led the President to tell Carter: 'I've been familiar with your music for years. I'm proud to have a cousin like you.'

Others heard were George Benson; Herbie Hancock backing Dizzy Gillespie; Chick Corea sitting in with Lionel Hampton; Sonny Rollins backed by McCoy Tyner, Max Roach and Ron Carter; Ornette Coleman with his son Denardo; and Cecil Taylor. Carter was so moved by Taylor that he leaped on to the bandstand and said: 'Wonderful! I wish I could play like that.'

George Wein called for a standing ovation for the ailing Charles Mingus, who was present in a wheelchair, and whom the President embraced. The programme proceeded with Stan Getz, Zoot Sims, Gerry Mulligan, Billy Taylor and Pearl Bailey. Finally, Gillespie and Roach persuaded the President of the United States to join in the vocal on Dizzy's 'Salt Peanuts'.

As President Carter commented, 'This concert is just as much a part of the greatness of America as the White House itself, or the Capitol building down the street.'

THE PRESIDENT AND MRS. CARTER

welcome you to a

JAZZ CONCERT

THE WHITE HOUSE
June 18, 1978

AFLOAT

'Another boring day in Paradise,' said Joe Williams with a wry smile as he lounged around the pool deck of the SS *Norway* sipping cool drinks and contemplating the sunlit ocean view.

We were somewhere in the Caribbean, in the autumn of 1984, relishing what must have been the most luxurious floating jazz journey of the many that had set sail since the shipboard festival concept was launched in the early 1970s.

Jazz musicians had been working at sea for several decades, but they were never hired in order to attract jazz fans. Bud Freeman played his way across to Europe on the *Ile de France* in 1928. In the late 1940s and early 1950s John Dankworth, Bruce Turner and others played in ship bands simply in order to reach New York and hear Charlie Parker in person.

The first full-scale indication of a significant new outlet for jazz was the hiring of Count Basie and his Orchestra for five Caribbean cruises, the first four aboard the *Queen Elizabeth*, annually from 1970 to 1973. Sailing on the first and third of these, I immediately realized the great advantages to musicians and passengers. The band, playing only one set a night, was enjoying a virtual paid vacation. Most of the musicians' wives came along. Along with the gambling, the deck games, swimming pools and abundant food and drinks, there were the ports of call in Jamaica, Barbados, St Thomas and Haiti.

Eubie Blake, just shy of his eighty-seventh birthday, and his wife Marian were along as paying passengers, as was Sarah Vaughan. Naturally, Eubie was persuaded to play at a jam session and Sarah sat in with the orchestra. The opportunity for musicians and passengers to mingle socially, the easy hours and the glorious weather added up to an experience such as no landlocked concert or festival could offer. Moreover, the audiences were attentive and there was none of the noisy carnival atmosphere that had ruined several events at Newport, Monterey and New York. These were mostly well-to-do, middle-aged jazz lovers; for many of them the presence of Basie's band was a bonus on a voyage they had probably already planned to take.

The next stage in the evolution of the seaborne jazz phenomenon came to my attention when, one evening in April 1974, Dizzy Gillespie came over for dinner. Asked about his summer plans, he said, 'Well, I'm going on this jazz festival on the *Rotterdam*.'

A jazz festival on a ship? My curiosity piqued, I asked Dizzy for the details and next day put in a call to Exprinter Tours. This company had been packaging classical music festivals for the Holland America Line and was now prepared to try out a similar project with jazz.

I arranged to join the company, bringing along some of my jazz-film collection for one or two lecture/screenings. With Jane, I arrived in New York on 24 May – only to learn from the headlines that Duke Ellington had died early that morning.

The next twenty-four hours were traumatic. Jane and I went to the funeral parlour to pay our last respects. Mercer assured me that a commitment Duke had made, to have his orchestra play at the IBM Convention in Bermuda whether or not he could be there himself, would be honoured. By an ironic coincidence, 'Showboat 1' (the official name for the first jazz festival aboard the *Rotterdam*) was due to dock in Bermuda on the day the band was set to play there. Mercer and I arranged to meet at his hotel in Hamilton and talk about the future of the Ellington ensemble.

We sailed from New York in a strangely mixed mood of sorrow and celebration. Oscar Peterson and Dizzy, setting the tone for the week, included enough Ellingtonia in their sets to establish that the festival had become a tribute to Duke's memory.

At our first stop in Nassau Ray Charles boarded the ship with his orchestra and the Raeletts in tow. Unlike the other artists, they did their show and left the *Rotterdam* without taking part in the journey.

Ella Fitzgerald, in magnificent form, dedicated her performance to Lucille Armstrong, Satchmo's widow, who was among the passengers during our week in the sun. Others were our good friends Red and Mary Lou Callender and Jake Hanna, all of whom had flown in from Hollywood just to be part of the audience. Much more than on the Basie trips I observed a substantial number of middle-class blacks – doctors, lawyers, business people – who related to this music in much the same way middle-class whites relate to Dixieland.

As he is at every event in which he takes part, Dizzy was the life of this moveable feast. Officially he made only one appearance, on our first day out, but before the week was over he had embellished everyone else's act. He joined with Ella for a Duke medley, surprised Oscar by walking in on him in mid-chorus, and in a kind gesture helped out the frail, ailing Bobby Hackett, whose chops were not up to tackling a whole hour (he died just two years later).

Gillespie had arrived on board armed with a large supply of firecrackers, a volley of which he detonated during a promenade-deck photo with a harried Exprinter photographer. Talent and comedy value aside, Dizzy was considerate: he arranged for a movie screening to be cancelled so that he could use the theatre to give a special recital for the crew.

The most adventurous music on board was supplied by James Moody, whose saxophone and flute had once been part of the Gillespie quintet. During a solo by his pianist, Mike Longo, two figures emerged from the wings waltzing onstage together – Moody and his ex-boss. Gillespie then brought on Peterson to take over from Longo; finally, Ella materialized from the audience to scat a few choruses of 'Now's the Time'.

During the Bermuda stop, a long talk with Mercer proved encouraging. 'I want a band Pop would be proud of,' he said. Of the old guard, only Cootie Williams and Harry Carney were left, but Mercer assured me that the faceless figures who had begun to inhabit the bandstand when Duke became too old, tired and sick to care would be replaced by men steeped in the Ellington tradition.

Festivals continued, usually every May and December, until 1979; I was aboard all but two. I have particularly fond memories of Showboat 2, which was preserved for television. Where American networks feared to tread, the BBC joined us with a staff of thirteen, among them two camera crews, to shoot footage of Sarah Vaughan, the Lionel Hampton and Count Basie bands, Joe Williams, the Cannonball Adderley Quintet, Cecil Payne on baritone sax and his sister, the singer Cavril Payne. As often happened on jazz cruises, there was a birthday to celebrate; Jillean Williams staged a surprise party for Joe, who hit fifty-six on the day of our arrival in Bermuda.

My sister Gweneth flew in from London to join us for Showboat

3, on which our table companions for meals were Earl Hines and his singer Marva Josie. The Ellington band, the Brubeck combo, Carmen McRae, Dizzy and the World's Greatest Jazzband rounded out that show. Six months later we were off again, this time with Stan Getz, Ahmad Jamal and Woody Herman among others. At dinner one evening I suggested to Woody and his manager that with 1976 coming up, they ought to think in terms of a fortieth-anniversary celebration for the orchestra. As a result, in November 1976 Woody and I were together onstage at Carnegie Hall, just as we had been thirty years earlier.

Cruising is not necessarily all jazz and joy and sunshine. There is always the possible occasional storm at sea with the attendant pitching and yawing. I remember one night when Ella had to clutch the curtain in order not be be propelled across the stage. Count Basie, in disgust with the weather one night, threw up more than his hands, stayed in his cabin and missed an entire show. I also seem to recall a night when Ahmad Jamal almost had to chase his grand piano across the stage; neither the instrument nor the piano bench had been nailed down, and the sight of the unplanned movements in mid-solo were no doubt more amusing to us than to him. But such nights, or days, were very rare; smooth seas and sunny days were the rule.

There was one unique interruption in Exprinter's regular New York–Nassau–Bermuda schedule. In 1977, on very short notice, we were informed of a new and unprecedented journey: we would sail from New Orleans on a Greek ship, the *Daphne*, and make our first stop at Havana, where no American tourist ship had dropped anchor since the rupture of diplomatic relations in 1961. On board were the Gillespie, Getz and Hines groups, David Amram and Ry Cooder, all of whom took part in a concert at a theatre in Havana, joined by several Cuban musicians.

By late 1979, cruises had become so popular that it was evidently decided not to go to the expense of hiring jazz musicians, all of whom occupied cabins that would otherwise be paid for. When the series ended, I missed these biannual experiences so much that I persuaded the Princess Lines to attempt something similar, out of Los Angeles down the Mexican coastline. Claiming budgetary limitations, they refused to buy live talent. On the *Pacific Princess* I gave a few lectures coupled with screenings of some jazz films; not until 1984 did the Princess Lines try live jazz, and then on a small scale, hiring Bill Berry and a sextet for a 'Tribute to Ellington' theme cruise. By that time, however, something far more ambitious was taking place on the Atlantic coast.

Hank O'Neal, who had operated Chiaroscuro Records, and his partner Shelli Mae Shier, convinced Norwegian Caribbean Lines that the time was ripe for a full-scale floating jazz festival. Our vehicle would be the *Norway*, one of the biggest ships afloat (at 70,000 tons outweighing the *QE II*), our point of departure Miami, and our ports of call St Thomas and Nassau.

The first time around confusion reigned. The talent had to be lined up on short notice. Jonah Jones, a fine trumpeter in the swing era, now led a lacklustre quintet playing 'muted jazz' – or perhaps one might call it doll jazz, since you could always expect 'Satin Doll' or 'Hello Dolly'.

There was, in fact, nothing on board representative of today's jazz scene except for the Polish pianist Adam Makowicz. Astrud Gilberto, of bossa-nova fame, had all the charisma of a wet firecracker. Joe Bushkin complained about the piano, refused to use a bass player (he needed one), sang a dismal song called 'Boogie Woogie Blue Plate', and, having become independently wealthy many years ago, was given to such remarks as: 'I don't have to do this, you know.' Bushkin sounded better playing trumpet, as he did in two jam sessions.

Wild Bill Davison led an agreeable Dixieland combo. Clark Terry and Zoot Sims provided what little valid mainstream jazz we heard, helped at times by the house band under the direction of Chip Hoehler, a former name-band trombonist.

This is the other side of the captive-audience picture: if you are stuck with an uneven bunch of performers (and some bad vibes among them), frustration can be the outcome.

O'Neal was frank in admitting that the music and the organization left much to be desired, but he was now ready to spend an entire year lining up the roster for 1984, when there would be two consecutive week-long cruises.

The payoff was total, artistically and commercially. With every cabin filled and an aggregate of 3,500 passengers for the two weeks, the multi-million gross ensured that new vistas were opening up for jazz. This time there was a far better mix of ages and styles, from Scott Hamilton, thirty, to Doc Cheatham, nearing eighty.

The loose, 'Who calls this work?' ambience again produced some intriguingly incongruous groups. At a jam session one afternoon Benny Carter, on trumpet and alto, was joined by Bill Davison's traditional-style trombonist, Bill Allred, and Sayyd Abdul Al-Khabyyr, Dizzy's avant-garde-leaning clarinettist, whose tonal paroxysms contrasted sharply with the orderly, swing-rooted clarinet of Kenny Davern.

Every evening there were multiple choices for the passengers: a jam session in the Club Internationale, a dance band in the Checkers Cabaret, perhaps with Carter or Dizzy or Clark or Zoot joining Chip Hoehler's band; and a concert in the 525-seat Saga Theatre.

In addition, there was the regular cruise-style entertainment: a scaled-down version of *My Fair Lady*, a Las Vegas-type revue called *Sea Legs*. Again there were the celebratory surprises: Maxine Sullivan, Benny Carter, Woody Herman and others singing 'Happy Birthday' for Dizzy to the tune of 'Night in Tunisia'. Mel Torme interrupted one of a series of 'Meet the Stars' round-table discussions to sing 'Happy Birthday Dear Zoot,' to which Zoot replied: 'I may be fifty-nine today, but I have the body of a fifty-seven-year-old man.' Zoot, who played with strength and conviction though we knew he was gravely ill, was booked to play the next cruise in 1985, but four months later we lost him.

Just after we left St Thomas, George Shearing, in stunning form, joined with his old friend Benny Carter to play 'When Lights are Low' and 'Nightfall', both written when Carter was a London resident. 'George must be the only musician in America who remembers "Nightfall",' said Carter.

Mel Torme, who had married Ali Seversen that afternoon in St Thomas with Shearing as best man, teamed with George for a bebop vocal duet that took in everything from 'Lemon Drop' to 'Airmail Special'.

Joe Williams was in his glory all week, singing with his own trio (Norman Simmons on piano) as well as with Shearing and, using his big-band charts, with Hoehler's orchestra.

The week's all-purpose virtuoso was Shearing's Don Thompson. In the course of a single evening I heard him performing impeccably not only on bass, but on vibes and piano and then, in another all-star ad hoc group, on drums. Torme also distinguished himself as a drummer of very professional calibre.

The ship made a third stop on our last full day, at Great Stirrup Cay, a small, deserted island that belongs to the *Norway*'s owners. All we had to do there was picnic on the beach, swim and listen to a steel band playing island music.

One particular set on board offered a reminder of the time span encompassed by the week's jazz cornucopia. Dizzy sat in with Doc Cheatham for 'Royal Garden Blues', written in 1919; then Mike Renzi and Paul Langosh, Torme's pianist and bassist, joined Don Thompson and Bucky Pizzarelli for a very contemporary treatment of Chick Corea's 'Spain'.

The 1984 results encouraged the Norwegian Line to double the schedule yet again: four consecutive cruises were set for the autumn of 1985, creating what could be termed the world's longest jazz festival. Al Cohn, Ruby Braff, Doc Cheatham, Benny Carter, the Scott Hamilton Quintet, Maxine Sullivan, Kenny Davern, Eddie Higgins and Clark Terry stayed aboard for all four weeks.

Sailing on the second and third of the four expeditions, I met several newcomers to the American cruise scene; my old friend Svend Asmussen, whose unaccompanied solo on 'Sweet Georgia Brown' brought one of the longest standing ovations of the festival; Gary Burton and Phil Wilson from Berklee, each leading a different group of promising young Berklee students; Cab Calloway, fronting both the Woody Herman Orchestra and Hoehler's band; Art Hodes, a few weeks shy of his eighty-first birthday, whose blues piano in a duo performance with Gerry Mulligan worked surprisingly well; and Mulligan's admirable fifteen-man band, in which he served as baritone and soprano saxophonist, composer, arranger and vocalist.

Torme and Joe Williams repeated their successes of the previous year. On one set Williams invited the twenty-two-year-old pianist Cyrus Chestnut, from Phil Wilson's group, along with Gillespie and Cheatham, to embellish his blues and ballads. Later that evening Torme, at the drums, saw Clark Terry placing a microphone near him, enabling them to conjure up a vocal duet on Ellington's 'Just Squeeze Me'.

The impressionistic Burton unit had an international cast typical of the Berklee student body: Tommy Smith, an eighteen-year-old saxophonist from Scotland; a French pianist and bassist, a flautist from Sweden, and the remarkable Kazu Michishita, a guitarist from Tokyo.

Mulligan, whose reed section included Seldon Powell and Jerry Dodgion, made the strongest big-band impression, though some of the Herman band's charts effectively displayed its broad palette from piccolo to bassoon.

Buddy Tate, one of our dinner-table mates this year (along with

Jane, my sister Gweneth, Benny and Hilma Carter and Dizzy), brought his warm tenor sound to several groups before surprising us one night with a fluent flute solo. (How many seventy-year-old jazz flautists can you name?)

Clark Terry played 'In a Mellotone' with his horn upside down, pushing the valves up. This novelty might have been dismissed as foolish gimmickry except that the solo was musically excellent. Benny Carter brought the timeless beauty of his alto sax (and, happily, on several occasions, his trumpet) to a few crystalline ballads.

Around midnight as we sailed from our last call, with the festivities drawing to a close, Dick Hyman played the organ while Ruby Braff evoked memories of Buck Clayton, Bunny Berigan and Louis. With Jake Hanna offering a subliminal backing, they reminded us of the vital significance of logical, formal melody, whether in pristine or improvised state. As their set ended, Hyman remarked, 'I'm sorry I only booked this gig for two weeks; I realize now I would have been happy to stay the whole month.'

The jazz-at-sea events over the past dozen years have provided the most potent proof yet of how central a role the setting can play in the appreciation of music. At an outdoor festival in, say, Nice, there is a human traffic jam as the crowds press against one another, trying to find a seat or at least a distant glimpse of the stage. The amplification often is atrocious, and the sound leakage from some nearby stage may bring you two concerts simultaneously in unwanted binaural sound.

At Monterey, particularly on the Saturday afternoons, pandemonium erupts as the milling thousands, dancing in the aisles or on top of the chairs, compete for attention with the deafeningly overmiked electronic blues blasters onstage. In order to escape, you may have to step through the debris of empty beer cans and walk a quarter-mile out of your way to an exit, because a stern-voiced usher insists that the conveniently nearby door is for entry only. In New York there are the external distractions: the walks through humid streets, the hopeless attempts to flag down a taxi before curtain time.

Aboard a seventeen-storey-tall, 1,000-foot-long ocean liner, you are removed from all the petty nuisances and disturbances of city life. You don't have to struggle to make your way to the music: in effect, the music comes to you. (This is true even if you stay in your cabin, for by 1985 O'Neal and Shier had put together an incredible set of rare jazz films and videos that were presented on the TVs almost around the clock.)

The music on shipboard is presented for the most part under superior acoustical conditions. You can come and go as you please. By the end of the week, an artist whom you admired from afar as an idol may have become a good friend. Best of all, because the jazzmen and -women are on hand twenty-four hours a day, you never know who will decide to sit in spontaneously to add to the aural pleasures.

After hearing jazz under every conceivable set of circumstances, I am unalterably convinced that the jazz cruise is the ideal way to go. Being in the right places at the right time, in the right climate, with the right artists and the right listeners under the right conditions can hardly fail to provide the ultimate listening experience. Notwithstanding which I shall always miss the Savoy Ballroom.

HOLY LAND JAZZ

Throughout the 1970s each year was marked by events that became mileposts: the annual visits to New York and Monterey for the summer jazz festivals, the Dick Gibson jazz party held every Labour Day weekend in Colorado and attended by a growing number of mainstream and bebop giants (Gibson's initiative had been imitated by innumerable other hosts who cater to fans for whom these semi-private parties have a special and delightful ambience), and, starting in 1974, the cruises. But there were opportunities to explore further afield: a festival I attended in Sao Paulo, Brazil in 1978, another in Sydney in 1980. One of the most intriguing possibilities came to my attention in 1982 when I heard from a promoter named Charles Fishman about a jazz festival he was lining up to tour Israel.

'I've also been putting together the jazz talent for the Rubin Academy of Music in Jerusalem,' he told me in a call from Washington, where he headed the Kinneret Foundation. Though it came as no surprise that Israel had fallen in line among the countries that recognize jazz as a serious subject for education, the details of the imminent festival were particularly fascinating. Although it meant sacrificing all but the first day of Dick Gibson's party, I decided to go along.

How does a country only thirty-four-years old relate to a music that originated at the turn of the century? The answer came into focus not long after I had completed the circuitous journey from Denver to Los Angeles to New York to Tel Aviv. Any of us involved with the festival (twenty-six artists in all) found an immediate chance to relax at the Tel Aviv Hilton, a Miami-on-the-Mediterranean luxury beachfront hotel where we were headquartered prior to leaving on a series of one-night stands.

In this minuscule country, one-nighters are no problem. None of the venues booked was as far from Tel Aviv as Philadelphia is from New York.

The first concert offered a stunning indication of how the settings would inspire the musicians. The scene was an oceanside amphitheatre at Caesaria, forty miles up the coast. Built by Herod the Great (Nero, I was reminded, trod these grounds), rebuilt twenty years ago, it now had great arced rows of stone benches, with a handsome stage for which the piles of amplifiers and electronic gear offered the perfect paradox.

As Les McCann remarked to me during the early evening, while the sun set behind us in the Mediterranean, 'If you can't play in a setting like this, you'll never play anywhere.'

The attendance was about 1,500, less than half a house. 'Not too bad,' said Fishman, 'considering the lack of publicity.'

The other participants on that first night were the Billy Cobham Quartet and a five-piece combo led by the trumpeter Allan Vizzutti. The next night, the other half of the show was presented in an amphitheatre near Beit Shan: the Jon Hendricks Singers, the guitar team of Larry Coryell and Brian Keane, and Airto's group with Joe Farrell on tenor sax.

We seemed to be in a forest, miles from anywhere. While the stage lights were off, before soundcheck time, we were in pitch-black territory, stumbling around and trying to find the band bus. There was only one electric source for the entire area. How, I wondered, could anyone find this deserted spot and attend a jazz concert?

I was wrong. Around 8 p.m. a steady stream of cars arrived, carrying visitors from many kibbutzim. Soon the Roman edifice had accommodated more than 1,000 patrons, each paying 250 shekels – almost $9, which seemed like heavy dues in a country with 150% inflation.

Jon Hendricks said, 'Just you wait and see. This is a hip country; we're going to break it up!' Sure enough, he went through a triumphant set with the help of his wife Judith, his enchanting daughter Michelle, and Bob Gurland, whose amazingly lifelike vocal impression of a trumpet had some of the fans on their feet, laughing and shouting.

Coryell and Keane, playing acoustic guitars, proved that a thumping electronic beat is not a prerequisite for success. Airto, closing the show, drew such an intense reaction that the crowd refused to let him go. Somebody shouted 'Blues!' Airto and the others then eased into 'Blue Monk', which impelled me to take over from Kei Akagi at the piano. Soon several others felt the spirit; Jon Hendricks began ad libbing some blues, Keane brought back his guitar, and we had a fifteen-minute jam session that had the audience near hysteria.

Back in Tel Aviv, I met Michael Handelzalc, a theatre critic who also writes about jazz. He reminded me that jazz has a fairly long tradition in Israel, that Lionel Hampton was an early visitor on tour with his orchestra, and that Dizzy Gillespie, Stan Getz and Ella Fitzgerald also had made powerful impressions during their visits some years back. But now tastes, he said, were more contemporary.

'The young people here today are listening to Chick Corea,' he said. 'The bass players are trying to sound like Jaco Pastorius. To them, the swing-era sounds are just an unneeded reminder of something their parents listened to – or even their grandparents.'

Corea certanly had established himself as a symbol of what the Israeli musicians and fans found relevant and stimulating. After a solo piano tour here in 1980, he had made a big breakthrough the following year when he returned with Gary Burton, Paul Horn, Michael Brecker and Corea's vocalist wife, Gayle Moran.

Jerusalem was a principal setting for every musician on these earlier visits, and it was there that Fishman presented, for the first time, a concert in which all six groups took part. The scene was the Sultan's Pool, a vast hole in the ground, dating from the Islamic period (seventh century). Here we found no creature comforts; instead of seats one looked for an available patch of grass, or a stone somewhere up in the hills. The weather was cooler and less humid here, and the presentation took place before a wall-to-wall audience of some 7,500, mostly in their twenties, wearing jeans and T-shirts.

Jon Hendricks scored heavily with the Middle Eastern sound of 'Caravan'. Vizzutti worked hard and fulsomely on his electric gimmicks, but the real treat for this crowd was Les McCann. During 'Compared to What?', he had the audience responding as if he had been singing the lyrics in perfectly enunciated Hebrew. McCann's soprano sax soloist, Bobby Bryant Jr, set up his own wailing wall of sound. The set proved too short in terms of the crowd's preference, but the show already had run inordinately long.

The next evening being the Sabbath, no concert was scheduled, but during the afternoon we all were invited to a party at the handsome oceanside home of the US Ambassador, Sam Lewis. Other performers involved with the Israel Festival, of which the jazz festival was just one segment, were among Lewis's guests: the Twyla Tharp Dance Company, the American Repertory Theatre, and a *West Side Story* group. Typically, Hendricks engaged the Ambassador in a political discussion, while equally typically, Les McCann examined the considerable female pulchritude around the gardens.

Out on the lawn, with the Mediterranean as his backdrop, Lewis made an amiable speech and presented souvenirs to the leader of each group involved in the festival.

The elaborate hors d'oeuvres and canapes contrasted sharply with the hastily grabbed food we had been accustomed to backstage at the concerts. It also differed from the home-grown lunch I enjoyed during a visit earlier that day to the Givat Haim kibbutz. To make this day of contrasts complete, many of us spent the evening at the home of a member of the production staff, who served a succulent pork barbecue.

The next night there were three shows. McCann was back in Jerusalem, Coryell played at Ein Hod, an artists' colony, and the Hendrickses, whom I joined, worked in the ballroom of the Tel Aviv Hilton. The difference from all the previous audiences was quite striking: the age level was much higher, the clothes were elegant, the women glamorous.

The next night, Coryell and Keane took their guitars to Jaffa, another artists' colony, just south of Tel Aviv. With its indoor and outdoor stages, its many restaurants and sidewalk concessions, it reminded me of Los Angeles' Westwood Village or New York's Greenwich Village.

All 500 seats were taken in the intimate outdoor arena where the duo played a delightful mixture of jazz, pop, classical and flamenco works. I noticed how right Handelzalc had been about Israeli tastes: Coryell drew applause merely by mentioning Al Di Meola or Chick Corea as the composer of the tune about to be played.

During this fast-moving week there was not much time to gather evidence about the local jazz scene: however, it was clear that by no means all the music here had to be imported from the US. I was able to hear, either in person or on albums given me, several groups or individuals whose contributions have been of more than localized interest.

Platina, a combo that took part in the festival, had been working together for eleven years; its principal members were Roman Kunzman, a flute and saxophone virtuoso who had immigrated from the Soviet Union, and the drummer Aron Kaminsky, who in 1979 had been one of three Israeli musicians in Manhattan Transfer's regular back-up group. The others were Yaroslav Jacubovic, a saxophonist who, like Kunzman, soon returned to Israel; and most notably Yaron Gershovsky, a keyboard player and arranger who has been with the Transfer continuously for seven years. Gershovsky even played piano with the Count Basie orchestra when it recorded two numbers with the Transfer for its *Vocalese* album.

'I found things too easy in Israel,' Gershovsky told me when we met later in Los Angeles. 'I did arrangements, studio work, radio, TV – there's only one television channel, so if you're on it, you become a celebrity. So, wanting more of a challenge, I went to Berklee, studied there from 1974–7, then got into New York studio work, wrote some music for a movie, and later spent six very rewarding months with Pharoah Sanders.'

Israel at the time of my visit had no perceptible jazz-club activity; big bands also were scarce and worked sporadically. The seventeen-piece Tel Aviv Jazz Orchestra, playing in a warm-up concert during the festival, was led by the pianist David Kirovshei, who had spent a few less than rewarding years in New York playing mainly Israeli music.

My greatest surprise, a record I did not hear until after returning home, was an album by Nurit Galron. Though heard briefly as guest singer with the band led by Kirovshei, she was best represented on a couple of CBS-Israel albums. Her oddest achievement was a Hebrew-language version of Annie Ross's 'Twisted', with lyrics translated for her by an Israeli friend.

Because the country's native culture was remote from the roots of jazz, it seemed arguable that Israel was unlikely to generate any talent of lasting importance. But couldn't this same assumption have been made, not too many years ago, about Japan? If Tokyo could send us Toshiko Akiyoshi and the numerous other musicians now visiting or resident in the US, Tel Aviv could well respond some day in kind. Israel, a country smaller than New Jersey, may yet provide the world jazz community with a new sound that is larger than life.

In fact, everything I have heard during the past twenty years of extensive travel in Japan, West and East Europe, Latin America, the West Indies, Australia, Israel, Cuba, Canada and Mexico has reaffirmed my view that jazz is now firmly established as a global music. When I made my first steps into the native land of the music in the mid-1930s, the mere idea of such a development would have seemed laughable, since more than ninety-nine per cent of the reasonably competent performers and composers were Americans; of these the vast majority were black Americans.

The reason for the inexorable spread of jazz around the world stems primarily from its obvious emotional appeal to musicians outside the United States, and from the growth of communications, either through live visits or such sources as the Voice of America.

As I write, an internationally acclaimed Soviet jazz group, the Ganelin Trio, credited by some critics as having found a new direction for the avant garde, is making its first tour of the US. The clichés of yesteryear – that jazz is a unifying force, a means of bringing together men and women from vastly different cultures – today are vibrant, exciting realities to which I have been, and hope always to remain, an active and enthusiastic earwitness.

APPENDICES

MUSIC

It was my good fortune to learn empirically, through close contact with musicians I admired, the aesthetic and creative essentials in the craft of writing music.

According to whatever requirements presented themselves, I wrote blues, pop-style songs, instrumentals, music and lyrics. Sometimes I wrote music for other writers' words ('Mound Bayou' with Andy Razaf); now and then I tackled the more demanding task of fitting lyrics to someone else's preset melody ('Whisper Not' with Benny Golson). I also gained, as an arranger, just enough experience to understand a little about this most exacting art.

As I mentioned earlier, some of my work now seems to me to have been trivial or inept while others have given me cause for satisfaction, even pride. Like countless writers before me, I found that those I considered most successful did not necessarily reach the broadest audiences. The following examples represent various aspects and approaches to several kinds of material; among them are some of the best-known and most performed, along with a few that are virtually forgotten. I wrote the music to them all, and the lyrics unless there is an indication to the contrary.

The recordings are listed according to the American labels on which they were most recently issued. Because of frequent deletions and reissues, no attempt has been made to state which versions are currently available.

I REMEMBER BIRD: This was written in 1962 as an elegy for Charlie Parker, to be played on a record by Vi Redd (United Artists). Like the five pieces that follow it in this chapter, it is based on a twelve-bar framework; however, it does not follow the conventional

I-IV-V-I pattern. Instead, it starts on a I mi 7 and IV 7, goes through a descending pattern of alternating mi 7s and 7s, returning to the I mi 7 at bar 5, and at bar 9 moves to an A Flat 7 before landing on the more predictable II 7 (G 7).

Much of the success of this piece is due to a magnificent arrangement by Oliver Nelson. He wrote it for a date by my own *Encyclopedia of Jazz* All Stars, featuring Phil Woods on alto (Verve), then recorded it again under the name of Oliver Nelson's Orchestra in a live session (Impulse) with Frank Strozier replacing Woods. He later wrote a new chart for an LP by the Three Sounds and the Oliver Nelson Orchestra featuring Gene Harris at the piano (Blue Note). Other recordings: Phil Woods' European Rhythm Machine (MGM), Cannonball Adderley Quintet (Capitol), Buddy De Franco–Tommy Gumina Quartet (Mercury), Night Blooming Jazzmen featuring Ernie Watts (Mainstream), Sonny Stitt as the title tune of an LP (Catalyst), Louie Bellson Orchestra featuring Pete Christlieb, tenor sax (Project 3).

I REMEMBER BIRD

Though this is essentially an instrumental work, I did set lyrics to it; they have been sung by Bob Dorough and others, but have never been recorded to my knowledge.

TWELVE TONE BLUES: Some themes seem to develop spontaneously at the piano (or even in a seat on a plane); others require careful premeditation. 'Twelve Tone Blues' belongs in the latter category. In effect it is the result of an exercise I set for myself. The challenge was to use Schoenberg's twelve-tone row concept and apply it to the twelve-bar blues structure.

The first requirement was a series of twelve tones that managed, rhythmically, to swing, and melodically to make sense while lacking a tonal centre. Bars 1 and 2 seemed to have this quality. The line also had to be changeable in a way that could correspond with the I-IV-V-I blues pattern, in effect combining the atonality with a hint of a tonal base. The only way this seemed workable was by using double-augmented chords throughout.

As the melody and the suggested bass line show, this enabled me to use a retrograde inversion of the tone row for bars 3 and 4, but with the phrase altered rhythmically; to shift the row up a fourth, again with a slight variation of the 1-2 rhythm pattern; then, from the last beat of bar 6 through the first beat of 9, to elongate the notes while using the tone row in its original place; then an inversion of the row (third beat of 9 through end of 10) and finally, to repeat 1 and 2 but with the last four notes an octave higher. Oddly, the melody ends as if it were in E flat; however, it is played against an E flat + 7 − 5, aiming toward a repetition of the entire chorus.

Some of the soloists on the various recordings attempted to adhere to the augmented feel of the lines; others essentially played blues choruses.

This piece might never have seen daylight had it not been for Yusef Lateef; as I said, it was written simply as an exercise. One day Lateef, visiting my home for a blindfold test, noticed the lead sheet on the piano. 'What is that?' he asked, and on examining it, asked to take it with him and recorded it soon after (in his *Live at Pep's* LP). This encouraged me to put it to further use: Oliver Nelson arranged it for the *Encyclopedia of Jazz* All Stars, featuring Nat Adderley (Verve); I recorded it with the Buddy De Franco group that included Art Blakey, Victor Feldman, Lee Morgan and

Curtis Fuller (Vee Jay), and with the Night Blooming Jazzmen, including George Shearing (alias 'Phil Johnson'), Joe Pass, Lew Tabackin and Blue Mitchell, on Mainstream.

TWELVE TONE BLUES

BASS REFLEX: This blues in 5/4 seemed so startling in 1956 that Oscar Pettiford, who was to play a solo on it as part of my 'Hi Fi Suite', recorded by the Dick Hyman–Leonard Feather Orchestra (MGM), insisted on taking his part home to study it before the session. Thad Jones, Frank Wess and Kenny Clarke were also on the date; Hyman arranged it and played a solo. There had been no 5/4 jazz records before, and there were no others until Dave Brubeck recorded Paul Desmond's 'Take Five' three years later. Hyman re-recorded 'Bass Reflex', retitled 'Space Reflex', for an electronic album, with a wordless vocal by Mary Mayo (MGM). Lyrics were later added by Milton Raskin and under the title 'Love is a Word for the Blues' it was recorded by Ann Richards (Atco).

BASS REFLEX

Bass Reflex (from Hi-Fi Suite: MGM Records E 3494)   FEATHER

EVIL GAL BLUES (EVIL MAN BLUES): Written for a Hot Lips Page date in 1940, with a Teddy Bunn vocal (RCA), this was the biggest hit of Dinah Washington's first session when I rewrote the lyrics for her in 1943 (Mercury); she also recorded it live with the Lionel Hampton band in 1945 (Decca). Other versions: Etta Jones (Black & White), Albinia Jones (National), Aretha Franklin (Columbia). Considerably updated with new lyrics, it was recorded by Joe Williams with the Thad Jones/Mel Lewis Orchestra (United Artists). Other versions by Jimmy Witherspoon (Impulse), Linda Hopkins (Palo Alto), Johnny Otis with Margie Evans (Epic), and, as 'Evil Gal's Daughter Blues', Vi Redd (United Artists) and Joan Shaw, aka Salena Jones (MCA).

EVIL GAL BLUES

HOW BLUE CAN YOU GET?: Written in 1949 and first recorded by Johnny Moore and the Three Blazers (RCA), this song earned its success through several lucky accidents with which I had no involvement whatever. A 1951 version by Louis Jordan (now on MCA) caught the attention of Jordan's perennial admirer, B. B. King, who began using it in his act and recorded it in 1963; it was included in his *Live at the Regal* album, for MCA, and the audience reaction to the climactic punch line ('I gave you seven children, now you want to give them back') helped establish it permanently in his repertoire. He recorded it again on another live album, *Live at Cook Country Jail* (MCA) and sang it in a film, *Medicine Ball Caravan,* a soundtrack album of which yielded still a third version (Warner Brothers).

Another link in this chain was the decision by Duane Allman to include it in a tribute to B. B. King in his album *An Anthology* (Capricorn). This was reissued in 1986. Other recordings: title tune of Linda Hopkins' album (Palo Alto); Chubby Kemp, accompanied by Duke Ellington and others (Mercer); Howard Tate (Verve).

HOW BLUE CAN YOU GET?

YOU COULD HAVE HAD ME BABY: As with 'How Blue Can You Get?', Louis Jordan, who recorded this with a big band in 1952 (as 'You Didn't Want Me Baby'), started a chain reaction. Subsequent records were by Sugar Cane Harris (Epic), Esther Phillips (Kudu), Lou Rawls (MGM), Linda Hopkins (Palo Alto), Anita O'Day (GNP-Crescendo).

You Could Have Had Me Baby

You could have had me baby, you threw your chance away
You thought you had a raincheck but there ain't no game today
Well good morning, Daddy, what can I do for you?
I don't seem to recall that we had any rendezvous.

You remember one night Daddy, I was standing in the rain
You never asked me in, I didn't even complain
I was broke, wet, tired and hungry, but you threw me out the door
Now it's my turn to tell you . . . I can't use you any more

The last time I was with you, you were evil as you could be
My sister had big eyes for you . . . you had no eyes for me
You could have had me baby, too bad you need me now
'Cause I ain't about to take you, no time, no place, nohow!

I used to love you Daddy, but you played so hard to get
So I found me someone else who made you easy to forget
You could have had me baby, back when the time was right
Now you're starving for some loving . . . but I've lost my appetite.

You could have had me baby, in 1963
Now I'm older and I'm wiser and you don't look so good to me
You could have had me baby, way back in 1968
But I got news for you baby . . . you came around too late!

YOU COULD HAVE HAD ME BABY

BORN ON A FRIDAY: Originally known as 'Unlucky Woman', this was recorded in 1942 under that title by Pete Brown with Helen Humes (Decca) and Joe Marsala with Linda Keene (Black & White). Many years later Cleo Laine heard the Humes vocal, gave it the new name and recorded it as the title tune of an album (RCA), then taped a new version in a *Live at Carnegie Hall* LP (RCA). Also recorded by Linda Hopkins (Palo Alto). The song is best known through a film version by Lena Horne, who performed it, accompanied by Teddy Wilson's small band, in her first musical movie short, *Boogie Woogie Dream*, in 1942. The clip of her rendition has been used in several television documentaries.

BORN ON A FRIDAY

BABY GET LOST: Like many of my songs, this was written under a pseudonym, and except for Dinah Washington (whose original version in 1949 reached the No.1 slot in the *Billboard* Rhythm & Blues chart), none of the artists who recorded it knew of its true authorship – not even Billie Holiday, who recorded it for Decca. Others were Donna Hightower (Capitol), Leslie Scott (RCA), Nancy Harrow (Inner City).

The success of the Washington record amazed me, since the lyrics, though based on the then popular theme of male–female antagonism, were not among my best; nor was the arrangement backing Dinah. Significantly, though, the songs she continued singing until the end of her life were 'Evil Gal', Salty Papa' and 'Blowtop Blues'.

BABY GET LOST

BLITZEN: This was the final movement of an eight-part suite, 'Winter Sequence', which I composed for a 1954 album by the Ralph Burns–Leonard Feather Orchestra. It is included here as an example of a simple long-note melody made interesting by challenging chord changes, and by a counter-melody played almost entirely in eighth notes (C, D, F *et seq.*). The theme was introduced by French horn, with reeds playing the counter-melody. I wrote this with a specific soloist in mind, the trumpeter Joe Wilder; this was his first real opportunity to display his improvisational talent on a record. 'Blitzen' was also recorded in a Benny Carter arrangement by Louie Bellson's Orchestra, featuring Conte Candoli (Roulette).

JUMPING FOR JANE: With its rhythmic hesitations, grace notes, and two-eighth-note end to each eight-bar stanza, this is a typical product of the bebop era; however, I wrote it on an unusual chord pattern. Though in the key of F, it begins with two bars on B flat and two on A before proceeding to the more conventional G Mi 7 – C 7 – F. The Coleman Hawkins version (RCA) showed that these changes proved quite compatible for Hawkins, Chuck Wayne, J. J. Johnson, Fats Navarro, Budd Johnson (on alto) and Hank Jones. There was also a version by the Jones Boys, with Thad Jones, Frank Foster and Jimmy Jones (Everest). Jimmy Raney recorded it in Stockholm (Metronome). The tune was dedicated to Jane Feather.

JUMPING FOR JANE

SIGNING OFF: This melody was set to a lyric given me by Jessyca Russell. Later I added another chorus of lyrics designed for use as a closing song for radio programmes; part of this later lyric was included in a version by Ella Fitzgerald (Verve) that sublimated the song as only she could. Sarah Vaughan made the original version in 1944; it is no longer available. Other versions by Helen Merrill (MetroJazz); Johnny Otis with Barbara Morrison (Jazz World), George Shearing (Capitol), the Night Blooming Jazzmen (Mainstream), and a superb arrangement written and played by André Previn (Columbia).

SIGNING OFF

Words and Music by
LEONARD FEATHER
and JESSYCA RUSSELL

* Radio-T. V. lyric

FSC 265

I REMEMBER DUKE: Originally titled 'Romeo', this is one of the themes I wrote for the ill-fated Johnny Hodges 'Great Lovers Suite' series. Hodges's Verve recording has yet to be released. Roy Ayers recorded it as 'Romeo' (United Artists); the Louie Bellson Orchestra made a version under the title 'I Remember Duke', featuring Joe Romano on alto with an expertly crafted arrangement by Tommy Newsom. The descending pattern of minor 7s and 7s seemed well suited to Hodges' caressingly legato style, and the bridge, with its octave jumps played off against lower notes that moved up a half tone at a time from E to G, supplied a dramatic contrast. The Bellson version, recorded live at Ronnie Scott's in London, was issued only on English Pye.

I REMEMBER DUKE

MEET ME HALFWAY: Like 'I Remember Duke', this was recorded by Johnny Hodges (Verve, unissued); Bob Wilber, hearing the Hodges version of which I owned a tape, arranged it to feature himself on soprano sax with the World's Greatest Jazzband (World Jazz), under the title 'Lovers'. André Previn scored it for a string ensemble featuring his piano (Columbia); his then wife wrote a fine lyric entitled 'Meet Me Halfway', but the words have never been used. I believe that melodically and harmonically, with its unexpected shift from A flat in the first eight bars to A in the second, this is perhaps the best example of my ballad writing. Note the forty-bar construction: A-A-B-A-C.

MEET ME HALFWAY

MUSIC BY
LEONARD FEATHER

LYRIC BY
DORY PREVIN

MOUND BAYOU: Written during a weekend spent at the New Jersey home of Andy Razaf. The words, comprising a sixteen-bar verse and sixteen-bar chorus, were not designed to fit the blues form, but suggested a melancholy, nostalgic melody. The first recording was made in February 1942 by Henry Levine's orchestra with a vocal by

Linda Keene (RCA), but a week later I included it on my Pete Brown session featuring Helen Humes (Decca, now MCA). This became the best-known version. In 1960 it was recorded by Ernestine Anderson (Mercury). Andy and I wrote several other songs together, but none of them was ever recorded.

TOURING: US 1958 AND
EUROPE 1972

(I have only twice had the chance to see the United States from the viewpoint of the touring musician on a series of one-night stands. On both occasions I was the MC of a show entitled *Jazz for Moderns*, assembled by the Detroit-based promoter Ed Sarkesian. Both tours began in late October and ran for about three and a half weeks. In 1958 the show comprised Dave Brubeck's Quartet, the Maynard Ferguson Orchestra, the Sonny Rollins Trio and the Four Freshmen; in 1959 Brubeck and Ferguson encored, along with Lambert, Hendricks & Ross and the Chico Hamilton Quintet, with Eric Dolphy. Following are some observations made during the first tour.)

For twenty-four days the bus was our only constant home as I found myself on the road with a typical jazz concert tour of the day.

When a group of jazzmen appears in your city for a concert, you may wonder who and what brought them there; what they were doing last night or this morning, where they are headed for later tonight or early tomorrow; and, possibly, why they didn't live up to expectations in their performance.

The bus personnel varied slightly, as Brubeck, the Freshmen and others occasionally took a plane, but generally it was as follows:

The Backer: Ed Sarkesian, an amiable, honourable, nervous man who bought the talents and made deals with promoters in each city (in a couple of cities Sarkesian himself rented the hall and promoted the show).

The Booker: An absentee partner, Joe Glaser's Associated

Booking Corporation, which booked most of the artists and lined up the routes and dates.

The Artists: Brubeck's Quartet, the Ferguson band (Bill Chase, Jerry Tyree, Larry Moser, trumpets; Slide Hampton, Don Sebesky, trombones; Jimmy Ford, alto; Carmen Leggio, alto & tenor; Willie Maiden, tenor; John Lanni, baritone; Bob Dogan, piano; Jimmy Rowser, bass; Frank Dunlop, drums); Rollins' trio, and the Freshmen. Ferguson's wife, Flo, was on the bus during half the tour; one or two other wives or girlfriends were aboard briefly.

The Management: 'Honest John' Srabian, Sarkesian's partner, who sold the $1 souvenir programmes at each show; Mort Lewis, Brubeck's manager; and Rick Gibbons, who worked on stage lighting for the Freshmen.

The Driver: The tireless and invincible Joe Walus, of the Raritan Valley Bus Company of Metuchen, N.J.

Thus there were in the bus up to thirty passengers as well as three basses, two sets of drums, thousands of programmes, clothes, instruments etc. Let's just say we were as comfortable as the conditions would permit.

SATURDAY: The tour began yesterday as we took the bus from Columbus Circle in New York City to Symphony Hall in Boston. Tonight, at Smith College in Northampton, a panic: Ross Barbour of the Freshmen was taken ill, and the hospital refused to release him. 'Only the third time in ten years that this has happened to us,' said Freshman Bob Flanigan. The Smith College students, reputedly great Freshmen fans, were presumably consoled when Rollins, to kill time, played a number with the Ferguson band.

SUNDAY: We were booked tonight in Allentown, Pa., in something called Agricultural Hall, compared to which the Holland Tunnel would be a model of acoustical perfection; moreover, the condition of the piano was such that Dave Brubeck concentrated on numbers featuring Paul Desmond.

We were all delighted to get out of Allentown.

MONDAY: Yesterday I asked Gene Wright, Brubeck's bassist, if he was growing a beard. 'No,' he said. 'I just decided to let it grow until we do a lousy show.' Tonight, after the performance, he shaved.

THURSDAY: Now the real heavy travelling has begun. Instead of fifty to 100 miles a day, it's climbing towards 300 or 400. After Harrisburg, Pa., on Tuesday, we drove straight through to

Pittsburgh, arriving at 5 a.m. and spending the day there. A good hall, fine acoustics and a wildly enthusiastic sellout house made Pittsburgh a happy night. Then we left early this morning for the long haul to Toronto, which involved an almost endless delay at customs as we entered Canada; we barely made the theatre on time and arrived starved. Good promotion and big house, thanks to disc jockey Phil McKellar.

SATURDAY: Mad, mad, mad! An all-night bus trip from Toronto, giving us a few hours' grace in New York before the two shows at Carnegie Hall. After the second show ended about 2.30 a.m. we had three and a half hours in which to get home, sleep, get up, dress and be at Columbus Circle in time for the 6 a.m. departure for Virginia. This was too much for me; after oversleeping and missing the bus, I flew ahead, arriving twenty minutes before the weary musicians unloaded from the bus.

Today we played two colleges 150 miles apart geographically, but separated by a million miles in every other respect.

The audience at the first, trudging in from a football game, was noisy and restless. Many of the students brought in bottles or checked them at the door. The setting was a huge gymnasium in which, not provided with seats, the audience squatted on a floor strewn with rugs and blankets. Though it was all but impossible to be heard above the uproar, the performance earned a vociferous reaction.

After Rollins' opening stint, and the Brubeck set that followed, these two groups and I sped ahead on the bus to the second college date, while the Ferguson band and the Freshmen, completing the show, followed us an hour or two later in a specially chartered second bus, arriving as the second show was half over.

Before we began the second performance, which was at Virginia Polytechnic Institute, one musician remarked: 'Will this evening be like this afternoon, or do we have to play good?'

As it turned out, VPI was a model audience. We had a concert hall with first-class sound, and in contrast with the afternoon show, the students were a sober, quietly attentive crowd. Our faith in the future of America was restored.

WEDNESDAY: A ghostly camp follower on parts of this tour was Jim Crow. We ran into him several times in a few days, notably when seven of the thirty of us were unable to check in at the same hotel.

Yesterday, an hour out of Indianapolis, where we had played the night before, we stopped at a diner for breakfast. The waitress, after keeping Gene Wright and me waiting for a long time before taking our orders, finally gave Gene a sidelong glance and said, 'I'm sorry, but we can't serve *you*.'

Happily there was enough *esprit de corps* and sense of humour to take these incidents in our stride. When a soft-drink machine outside a St Louis diner failed to cough up a bottle, somebody cracked, 'Even the machines down here discriminate.'

There was a general laugh-it-up atmosphere during the long days on the bus, as if it were tacitly admitted that the one-nighter grind is tough and the only thing to do is pretend it isn't happening.

Motion pictures notwithstanding, there is no such thing as a jam session on a bus. The only time music even comes under general discussion is when somebody (usually Ferguson) reads some review of the show from a newspaper that has caught up with us, with sarcastic interpolations and changes in the script and with frequent reactions from the bus audience.

The conversational sparkplug of the bus is Willie Maiden. Gaunt, bearded, spectacled, an incessant and hilarious gabber, Maiden apparently is the world's foremost authority on beer and the liquor licensing laws of every state.

If Willie's personality is the most extrovert, his antithesis must be Sonny Rollins' bashful bassist Henry Grimes, who exchanged about ten words in the first twelve days and earned himself the nickname Loudmouth.

The personalities of the others slowly came into focus en route. Various senses of humour were at play.

Ferguson based much of his kidding on a pseudo-stern-leader role; Joe Morello joked about his poor vision; Paul Desmond's is the quieter, more intellectual brand of humour. Desmond, who spent most of his time playing chess with Morello or Scrabble with me, is tough to beat at either. Gene Wright was the unofficial pinochle king of the bus. As in record reviews or items in a Blindfold Test, ratings from one to five stars were accorded to everything from a bowl of soup to a men's room.

The Four Freshmen broke it up at 2 a.m. one night on the bus by unveiling their Homer-and-Jethro-like versions of such songs as 'Angel Eyes' and 'The Nearness of You', which they reduced to three chords apiece, with extra beats thrown in here and there for bad measure.

There was a real camaraderie, strong enough to keep everybody's spirits at a high level. As Ferguson said one day, 'We've got to get some hate going around here. There isn't enough good, healthy hate around this bus.'

THURSDAY: To relieve the monotony of a tour of this kind, musicians will do just about anything for a laugh, no matter how trivial. Typical was the scene when, on our way to Iowa City, we stopped off for lunch at a town called Keokuk, Iowa.

Bob Dogan, Ferguson's new pianist, is a tall, handsome, blond fellow who looks vaguely like Van Cliburn. Hearing that Cliburn had been appearing in the area, some of us planned a man-in-the street interview, with Dogan as 'Cliburn'. I took along my pocket tape recorder, and as I stood on a street corner, Rick Gibbons, microphone in hand, introduced me, and I began my interview with 'Cliburn'.

While I asked such questions as 'Is your real name Sam van Cliburn or Max van Cliburn?' or 'How does Moscow compare with Keokuk?' a group of teenagers surrounded us. Soon local business-men, eager to get publicity, were introducing themselves, and Paul Desmond had climbed up a fire escape to take photographs while Willie Maiden brushed back the crowds with 'Gangway! This is a photographer from *Life* magazine!'

After my interview with 'Cliburn' ended, Flo and Maynard Ferguson walked up and were introduced as singer Lizzie Schwartz and her manager. Lizzie graciously acceded to requests for her autograph.

SUNDAY: Poor Ed Sarkesian's nerves were stretched to the breaking point tonight. The Freshmen and Brubeck, deciding to save time by flying to Detroit from Chicago, got all the way to Detroit, circled around the airport for ninety minutes in the fog, then turned back. Our concert was due to start 8.20 p.m. At 5.10, Brubeck called to tell us he was back in Chicago!

Starting the concert a half-hour late, we stretched it every conceivable way. Ferguson brought things out of the book that hadn't been heard on the whole tour. He doubled not only on valve trombone but also on baritone horn. Jimmy Ford sang. After the intermission, Maynard went on again and, exhausted, ceded to a Brubeckless quartet, which I introduced as the Paul Desmond trio. They had been onstage some ten minutes when Dave strode on in the middle of a tune, glasses missing, and dressed in rumpled travelling clothes, and started playing. ('Paul called out to me that they were on the release,' he told me later, 'but he didn't say the release of what.')

This happened at 11.25 p.m.; by the time the Freshmen had added their stint, the concert ran almost to 12.45 a.m., yet very few patrons left, and none asked for refunds.

MONDAY: Our only day off during the entire twenty-four, and this by accident, because a booking was cancelled. Since it happened to be the birthday of Sarkesian's partner, Srabian, we devoted much of the day to a celebration in his house. Preparing to leave the party, Carmen Leggio almost cut off his right forefinger closing a car door and was rushed to a hospital. How were we going to make out with a three-piece sax section the next night? You can't make replacements in the middle of a road tour.

TUESDAY: A brutally long trip from Detroit to Rochester, N.Y. We arrived at 8 p.m. – too late to eat, check into a hotel, or do anything but look for current outlets for our electric shavers. The concert went on at 8.28 p.m. Somehow Leggio managed to get his bandaged finger to do most of the work required of it.

WEDNESDAY: Srabian this morning kiddingly issued the following announcement: 'During the last three days of this tour, a psychiatrist will be on the bus for reorientation.'

SATURDAY: After an all-night bus trip from Cleveland, we arrived tonight in Buffalo, N.Y., and were happy to find a beautiful, acoustically perfect hall, Kleinhans Auditorium. Splendid promotion by Joe Rico assured two big houses. Everybody played a great show.

A curious thing through the tour was the similarity of audience reactions. All the artists played much the same tunes every night and got almost consistently big hands. Rollins' best was the frantic-tempoed 'After You've Gone'. Brubeck gassed them with extracts from the *Impressions of Eurasia* album, with the Morello solo used as a finale; Ferguson had two brilliant Slide Hampton arrangements, 'My Man Chopin' and 'Fugue', both of which drew tremendous hands. And the Freshmen, of course, broke it up with Ross Barbour's falsetto 'Sweet Lorraine' and with their biggest record hits, 'Day by Day' and 'It's a Blue World'.

SUNDAY: This was parting-is-such-sweet-sorrow day as we closed the tour with a matinee and evening show in Philadelphia. All the musicians were running around backstage asking each other to autograph copies of the souvenir programme. A genuine air of regret enveloped us as we prepared for the trip back to Columbus Circle.

All of us learned some lessons from the experience of this tour. A few of them are incorporated in the constructively meant suggestions that follow.

First, there must be much earlier planning of jazz tours. Ours was booked so late that there was an absurd waste of bus mileage and of our physical energies in the way it was routed. For example, Detroit and Toledo are only fifty-eight miles apart, yet between these two dates we played Rochester, N.Y., which is 300 or 400 miles from both! Similarly the Toledo and Cleveland dates, instead of being played consecutively, were separated by a booking in Louisville, Ky. No wonder agents are accused of routing bookings by throwing darts at the map.

Earlier planning and better routing could have done much to improve this tour; would have saved the wear and tear that affected even Ferguson's granite lip, which could not be expected to hold up under such conditions; would have enabled everybody to be in good enough physical shape to feel like *wanting* to play instead of *having* to, and would have enabled the leaders, and me, to arrive in some towns early enough to appear on disc-jockey shows and thus help promotion.

Second, a questionnaire should be sent to every musician months in advance of the tour to determine how much he is willing to spend on hotels. Reservations then should be made in advance for everybody so they won't arrive in a town with no idea of where to stay, as we did so often.

Third, as the sensitive Sarkesian pointed out, the South must be eliminated from future tours.

Fourth, with a little consultation among the leaders of the various groups, it would be possible to work out a few collaborations – in our case between Ferguson's band, say, and Brubeck or Desmond or Rollins – so that the show could consist not simply of four acts, one right after the other, but of a carefully integrated production.

Fifth, it would be better not to play a town at all than to play in a hall where the sound bounces back so hard that you can return the next night and hear the same show still reverberating. Better, too, to skip a date than assign it to the type of local promoter who figures a jazz show should be handled along the same lines as Fats Domino, whom he played last week.

Six, I'm sure all the artists would agree to work for slightly less, or prorate their salaries, if they could have one day off each week to catch their breath. Our thirty shows in twenty-four days represented a hardship that could and should be avoided.

Aside from these points, I have only one suggestion, and I am sure it will meet the approval of any musician who ever has made a jazz tour: buses should be equipped with DC-7 engines and should have a cruising speed of 400 m.p.h.

(Postscript: In close to thirty years since this tour, there has been only one change for the better: segregation was outlawed at the federal level more than twenty years ago. On the other hand, though they can now stay in the same hotels and eat in the same restaurants, black and white musicians alike find it impossible to go on the road, because of the high cost of accommodations and food; in fact, because the promoters found that bus travel is impractical and plane fares are unmanageably high, tours of this kind have long since been abandoned in the US.)

WEIN'S WORLD

The expansion of George Wein's festival promotions was in full swing by the early 1960s. Though he staged sixteen annual festivals at Newport between 1954 and 1971, he had expanded into other areas: French Lick, Indiana, New Orleans and a regular summer touring group that visited eight or more cities. Beginning in 1964 he had a European Newport Festival in the autumn that presented concerts in every major European country except the USSR.

I attended parts of these tours in 1967 and 1968. In late October 1972 Jane and I took off on a journey that offered a full picture of the travelling jazz life on the Continent. What follows is rewritten from an account I wrote for *Down Beat* at that time.

DRAMATIS PERSONAE

The Cannonball Adderley Quintet, with Nat Adderley, George Duke, Roy McCurdy, Walter Booker.

The Dave Brubeck Quintet with Paul Desmond, Gerry Mulligan, Alan Dawson, Jack Six.

The Giants of Jazz: Dizzy Gillespie, Sonny Stitt, Kai Winding, Thelonious Monk, Art Blakey, Al McKibbon.

Elvin Jones' quartet with Dave Liebman, Steve Grossman, Gene Perla.

Charles Mingus Quintet with Joe Gardner, Hamiet Bluiett, John Foster, Roy Brooks; guest soloist, Cat Anderson.

Jimmy Smith Jam Session with Clark Terry, Art Farmer, James Moody, Illinois Jacquet, Kenny Burrell, Roy Haynes.

George Wein; his aide, Bob Jones; Harriet Choice, a reporter from Chicago; sundry road managers, local promoters, critics, disc jockeys, and a scattering of orchestra wives.

The logistics and transportation problems were staggering. The Brubeck and Smith groups had started in Australia, New Zealand and Japan before the European venture got under way. The Wein peregrinations had grown both in the number of groups used and in the territories: since 1971 Iron Curtain countries had been on the itinerary.

No two combos had the same route, though sometimes two or more would be in the same city on the same day or successive days. A few cities hired all six groups and spread them over a three-day festival period.

The Adderley and Smith units kicked off the celebrations on 18 October as part of a five-day Polish jamboree. European musicians were added to some shows; the Lungstrem big band from Moscow and Kurt Edelhagen's orchestra helped induce sold-out houses every night.

Jan Byrczek of the European Jazz Federation said, 'It is encouraging to observe how young the audiences are. Kids who used to go exclusively for rock now admire all kinds of jazz. Cultural recognition is expanding in many countries: Graz, Austria has a jazz school, supported by the local government, along the lines of Berklee in Boston.'

Byrczek was then editor in chief of *Jazz Forum*, the organ of the International Jazz Federation, which published, then as now, English and Polish editions, bi-monthly, served by correspondents around the world.

SATURDAY, 28 OCTOBER: The Newport tour had been under way ten days when I joined it in London, where the Giants of Jazz were playing at the Odeon in Hammersmith. George Wein, though not travelling with the tour, was within reach for the duration, in London or Paris, available for trouble-shooting. Wein was his perennial, indomitably optimistic self. 'Rotterdam is a sensation. We're sold out for the entire weekend – it's the greatest ever. Paris was disappointing, and so is London, but we'll bounce back next year with some new talent.'

Robert Paterson, Wein's co-promoter on the London dates, struck a note as gloomy as Wein's was cheerful. 'Jazz is dying. The more fanatic fans came all the way from Scotland and Ireland, but there aren't enough of them. It's an expensive hobby for me. Why should I use my profits from Nana Mouskouri and Shirley Bassey to subsidize it?

'Cannonball and Mingus got big notices. Brubeck is a darling. The Giants are doing pretty good business this evening, but disappointing when you consider it was fifty per cent better last year. Jimmy Smith had the nerve to tell the audience: "We're lowering ourselves to play here at the Odeon. Last time we played at the Festival Hall." I never want to see him again.'

According to Paterson, the BBC was then putting its jazz in Siberia-type time slots. One radio reporter, airing between 1 and 2 a.m., expressed wonderment at the apparent absence from the concerts of so many fans who had been complaining about the lack of live jazz.

Whatever the facts, the music at the Odeon showed that the Giants had not recovered from their jet lag. After one-night stands in Brussels, Sheffield, Paris and a last-minute arrival here, they put on a lacklustre show, the only sub-par one I was to hear throughout my travels.

SUNDAY, 29 OCTOBER: Wein tells me the concerts in Bucharest, set for next Wednesday and Thursday, are cancelled for reasons that seem to be wrapped in mystery. The explanation from Bucharest officials (this was to have been a bi-governmental subsidized venture) was that the hall had become unavailable. So the musicians will all have an unexpected day off.

MONDAY, 30 OCTOBER: Flew to Budapest, where the Giants and the Elvin Jones group had checked in at the spacious Intercontinental Hotel. We had rooms overlooking the Danube, but were dismayed to find that the waltz-famed waters have long since turned grey. Beyond the bridges in Buda we could see the mountains where, with my wife and Harriet Choice of the *Chicago Tribune*, we went on a sightseeing tour the next morning.

Imre Kiss, in charge of jazz and State Radio for six years, told me of the slow but sure upsurge in interest. 'When I began we had a one-hour record programme a week. Currently we have live performances weekly for an hour or two, also an official Hungarian radio jazz club that holds a monthly concert.

'The Albareggio Jazz Festival, organized by the Hungarian Radio, is held in Szekesfehervar, a town of 80,000. Musicians from Budapest make the pilgrimage there every year, and the concerts are always sold out. At the last one we had the Dutch Swing College Band, a group from Czechoslovakia, a big radio band from Warsaw – the big band sound is popular. We also had Keith Jarrett and Attila Zoller with a quartet.

'Avant-garde and free jazz is popular with the young people, but there aren't enough of them to fill a big room.'

The concerts at the 2,200-capacity Erkel State Theatre showed that Elvin's quartet was not too far-out for the Hungarians. Some of their less abstract works were well received: David Liebman's lyrical flute on 'Yesterdays' and 'A Time for Love' and the flute–soprano blend of Liebman and Steve Grossman. A march number, written by Elvin in honour of his wife Keiko, brought that special brand of heavy unison applause in which some of the European audiences like to indulge.

Elvin's sidemen are the youngsters among Wein's thirty-three emissaries: Grossman is twenty-one, Liebman twenty-five and Gene Perla thirty-two. When I asked Perla how he was adjusting to the rugged schedule, with its daily changes of language, money and hotels, he said: 'It beats going to engineering school – and, before that, pumping gas.'

The Giants are almost a generation older than Elvin's colleagues, but their spirit of enthusiasm and the reception accorded them differed not at all. Everyone shone on Dizzy's 'Blue 'n' Boogie', but Sonny Stitt stole the evening with his alto on 'I Can't Get Started' – despite the fact that his horns had been stepped on and damaged during the Paris concert.

TUESDAY, 31 OCTOBER: Cannonball, in his first appearance in this country, left the audience numb with excitement. With the State TV cameras rolling onstage, George Duke and the rhythm section got the show under way with some inspired vamping. The quintet was in estimable form playing Joe Sample's 'Dr Honoris Causa'. An extended 'Autumn Leaves' offered suave bowing opportunities to Walter Booker, with sensitive muted work by Nat and an unpredictable range of moods, from free jazz to ballad to mambo. Cannon himself played superbly; Nat crashed through the language barrier with his blues singing.

An unaccompanied, improvised concerto, on which Duke

alternated between acoustic and electric piano, was announced straight-faced by Cannonball. 'There'll be no horns, no bass, no drums; you will now be exposed to the sound of George Duke playing with himself.' Nobody seemed to get it.

At the end of a wildly acclaimed set, Cannon was awarded a kiss on each cheek, and a floral bouquet from a fetching Hungarian brunette – a courtesy accorded to each leader.

The slow, stately, evocative grandeur of a Jimmy Smith solo provoked one fan to comment: 'This man is a tiger. The Hungarian artists are mice.' The tiger began his jam session with 'Walkin' ' and ended it with a Latin blues. The two were separated by a long medley, mostly ballads, by Burrell, Jacquet, Terry, Moody, and most notably Farmer, on an 'Ill Wind' that blew everyone some good.

Backstage, it was Jacquet's fiftieth birthday – celebration time – starting officially at midnight; but there had been a champagne party on the Budapest-bound plane and, as Moody pointed out, 'We've been celebrating his birthday ever since Australia.'

WEDNESDAY, 1 NOVEMBER: An example of the transportation pressures that can affect musicians' nerves (and in some cases their performances) was our trip from Budapest to Berlin. On paper it was a two-hour flight, but from door to door it took nine hours. First, a two-hour wait at Budapest airport, fogged in. Then, during the prop-plane flight, we learned that we were headed for East Berlin airport. At that dismal outpost (in stark contrast with West Berlin airport, which is efficient, large and close to midtown) the Adderley group, the Smith sidemen and the rest of us were delayed by slow customs clearance, then by waiting for a limousine to take us across town, thirdly by an East German petty bureaucrat at the checkpoint, who seemed to take forever, walking through the bus, checking each passport photo against its owner. Finally a briefer stop at the West German checkpoint, then clear across town to the Hotel Schweitzerhof.

Luckily, the Adderley and Smith groups had no concert that night, but we all missed a chance to catch what must have been an interesting performance by British avant-gardists that launched this year's five-day-long 'Berliner Jazztage' (Berlin Jazz Days) at the jauntily mod Philharmonic Hall. The Jazztage had become an institution, thanks to the tireless efforts of Joe Berendt, but the noted German entrepreneur/critic/world traveller was absent, hospitalized after a nervous collapse following on the heels of an article in a national magazine, *Spiegel*, attacking him for allegedly playing angles and bad-mouthing the festival.

Whatever the facts, Berendt annually since 1964 had mounted a series of festivals that were notable for artistic originality and for the efficiency with which details were carried out. The piano workshops in 1965 and 1969, the violin summit in 1971, the history of soul in 1968, a guitar workshop which I saw personally in 1967, even a tap-dance festival in 1966, were all Berendt brainchildren.

In his absence George Gruntz, a fine pianist and organizer, took over the artistic direction. He has been in charge of it ever since.

In the hotel restaurant I was astonished to run into Eubie and Marian Blake.

'I thought you didn't fly, Eubie,' I said.

'I don't. Took a boat on an eight-day sailing to Genoa, then got here by train. I haven't been to Europe since 1924, and you know something? I kind of missed it.' (As it turned out, Eubie subsequently took his very first plane trip, from New York to Buffalo, in May 1973, at the age of ninety.)

In Berlin, Eubie stayed at the restaurant until long after midnight, chatting with old and new friends, until I had to excuse myself. I can't keep up with these energetic youngsters. After telexing a story to the *Los Angeles Times*, I got to bed at 2 a.m. after a day that seemed to have lasted forty-eight hours.

MONDAY, 6 NOVEMBER: The dates in Munich and Vienna went off reasonably well, though there seems to have been an ongoing problem with Jimmy Smith. He is unhappy with the organ provided for him in just about every city, and in Vienna wound up playing his whole set on piano. Aside from this, there is obvious resentment among certain musicians working under his nominal leadership, who are respected leaders themselves, and who are not too happy with his repertoire, which consists largely of endless variations on the blues, plus the ballad medley. In fact, things became so tense that George Wein had decided to send for Lola, Jimmy's lady, to fly over and act as troubleshooter. After her arrival things seemed to calm down.

When we checked in at the hotel La Fenice in Venice I found a telegram waiting for us: 'Look forward to joining you there tonight. Hold a seat for me and give my regards to Dizzy. Signed Romano.' That was Romano Mussolini, whose late father was somewhat better known than Romano, and who himself had a checkered career as a jazz pianist, partly because he was reluctant to appear in public for many years after the end of the war. Romano had visited Los Angeles for an all-Italian concert a year or two earlier, and had spent a pleasant evening at our house. Though not the greatest pianist around (he was clearly Oscar Peterson-influenced, however), we found him amiable and completely wrapped up in music.

Mussolini did indeed show up in time to join us at the ornate, almost 200-year-old Teatro La Fenice, with its several mezzanines and beautiful decor. The concert was by the Giants, who are getting along reasonably well despite the fact that Thelonious Monk is not the easiest person in the world with whom to communicate.

WEDNESDAY, 8 NOVEMBER: We had trouble getting out of Venice, since the heavy fog prevented us from taking off on the flight to Belgrade. Romano had a suggestion for Jane and me: 'Why don't you just jump into my car? We can drive to Rome, you can catch a plane from there to Belgrade.' Not wanting to wait around any longer in fog-bound Venice, we agreed, and the four of us (Mussolini had his girlfriend along) somehow managed to squeeze our baggage into his smallish car.

The journey to Rome, which started out pleasantly enough, almost turned into a nightmare. Romano had no respect for whatever speed-limit laws may have existed; we seemed to be doing close to 200 kilometres an hour most of the way.

When we finally hit the outskirts of Rome it occurred to us that we had no hotel reservation. It was by now very late at night, and the first hotel we tried was full. So was the second. Tirelessly and without any show of impatience, Romano took us to a third, where we were finally able to check in, wash, then rejoin Romano at a disco owned by his girlfriend.

The first person I ran into there was Tony Scott. We had known him in New York during the 1950s as a respected and handsome young clarinettist, but he had become disillusioned, and for many years had been a world traveller. He had put on a tremendous amount of weight, was now totally bald, and we had been sitting together only a couple of minutes when he begun one of his typical tirades, putting down some of his old American associates.

We left the disco and were taken around on a brief tour of the city by Romano, who seemed determined to act as friend, escort and tour guide. It was somewhat eerie to be in his company as we would drive into a large piazza and he would point to a balcony with some remark such as: 'That is where my father used to make his speeches.' This was the closest we came to anything political.

Romano was very apologetic about not being able to drive us to the airport the next morning, but his quartet, which included Tony Scott, had a gig, playing at a high school.

We were greeted early Wednesday by huge headlines in the papers with the shocking but not unexpected news that Richard M. Nixon had been re-elected by a landslide.

FRIDAY, 10 NOVEMBER: We did succeed in making our way from Rome by plane to Belgrade, touching down at Dubrovnik on the way. The Belgrade concert at the Dom Sindikata went well, and brought together most of the groups. We ran into a couple of old friends, among them Ed Thigpen, who had recently left the United States to take up residence in Copenhagen.

From Belgrade we flew to London and thence to New York and Los Angeles, a heavier flying schedule than either of us would have wished. In fact, in retrospect, I don't envy any of the participants in tours such as this. For George Wein they represent a tremendous responsibility in the juggling of dates, logistics and quite a few artistic temperaments. For the musicians, the almost total inability to see anything of a city except the airport, the hotel and the concert hall was a frequent source of frustration. In fact, for Jane and me the pleasantest day of all was our visit to Vienna, where Art Farmer lives, and where we were able to do a little sight-seeing, and share some Sachertorte with him and his attractive Viennese wife Mechtilde.

Postscript: Jane and I decided that this would be our last moving jazz festival for a long, long time. As it turned out, in 1973 we attended the non-moving Onda Nueva Festival in Caracas, Venezuela's supposed answer to Brazil's bossa nova (but with a 5/4 metre); I made my first and only visit to the Montreux Festival in July, finding the concerts too long, lasting far too late into the night, and too strongly dominated by the control of various record companies, one of which seemed to be in charge of a concert each night. I was also at Concord (East of San Francisco) for an agreeable mainstream festival there in which Carl Jefferson of Concord Jazz Records was a key organizer; and, as usual, there was Monterey in September. But the real excitement was to come a year later when we would make our visit to the first in a series of jazz festivals in Nice and, even more auspiciously, would sail on the first jazz festival cruises.

A YEAR IN THE LIFE

1946

Living at 1 Sheridan Square, New York 14 (over Cafe Society)

2 JAN. Recorded Pete Johnson with Etta Jones for National

3 JAN. Recorded Hot Lips Page for Continental

5 JAN. Broadcast with Woody Herman; interviewed P. Candoli

10, 14 JAN. Recorded *Esquire* All Stars for RCA (Ellington, Armstrong, Strayhorn, Hodges, Byas, Norvo, Hamilton *et al*)

16 JAN. *Esquire* All Stars Concert from ABC radio studio: Ellington, Herman Orchestras, King Cole Trio

18 JAN. Recorded Hot Lips Page for Continental

19 JAN. Weekly broadcast with Woody Herman

21 JAN. Met Igor Stravinsky at Herman rehearsal

21 JAN. Jane, Linda Keene to Blue Angel to hear Mildred Bailey

23 JAN. Three Deuces, Downbeat with Steve Sholes

25 JAN. Broadcast with Herman; interviewed Red Norvo

26–31 JAN. Minneapolis with Jane to visit her family

1 FEB. Herman; interviewed Chubby Jackson

4 FEB. Count Basie recorded 'Lazy Lady Blues'

7 FEB. Herman recorded 'Panacea'

8 FEB. Dinner with Dizzy G., Max Roach

18 FEB. Recorded Edmond Hall for Continental

19 FEB. Recorded Kirby Walker for De Luxe

21 FEB. Recorded Clyde Bernhardt for Musicraft

22 FEB. Recorded Dizzy Gillespie for RCA (Byas, Milt Jackson, Al Haig, Ray Brown, Bill de Arango, J. C. Heard)

25 FEB. Recorded Mary Lou Williams for Continental (Margie Hyams, Mary Osborne)

1 MAR. Broadcast with Herman; dinner with Bob Thiele

3 MAR. Played at Kelly's for Linda Keene

10 MAR. With Mary Osborne, Allen Eager to Cafe Society Downtown

12 MAR. To Boston to hear Sabby Lewis band

15 MAR. New York: Recorded Sabby Lewis for Continental

18 MAR. Recorded Mercer Ellington for Aladdin

20 MAR. Recorded J. C. Heard Sextet for Continental

25 MAR. Woody Herman concert at Carnegie Hall

26 MAR. ASCAP banquet

10 APR. Ethel Waters here to discuss session

13 APR. Dizzy G. Town Hall concert

19 APR. Recorded Ethel Waters for Continental

22 APR. To Miami Beach with Jane – vacation

28 APR. New York: WABC broadcast, accompanying Louis Armstrong singing 'Long Long Journey'

29 APR. Back to Miami Beach; home 15 May

17 MAY. Basie at Apollo

20 MAY. Charlie Barnet recorded 'Lonesome as the Night is Long'

27 MAY. Jazz at the Philharmonic, Carnegie Hall

30 MAY. Apollo (Barnet), Downbeat (Billie Holiday), Three Deuces, Spotlite

4 JUNE. Evening with John Hammond

5 JUNE. Apollo (Ella F., Willie Bryant)

11 JUNE. Recorded Etta Jones for RCA

18 JUNE. Helen Oakley to Spotlite, Three Deuces

5 JULY. Final broadcast in W. Herman series

5 JULY. Weekend with Andy and Jean Razaf in Englewood, N. J.

14 JULY. Weekly radio show on WNEW; Ch. Barnet, guest

24 JULY. Recorded Mary Lou Williams Girl Stars Quintet for RCA

1 AUG. Helen Oakley to Aquarium (Basie), Kelly's Stable (Pete Brown)

2 AUG. Remo Palmiers here and to Spotlite (Roy Eldridge)

14 AUG. Party for Peggy Lee & Dave Barbour; 53 people

22 AUG. Left NY; arr. Los Angeles 3 a.m.

24 AUG. Lighthouse with Arv Garrison, Vivien Garry

26 AUG. Ellington record session

28 AUG. Dinner at Lena Horne's

2 SEP. To Boyd Raeburn broadcast and to Billy Berg's (Erroll Garner)

3 SEP. Ellington session: 'Esquire Swank', 'Midriff' etc.

5 SEP. Recorded Vivien Garry Quintet, morning, for RCA; André Previn, afternoon, for RCA

6 SEP. Recorded Louis Armstrong for RCA (sat in on own two blues numbers)

7 SEP. Recorded Leo Watson for Signature

8 SEP. Denver

9 SEP. Chicago

11 SEP. NY

13 SEP. Birthday: Jane and her mother, Tody, to Copacabana, Three Deuces, Downbeat, Kelly's Stable

23 SEP. Coleman Hawkins to dinner

3 OCT. Ellington at Aquarium

4 OCT. Sweethearts of Rhythm at Apollo

7 OCT. Recorded Mary Lou Williams Trio for RCA

8 OCT. Recorded Beryl Booker Trio for RCA

14 OCT. Recorded Sweethearts of Rhythm for RCA

31 OCT. Broadcast on: 'Author Meets the Critics' – *Really the Blues*, discussion with the author, Mezz Mezzrow

4 NOV. Mary Lou's for dinner

12 NOV. *Down Beat*: Billie Holiday

20 NOV. Mae and Mezz Mezzrow to Eddie Condon's

21 NOV. Susie and Brick Fleagle, Linda Keene, Django Reinhardt, Chubby Jackson, Allen Eager here

22 NOV. Lionel Hampton Orch., at Aquarium

23 NOV. Ellington concert Carnegie Hall

28 NOV. Thanksgiving dinner at Fleagles'

30 NOV. Recorded Wynonie Harris for Aladdin

4 DEC. Recorded *Esquire* All Stars for RCA (Shavers, Clayton, Hawkins, J. J. Johnson, Carney, T. Wilson, J. Collins, Chubby Jackson, Shadow Wilson)

10 DEC. To Camden, N. J. (RCA officies)

16 DEC. Django Reinhardt at Cafe Society Uptown

18 DEC. Leave NY for Minneapolis, home 26 Dec.

28 DEC. Town Hall concert

30 DEC. Shearing here

31 DEC. Newark: repeat of Town Hall concert with Mary Lou, Ch. Ventura *et al*

Blindfold test subjects in *Metronome*: Sept.: Mary Lou Williams; Oct.: Mezz Mezzrow; Nov.: Coleman Hawkins; Dec.: Dave Tough

CODA

Looking back over more than a half-century of involvement with jazz, I realize that no other art form has ever undergone such drastic changes or made such profoundly significant advances in a relatively short time span.

When the music first came to my attention, there was no difficulty in identifying it, since it took only two or three forms. Big-band jazz was an orchestral form that left room for improvisation; solo or small-group jazz was for the most part spontaneous, a theme-and-variations form in which the participants often improvised collectively on a pop song or jazz standard. These guidelines applied both to all-black and all-white groups; for a long time, except for record sessions, there were no others. The few exceptions – Teddy Wilson and Lionel Hampton with Goodman, Billie Holiday with Shaw – came later in the decade.

During the first years of my participation jazz was played only in nightclubs, dance halls or hotel rooms. Concerts were a rarity and festivals non-existent. Media coverage was minimal; the press all but ignored it, and there were perhaps three or four people in the world who made their living writing about jazz. Even John Hammond was not a full-time writer, devoting himself primarily to producing records. Robert Goffin was involved in many other areas; Charles Delaunay and Hugues Panassié were writing, running the Hot Club de France, and later had their Swing Records company.

The picture today is vastly different. The number of jazz critics, historians, journalists and/or reporters is somewhere in the thousands, if one includes those who write part-time; even the full-timers by now are well into the hundreds. More significantly, the approach to the music began to become more serious and scholarly with the emergence during the 1950s of such writers as Nat Hentoff, Whitney Balliett and, a little later, such musician-writers as Gunther Schuller.

That jazz now enjoys this tremendous volume of press coverage, that there are now hundreds of books dealing either with the art form as a whole or with particular artists or phases, does not connote the existence of any unanimity of opinion. We are, in fact, poised today on what might be called the dilemma of our horns.

The jazz community is sharply divided into three areas. There are the merchants, the observers and the musicians. Some men and women overlap into two or all three areas, but for the most part they can be defined as follows:

The merchants are the essentially money-minded figures who own record companies or produce albums. They are also in charge of the trade publications responsible for the listings of best-selling jazz albums. Reading a typical list, one begins to wonder whether the term has any real meaning at all in today's commercialized market. Among the best-sellers are funk bands led by, say, Roy Ayers, George Howard or even the current Miles Davis; pop vocal and instrumental groups or soloists such as Spyro Gyra, Joe Sample, Earl Klugh, Sadao Watanabe, and the Nigerian singer Sade. There are also the quasi-classical, impressionistic sounds of George Winston, whose music has started a whole new idiom that the merchants choose to classify as jazz or New Age.

The critics look at these lists in amazement, since to most of them, anywhere from half to ninety per cent of the records listed do not qualify as jazz. The artists will be given short shrift in jazz history books if they are mentioned at all.

This is not to imply that the merchants are entirely ignorant or the critics always correct. The jazz world is now populated by a substantial body of writers who were obliged to learn about the music's history backwards. Perhaps the sounds came to their attention through one of the electronic funk bands, after which they began to investigate Wynton Marsalis, then Sun Ra, then John Coltrane, then Lester Young, then Coleman Hawkins, finally making their literary romp through Harlem and 52nd Street in the 1930s and 1940s without the ability to understand what it was like to hear that music in those times and places – to hear jazz in person, in those days when it was restricted by the three-minute time limit on the phonograph record, to study it as it evolved in orderly succession, from Louis and Bix to Roy Eldridge to Dizzy and Miles and Clifford Brown and Freddie Hubbard and Wynton (to take just one line of succession at random). Those of us who came up through those years were more fortunate than we realized; we saw those flowers bloom, we observed every chrysalis becoming a butterfly.

In the final analysis it seemed to me that the musicians, or at least most of those with whom I had close, extensive contact, had a more intelligent sense of where jazz was heading, of its realities and potentialities, than either the merchants or the critics. Ultimately it was they who proved my point in every controversy, starting at the very beginning when I made my first appearance in print in the English language, arguing about the possibility of jazz in 3/4 time.

It seems a little ridiculous today that what the editor of the *Melody Maker* derided as a request for a 'red piece of green chalk' has now become so commonplace that it is almost impossible to listen to a single set by a typical jazz group without hearing at least one number in waltz time. 'Bluesette', 'Waltz for Debby', 'A Child is Born' and many other compositions by jazz musicians have become jazz waltz standards. Even 5/4, which seemed so weird to Oscar Pettiford (see Music section) when I handed him his part to 'Bass Reflex' in 1956, is by now far from uncommon.

Controversy played a significant and in some ways helpful part in establishing my credentials; however, I lean towards the view that the intramural fights of the 1940s were foolish and avoidable. To dignify the attacks on me and on the musicians of the swing, bop and all subsequent stages by counter-attacking them served only to escalate the feud. Ignoring the reactionaries and their false gods might have been a wiser course to follow, since in due course they fell of their own weight. Critics of a later generation have seen the picture from a more realistic vantage point. James Lincoln Collier, in *The Making of Jazz*, wrote in 1978 of Bunk Johnson and his followers: 'The fact that Johnson and his fellows played badly out of tune, muffed notes constantly, and played with little rhythmic ease did not seem to matter . . . [Johnson] grew progressively more arrogant, drank heavily and caused endless squabbles within the group.'

By the same token, controversial artists who came to prominence in later decades have elicited a similarly outspoken reaction from several scholarly observers, most notably Grover Sales, author of *Jazz – America's Classical Music*, who made the following comments in 1984:

The slowly mounting suspicion, which I have come to share, that the music of (Cecil) Taylor, (Anthony) Braxton, (John) Coltrane during his *Ascension* period, and much of (Ornette) Coleman has a rendezvous with oblivion, runs counter to the conventional wisdom of the day. These musicians enjoy, if not large incomes, the plaudits of widely-read and influential critics. Without second-guessing the motives of such writers, one can see the familiar pattern of 'once bitten, twice shy'. Dogged by painful memories of the 1940s when nearly every established jazz writer except Leonard Feather dismissed Parker and Gillespie as fakes, critics later thought twice before rushing into judgement on the apostles of free jazz and atonality for fear of repeating past mistakes.

Gene Lees, the respected lyricist, author and editor of the *Jazz Newsletter*, shares Sales' point of view. 'Where is jazz going?' he asked rhetorically. 'Nowhere – it's *there*. Jazz has the capacity, not seen in classical music to nearly the same extent, to renew itself from its own past.'

Sales actually gave me too much credit; although I was the principal target of the moldy figs, I was by no means alone. Charles Delaunay's prompt championship of the new music was of great significance. Robert Goffin was quick to grasp the importance of the new sounds. Most important of all, it seems to me, was Barry Ulanov's tenure at *Metronome* during the transitional years. His move from jazz to the world of academe (he has been a professor in the Department of English at Barnard College for many years) robbed our community of one of its most articulate voices.

In early 1986 Barry and I reminisced about the years we shared. Not long afterwards he put some of his reflections in writing.

What we fought for was right and the way we fought was right, too, I am still persuaded. We were up against extraordinarily thick heads and tin ears.

It still astonishes me that anyone who had any feeling for jazz could have failed to hear what Bird and Dizzy and all the rest of them were accomplishing or, even worse, could have been put off by it. I was simply knocked over by Bird the first time I heard him, playing with Jay McShann's band at the Savoy, and I remembered pushing to make the point by putting my review of the McShann band and Bird opposite my review of the Jimmy

Dorsey band in a double-spread – a fair contrast in altos.

Bird was the Mozart of jazz; he had an endless supply of melody; his rests were more eloquent than four choruses by anyone else. He was also, I think, in the curious way that Billie Holiday was too, an innocent. He was simply unequal to the pressures of the jazz world and, more frightening still, the tortures of being taken up, especially by those who had what looked like money and position. It remains extraordinary that he was able to do so much, to make what had become a tired and cliché-ridden music come alive again, and to do so through breakdowns and heavy drugs and a ridiculous playing and recording life.

What we have on records is splendid – the lines themselves, his sound, his beat, his never-failing freshness – but it doesn't quite catch what I heard in person, the sweetness, the strength, the musical wisdom, even when he was stoned and there was no mistaking that he was. How could we help but snarl and mock and be appalled by those self-appointed guardians of the 'real jazz' who were working overtime to attack a genius and the superb music he was bringing into being?

Please say it strongly in your memoir – and keep in touch.

The best,
Barry

More than four decades have gone by since Charlie Parker reached the zenith of creativity recalled by Barry Ulanov. Though a few hopeless, helpless right-wingers survive, the battle he mentioned has long since been won; yet the jazz world is far from united. Opinions concerning free jazz, electronic jazz-rock and other developments of the past two or three decades remain stubbornly divided, but at least today there is a profusion of healthy outlets both for the music itself, no matter what form it may take, and for the views of those who seek a sizeable audience for their statements.

My journey through jazz has been and continues to be marked by excitement and disappointment, agreement and contention; above all, it is never dull.

The train has been running for a long time. The ride, though not without its occasional violent bumps, has been smooth and satisfying much of the way. I have seen far too many passengers dismount at too many stops en route, many of them gifted men and women who had evolved from names on a record label into friends, whose departure left me irreversibly poorer. Fats left early; so did Mildred, and Lips Page and Prez and Billie and Swee' Pea and eventually the very men who unknowingly had been responsible for my taking the ride: Louis, Duke, Don Redman, Fletcher, Venuti, Basie, Benny Goodman.

The consolation, of course, has to be found in the innovative artists who came aboard later and who have shown new directions to be taken, refusing to be deflected from the path of genuine artistry by the eternal search for the dollar. Thanks to them my enthusiasm remains unquenched; I hear validity, vitality and creativity in the World Saxophone Quartet, JoAnne Brackeen, Stanley Jordan and Wynton Marsalis just as I did in Louis Armstrong's Hot Five, in Earl Hines and Joe Venuti and Eddie Lang and Duke Ellington in 1929 when I started collecting records.

Will the young lions of the 1980s – the Michel Petruccianis, Terence Blanchards, Makoto Ozones, Courtney Pines, Mulgrew Millers – fill some of the most conspicuous voids? Perhaps it is too early to be certain, yet their presence, and their apparent desire to keep this journey in motion on an unswerving path, encourages me. I believe that new challenges will be met, fresh ideas discovered and unexplored territories negotiated.

Getting there, the cliché tells us, is half the fun. But simply being along for the ride is pleasure enough for a lifetime.

HONOURS AND AWARDS

1964 Received first Grammy award given by NARAS (National Academy of Recording Arts & Sciences) for album notes (*The Ellington Era*)

1971 Nominated for Emmy award for producing 'The Jazz Show', a series seen on KNBC, Los Angeles

1978 Corporation for Public Broadcasting award for excellence in local programming on 'The Leonard Feather Show', KUSC, Los Angeles

1981 Citation from Mayor Tom Bradley and LA City Council at banquet organized by Harold R. Udkoff to establish Leonard Feather Scholarships at the Duke Ellington School of the Arts in Washington, DC

1983 International Critics' Poll, *Down Beat* magazine: Lifetime Achievement award

1984 Awarded honorary doctorate of music at Berklee College of Music in Boston

1985 Greater Los Angeles Press Club Journalism award: Certificate of excellence in entertainment reporting, *Los Angeles Times*

1986 National Association of Jazz Educators award for fifty years of contribution to jazz education and journalism

INDEX